D0294353

BOXING'S HALL OF SHAME

BOXING'S HALL OF SHAME

THE FIGHT GAME'S DARKEST DAYS

THOMAS MYLER

MAINSTREAM
PUBLISHING

EDINBURGH AND LONDON

To my wife Betty who is and
always has been in my corner

Copyright © Thomas Myler, 2006
All rights reserved
The moral right of the author has been asserted

First published in Great Britain in 2006 by
MAINSTREAM PUBLISHING COMPANY (EDINBURGH) LTD
7 Albany Street
Edinburgh EH1 3UG

ISBN 1 84596 081 5

No part of this book may be reproduced or transmitted in any form
or by any other means without permission in writing from the
publisher, except by a reviewer who wishes to quote brief passages
in connection with a review written for insertion in a magazine,
newspaper or broadcast

A catalogue record for this book is available from the British Library

Typeset in Caslon and Meta Bold

Printed in Great Britain by
William Clowes Ltd, Beccles, Suffolk

ACKNOWLEDGEMENTS

The author would like to thank a great many people whose invaluable help made this book possible, including the many boxers who kindly granted interviews over the years. Many individuals did not want any credit but mention must be made of Alexander G. Skutt of McBook Press, New York, for permission to use an edited version of an article by James B. Roberts in the *Boxing Register*, the official record book of the International Boxing Hall of Fame in New York, as the foreword, *Ring* magazine editor Nigel Collins, *Boxing News* editor Claude Abrams, the British Library in London, the National Library of Ireland, Independent Newspapers in Dublin, the World Boxing Organisation, Lonsdale International Sporting Club chairman Bernard Hart and boxing writers Jack Hirsch, Reg Gutteridge and Bert Blewett. Thanks also to Mainstream Publishing, including director Bill Campbell for his enthusiasm and faith in the project from the outset, editorial coordinator Graeme Blaikie for his help and guidance, editor Paul Murphy for his skill and patience, sales administrative manager Elaine Watt for her efficiency, Emily Bland for the attractive cover and publicity manager Lindsay Farquharson for keeping the author in touch with Mainstream's current and upcoming books. Last, but certainly by no means least, thanks to my wife Betty and family for their continued support and encouragement.

CONTENTS

'All I've ever heard is how some scandal is another nail in boxing's coffin. You know, this coffin's got nothing but nails.'

Bruce Silvergrade, owner of Gleason's Gym in
New York, 1999

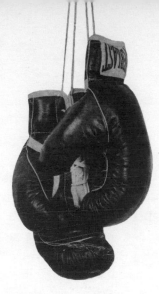

FOREWORD

Throughout its colourful history, boxing has had more than its share of scandal, both inside and outside of the ring. Almost from its very beginning, the sport has attracted a criminal element, and many boxers and non-combatants have risen from environments where obeying the law is less relevant than economic or physical survival. The violence that is prized in the ring has at times erupted in boxers' private lives, and stints in reform school or prison are woven into several champions' histories.

A continuing theme in boxing's chequered history is the fixing of fights. The sport is very susceptible to rigging. First, it involves only two active participants and only needs one to be convinced to throw a fight. Fixing team sports, in which there are many players and where events can occur more haphazardly, is much less practical. Furthermore, boxing is essentially an entrepreneurial endeavour in which individual boxers must guard their own financial interests.

Lacking the kind of central authority established in other professional sports, boxing does not have rigorous procedures for self-regulation. Certain boxers, with the control of their careers in the hands of trainers and managers, and perhaps living from purse to purse, have been vulnerable to manipulation.

While no one can say for certain when the first fight was thrown, the first known fix by a Hall of Famer took place in 1822 when Englishman Jem Ward threw his fight with Bill Abbott. In more modern times, allegations of fixed fights have risen many times, although the charges have rarely been proven.

For instance, it was rumoured that Stanley Ketchel was to allow the great black heavyweight Jack Johnson to beat him, and in return, Johnson would take it easy on the lighter Ketchel. When Ketchel knocked Johnson down, some say Johnson was outraged at the betrayal. In any event, he responded with a ferocious attack which ended the fight quickly.

Action in other heavyweight boxing matches has raised cries of 'fix' as well. Many suspected Hall of Famer Jack Sharkey of giving less than his best when he lost the world heavyweight championship to the ungainly giant Primo Carnera. Sharkey vehemently denied the charges for the rest of his life, but Carnera had well-known underworld connections and won other fights in which his opponents took dives. Reportedly, Carnera's handlers arranged the fixes without his knowledge.

In the 1960s, the two Muhammad Ali–Sonny Liston title fights raised some eyebrows. In the first, the then champion Liston quit between rounds, refusing to get up from his stool because of an injured shoulder. Although the examination after the fight did reveal an injury, the seeming invincibility of Liston and the shady figures with whom he associated cast doubt on the legitimacy of the fight's outcome.

In the second fight, Ali floored Liston with a short right which Ali dubbed 'the anchor punch' but some at ringside called it 'the phantom punch' because they never saw it. Confusion over the count by referee Jersey Joe Walcott contributed to the perception that the fight was not on the level. As with most boxing fix stories, the charges were never substantiated. It was never implied that Ali himself was involved.

Publicly confirmed fixes include middleweight Jake LaMotta's

admitted fall to Billy Fox in return for a pr~~o~~
Middleweight Rocky Graziano was suspended by
State Athletic Commission for not reporting a br.
heavyweight Harold Johnson had his licence suspended
against Julio Mederos without being hit. Fans
commissions alike have undoubtedly been duped at othe
unscrupulous figures whose influence on boxing has dimin..~~i~~ed the
sport's integrity.

With some notable exceptions, boxing has always tended to draw
its participants from the lower socio-economic strata. The streets of
urban neighbourhoods have been a wellspring of aspiring boxers.
Factors which discourage more affluent youths from taking up the
sport – the risk of serious injury or disfigurement, the availability of
many other forms of recreation and the lack of violence in everyday
middle-class life – mean very little in dangerous neighbourhoods
where violence and fighting are often a part of growing up.

Historically, youngsters particularly adept with their fists have
been urged to channel their aggressiveness through formal boxing
instruction. Unavoidably, the type of environment which fosters a
career in boxing may also lead to tangles with the law. Several great
boxers served time in youth detention centres or prison.

In his autobiography, *Somebody Up There Likes Me*, Rocky
Graziano details the many youthful misdeeds that landed him in
reform school. Sonny Liston learned to box in prison, and the young
Mike Tyson was discovered by trainer Cus D'Amato while serving
time in an upstate New York detention centre. Even boxers who came
to be highly respected for strength and character, such as Archie
Moore and Floyd Patterson, served time in reform schools.

Some boxers have been involved in criminal activities in their adult
lives as well. Liston, who was strongly linked to St Louis racketeer
John Vitale, was arrested numerous times, although sometimes he
may have been the victim of police harassment. Hall of Famer Kid
McCoy, whose gradual decline ended with suicide, was convicted of
killing a woman with whom he lived and shooting three other people.

Carlos Monzon, former world middleweight champion and a
national hero to Argentinians, was convicted of killing the mother of

his youngest child by throwing her off a second-storey balcony, and Hall of Fame trainer Jack Blackburn killed his wife and shot two other people. In a case which received worldwide attention, Tyson was convicted of rape and served over three years in prison before his release in 1995.

Criminality is by no means the norm for successful boxers. Many have had stable home lives or followed their boxing careers with public service or youth work, but for some, the violence that defines the sport is not confined to the 'squared circle'.

Boxing has been tainted with widespread corruption at various times in its history. From the end of the 1940s to the late 1950s, the International Boxing Club (IBC) dominated the promotion of boxing in the US. Though primarily owned by James D. Norris, who controlled Madison Square Garden and owned three other major arenas, the IBC fell under the influence of mobster Frankie Carbo. Carbo and his associates also controlled the Boxing Managers' Guild, which gave them strong influence over two aspects of the fight game: staging fights and controlling fighters.

The reputation of premier fight promoter Don King, a hugely successful figure on today's boxing scene, makes many observers uneasy. King, convicted of manslaughter in 1967 in connection with the death of a rival in the Cleveland numbers racket, has survived numerous scrapes with law enforcement authorities. An FBI sting operation, three grand-jury probes, an income tax evasion case and prosecution for insurance fraud all failed to prove King guilty of wrongdoing.

Questions about King's complex dealings seem to arise from an apparent conflict of interest when he acts as both promoter and manager. Although rumours indicate that boxers have been underpaid, few have complained publicly. According to a 1991 *Sports Illustrated* article by a former FBI agent who investigated King's alleged mob connections, the then world heavyweight champion Larry Holmes, managed by King, said in private that he feared for his safety if he cooperated with the government.

At its best, boxing is an unparalleled physical art. At its worst, it is a killer and maimer of good men. Blindness, hearing loss, mental

12

impairment, respiratory or speech difficulties, paralysis and death are among the possibilities that lurk behind the glory of being a star in satin trunks. While serious injuries and deaths do occur in other sports – skiing and motor racing, for instance – boxing is perhaps the only sport where death and injuries are viewed as 'part of the game'. Financial or other pressures have led to more than one hurt or sick boxer fighting at extreme risk to his health.

The well-publicised case of Gerald McClellan, a 27-year-old boxer who received very severe injuries in his super-middleweight title fight with Nigel Benn in 1995, renewed calls for the outright abolition of boxing. A six-inch blood clot was removed from McClellan's brain in emergency surgery following the title bout. The young boxer suffered almost total hearing and sight loss, cannot walk and will need lifelong care.

One of the most distasteful aspects of boxing injuries is the long-term effect on the brain of numerous blows to the head. The once-comic image of the punch-drunk fighter is a tragic reality for some ring veterans. The plight of one-time heavyweight contender Jerry Quarry came to light in both the boxing press and in the general media.

At the age of 50, Quarry had lost many physical and mental capabilities and could no longer care for himself as a result of the beatings he endured in the ring. Sports fans are also very familiar with the transformation of Muhammad Ali from a quick-witted, swaggering champion to a soft-spoken, slow-moving figure because of Parkinson's disease, perhaps exacerbated by his ring career. Brain injuries have shortened the productive lives of many other boxers and former boxers.

The dangerous nature of boxing has periodically led to calls for reforms, ranging from more thorough and frequent examinations to protective headgear. At various times, the US Congress has held hearings to discuss federal control of boxing, and, from time to time, movements to ban the sport have arisen. One of the most outspoken proponents for the abolition of boxing was announcer Howard Cosell, who, after many years of commentating on fights, became disgusted by a particularly brutal match.

Boxing has been part of human history for centuries, however, and it may never be 'civilised' out of existence. The promise of prize money, as well as the possibility of being the very best at something excruciatingly difficult, is a timeless lure to many talented young men.

James B. Roberts
Co-editor of the Boxing Register,
official record book of the
International Boxing Hall
of Fame, Canastota, New York

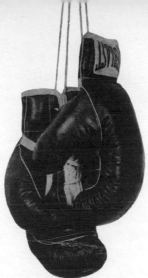

1

FIXES, FAKES AND FINANCES

Boxing's appeal crosses all barriers, race, religion and, today more than ever, the sexual divide, with women's boxing gaining more momentum than at any other time in the sport's long and colourful history. Kings and commoners, princes and paupers, movie stars and mobsters, guys and dolls have all been brought together by the sport's indefinable glamour.

The 'Sweet Science', with its origins dating back over 8,000 years as a leisure-time activity in the Nubian valley of what is now Egypt, has a culture all of its own, and, it must be said, a chronicle of events littered with scandals and controversy.

Mind you, boxing is not the only sport smeared by disgrace and wrongdoing. Horse racing has not been free of doping and bribery. Track and field, cycling and swimming have all had their scandals, while soccer has also come under fire with allegations of match-rigging.

Drug taking has also stalked rugby, while racism and homophobia are very much a part of ladies' tennis. Bribery, corruption and that recurring old enemy, drugs, have scarred the world's greatest amateur sporting event, the Olympic Games. Baseball has had its 'Black Sox' rigging scandal and golf its infamous 'Brookline 1999' tournament during which both the US Ryder Cup team and drunken fans shamed the game. Even that most aristocratic of sports, cricket, has been linked to drugs.

Boxing, the noble art, however, would appear to have come off the worst. Hardly a month passes without some new scandal breaking out, with seemingly ongoing investigations and probes. Then again, the underworld, particularly in the US and to a lesser extent Britain, has always flirted with the sport – and the sometimes sleazy, often raffish glamour of the 'squared circle' would appear to be part of its attraction.

Today, the sport has been cleaned up considerably; however, there is still a lot to be done. Although any true and accurate comparison between the bad old days and today is almost non-existent, frightening mismatches still mar the sport, and boxers long past their sell-by date are still pushing their hands into gloves and climbing wearily into rings around the world, risking life and limb. The last chance saloon is always open.

There are also far too many boxing organisations around the world, each with their own 'world' champions, and they rarely agree on anything. Nevertheless, the 'Mob' days of the 1950s, when the gangsters virtually controlled the sport in the US, would seem to be over.

Since America dominated the world championship scene during those years, it followed that titles were at the disposal of the mobsters and more or less freely available for them to manipulate. Boxing people scoffed at Hollywood movies like *Champion*, *The Set-Up* and *The Harder They Fall* for depicting the sport in a poor light and implying that it was as straight as a winding mountain road. In truth, hoodlums and gunmen were very much a part of the sport in an age when guns and threats were as important as the ring and the ropes.

Though US boxing was officially controlled by the two major bodies at the time, the New York State Athletic Commission (NYSAC) and the National Boxing Association (NBA), which would later become the World Boxing Association (WBA), the underworld held power. Earlier, in the 1920s and into the 1930s, gangsters like Al Capone, 'Lucky' Luciano, 'Legs' Diamond and John Dillinger had an enormous influence on the sport, and there was considerable evidence of fixed fights.

In the mid and late 1930s, promoter Mike Jacobs was frequently accused of having associations with the underworld, but his links with contender and later world heavyweight champion Joe Louis appeared to halt any spread of corruption.

Nevertheless, one of Louis's early managers, Julian Black, was a numbers racketeer and his first trainer, Jack 'Chappie' Blackburn, had served four years of a fifteen-year prison sentence on a manslaughter charge. Blackburn's most distinguished feature was a long scar that creased the left side of his face from ear to lip, a souvenir from a knife fight in a Philadelphia bar.

Later, when training Louis for his first fight with Max Schmeling in 1936, Blackburn was tried on a murder charge but was freed six days into the trial in Chicago when the prosecution abruptly decided not to go through with the case. Exactly whose influence or money was at work remained a mystery, but it certainly did not hurt matters that Blackburn was a top trainer who was needed to prepare Louis, a potential gold mine, or that the murder victim was black.

With most of the world champions in uniform during the Second World War, there was little activity among the boxing underworld, but in the immediate post-war years a new breed would come to the fore, such as Frank 'Blinky' Palermo, Felix Bocchicchio, Truman Gibson, Joe Sica and the man considered the ringleader, the notorious Frankie Carbo.

There is little doubt that Carbo had more power and influence than any other individual in boxing, including the members of the two leading commissions. He was able to control the movements of several world champions and top contenders through their managers, even though the boxers themselves, in many cases, were not consulted in the negotiations.

Carbo, who dressed in expensive grey suits, was also known as 'Mr Grey', or simply 'The Man In Grey'. He was born John Paul Carbo in a tenement on New York's teeming East Side in August 1904, and in such an environment it was not the most difficult thing to get involved in crime. At the age of 18 he was arrested for assault and grand larceny. When he was 20 he was charged with shooting a butcher to death in a poolroom on East 106th Street. Carbo and the butcher, a man named Albert Webber, were apparently arguing over possession of a stolen taxicab. At the time, Carbo was known variously as Frankie Carbo, Frank Fortunato, Frank Martin, Jimmy the 'Wop' and 'Dago' Frank.

To avoid arrest on the shooting charge, Carbo relocated to Philadelphia but was soon arrested there after a hold-up and sent back to New York to confront the consequences of Webber's demise. He was convicted of first-degree manslaughter and received a sentence of two to four years in Sing Sing Correctional Facility in New York. He absconded, however, and was a fugitive for four years before being apprehended once again.

Carbo served two years before he was paroled in 1930 when he became a fully fledged triggerman during the Prohibition wars, working most prominently for the Brooklyn division of Murder, Inc. In 1931, he was arrested for homicide on a charge of killing a Philadelphian beer baron known as 'Waxie' Gordon in a hotel in Atlantic City, New Jersey. He was released on $10,000 bail but nothing came of the investigation.

In 1936, he was arrested during a boxing card in Madison Square Garden, New York, for the underworld murders of Max Hassel and Max Greenberg, henchmen for Waxie Gordon. Again, nothing more came of it.

Carbo's most notorious homicide was in November 1939 when, on Thanksgiving Day in Los Angeles, he was one of five arrested for the gangland slaying of Harry 'Big Greenie' Greenberg, a former member of Murder, Inc. Greenberg, whose real name was Harry Schachter, was also a member of Louis 'Lepke' Buchalter's gang in Brooklyn. The other four were Buchalter himself, Benjamin 'Bugsy' Siegel, Harry 'The Champ' Siegel and Emanuel Weiss, also known as 'Mendy'.

Big Greenie had been shot five times as he sat behind the wheel of his car on a quiet residential street. At the subsequent trial, Albert

'Tick Tock' Tannenbaum, a member of Murder, Inc., testified that Carbo fired the five bullets into Greenberg and that Bugsy Siegel drove the getaway car. He also named Mendy Weiss and Lepke Buchalter as accomplices. The case against Carbo seemed particularly strong, especially as there were several other witnesses, including Abe 'Kid Twist' Reles, another hoodlum, who said he saw Carbo heading towards the scene of the shooting and running away afterwards.

The trial in 1942 resulted in a hung jury, but the case for the prosecution was weakened in the second trial when Kid Twist, while under police protection, either fell or was pushed from his fifth-storey hotel window to his death. Carbo said he knew nothing of the incident. The jury decided that while they doubted Carbo's meandering and innocent gestures, they could not entirely trust Tick Tock Tannenbaum as a reliable witness. After 53 hours of deliberation, Carbo was acquitted.

Carbo's name was also linked with the slaying in June 1947 of Bugsy Siegel in Los Angeles when mobsters sent a burst of gunfire through the living-room window of his palatial home in Beverly Hills. Two years earlier, Bugsy had built the Flamingo Hotel and Casino in Las Vegas after realising the potential of the desert town in Nevada as a gambling oasis. Indeed, he is credited as the man who started the Las Vegas gambling boom. The money for the Flamingo was raised from funds accrued by the Mob and loaned to Bugsy. When he reneged on his creditors, Mob boss Meyer Lanskey put the finger on him and, allegedly, named Carbo as the man to finish him off. Carbo always denied any direct or indirect link to the killing, and like so many gangland murders of the period, it went unsolved.

Some years earlier, Carbo had become involved in the boxing scene. In 1936, the mobster Gabe Genovese, a barber by profession, was managing world middleweight champion Babe Risko, and he brought in Carbo as a partner. In the mid-1950s, Genovese would be cut in on the purses of world welter and middleweight champion Carmen Basilio and lightweight contender Ludwig Lightburn. He also collected money by force from New York promoter Norman Rothschild.

The law eventually caught up with Genovese in 1959 when he was sentenced to two years in a state penitentiary on Rikers Island in New York for operating as an undercover manager. New York's Assistant District Attorney, John G. Bonomi, described him as 'an evil and degrading influence on professional boxing for over two decades'. Genovese served a little more than a year and died soon after his release.

In the late 1940s, Carbo became a major influence in the fight game. He was freely acknowledged as the 'underworld commissioner of boxing'. From his New York offices in the Forest Hotel on West 49th Street, Carbo used any method – bribery, bullying, threats, blackmail – to get his message across. He used his associate Frank Blinky Palermo, who managed world champions such as lightweight Ike Williams and welterweight Johnny Saxton, as a front man, and there were always willing managers like Bill Daly, known as 'Squire' and 'Honest Bill', and Willie Ketchum to help him manipulate other boxers.

When Ike Williams threatened to sack Connie McCarthy, one of his earlier managers, and manage himself because McCarthy was continually drunk and incapable of looking after the boxer's interests, McCarthy went to the notorious Boxing Managers' Guild, and they blacklisted Williams. Ike, however, soon came into contact with Palermo, who told the boxer he would 'straighten everything out'.

Palermo, with offices in the Schubert Building on South Broad Street in Philadelphia, took over Williams' contract from McCarthy, who got a 'pay-off' from Blinky. Ike got the fights he wanted, although Williams would later admit, 'Palermo just robbed the hell out of me for my money.'

To his friends and associates, Palermo was simply Frank or Mr Palermo. He hated the Blinky nickname given to him by the media because of an eye infection, though some said it was because he could not look anybody straight in the eye. He had legitimate licences to manage boxers in New York, Pennsylvania, Illinois, Maryland, California and Florida, but he would eventually lose them one after the other, even in his native Philadelphia. It was just that he did not really need a licence, as his alliance with Carbo meant that his power as an undercover manager was greater than that of any licensed manager.

Palermo's police record was also extensive, with various misdemeanours dating back to 1928. As a bookmaker in 1950, he staged a running gun battle through the streets of Philadelphia in pursuit of a numbers runner who pocketed the pay-off on a big bet. He also operated a restaurant in partnership with Sam Margolis, who had gangland connections and was not adverse to pulling the trigger on anybody he thought was trying to double-cross him.

In December 1942, Sugar Ray Robinson, then the uncrowned world welterweight champion, was supposed to carry Al Nettlow, who was handled by Palermo, for the full ten rounds in a fight in Philadelphia. In the third round, however, Nettlow landed a hard right hand, and Robinson lost his temper. He hit Nettlow with a powerful left hook which had him in so much trouble that the fight was stopped. That night Sugar Ray went down to the news-stand where Blinky hung out and tried to explain what happened. 'It was an accident,' he told the manager. 'I just happened to catch him.'

Blinky smiled, shrugged his shoulders and said, 'It's all right, Ray. Nothin' we can do about it now.'

Like lightweight Ike Williams, heavyweight contender Coley Wallace claimed he too was ripped off by Palermo. He recalled in 1996 that he was never paid for two fights: his fourth-round win over Bill Gilliam in New York in December 1953 and his knockout in ten rounds by former world heavyweight champion Ezzard Charles in his next fight three months later in San Francisco.

'I don't recall what my purse was for the Gilliam fight, but I was supposed to receive $20,000 against Charles,' he said. Palermo paid him $3,000 and did not offer any explanation. When Wallace pressed him for an answer, Blinky said the missing money had in fact been accounted for by 'unforeseen expenses'. Wallace also claimed he was drugged before the Charles fight, although he could never prove it.

Wallace had turned professional in 1950 after beating Rocky Marciano in a national tournament. Securing a title fight with Marciano after Rocky became world heavyweight champion, however, turned out to be impossible. 'I beat Marciano easily in the amateurs, but they wanted a white champion,' remembered Wallace.

21

'Blinky told me if I wanted to fight Marciano, I would have to take a dive. I told him, "No, forget it."

'That was the fight game in the 1950s. You kept quiet or you didn't fight. I just let it go. That was boxing. I didn't fight for the title, but I have my pride. Frankie Carbo controlled boxing. You had to go to him, and the way to Carbo was through Blinky. I could have gone to somebody else, but without Carbo, you didn't get the big money or the big fights. Carbo controlled all the champions.'

Wallace's career eventually petered out and he retired, although he is probably best remembered by boxing fans for the 1953 movie *The Joe Louis Story* in which he played the 'Brown Bomber'. He also portrayed Louis in the classic 1980 film *Raging Bull*, although it was only a small part.

Up to the time of his death in January 2005 at the age of 77, he still talked fondly about *The Joe Louis Story*, which received strong promotion by United Artists, although it was not a commercial success. Coley had less happy memories of his association with his former manager. 'I get angry when I think about Blinky Palermo,' he remembered. 'He could have done better for me. He ruined boxing for me.'

The Boxing Managers' Guild was the brainchild of Carbo, and it allowed him to move in on the huge fees boxers were getting from television. Unofficially it was a kind of managers' union, but, in reality, it was a dictatorial organisation which threatened and bullied managers as well as boxers who refused to join. The message was clear: if you want to get the fights that matter, join the guild; otherwise, you're out.

Promoters were blacklisted, too, and sometimes beaten up if they did not cooperate or make the 'right' matches. Sam Silverman, for many years the leading New England promoter who put on most of Rocky Marciano's early fights, started to operate independently in the Boston area – and paid a high price.

One night a bomb was dropped into the basement of his home. Luckily, Sam was out at the time. A few days later, his wife was fortunate enough to be called to the phone when a bullet whizzed through a kitchen window. In the end they got Sam, who wasn't exactly a robust type of man. In a lonely back alley near his home, he was beaten up with a lead pipe wrapped in sackcloth. He survived but got the message.

One of Honest Bill Daly's boxers in the 1950s was the talented Vince Martinez, a leading contender for the world welterweight title. On 1 July 1954 in Los Angeles, Martinez outpointed Art Aragon, billed as the 'Golden Boy', and took an important step up the ratings. Five days later, Daly went to Martinez's home in New Jersey to split up a purse of $27,000.

When Martinez saw that Daly was adding $3,000 to the managerial expenses, he exploded. 'It's a rip-off,' the boxer yelled.

Daly barked back, 'What do you mean? What are you talking about? The money was spent wisely: $1,000 was for air tickets and $2,000 was for taking care of the referee and judges.'

In the ensuing argument, Daly stormed out and refused to meet again with Martinez. Vince appealed to the International Boxing Club (IBC), a blatantly monopolistic organisation but, at the same time, the leading promoters. The IBC offered to sign him to an exclusive contract. Martinez signed with them, but the IBC went back on their word after they got him just two fights at Madison Square Garden.

Shortly before the first one, against Carmine Fiore in October 1954, an unnamed source offered Martinez a straight $20,000 to take a dive. He refused and reported it to the New York State Athletic Commission. 'The commission gave me police protection during the fight and even a motorcycle escort to the New Jersey line after the fight was over,' he recalled. 'Nothing happened, except that I knocked out Fiore in the seventh.'

After the second fight, a ten-rounds decision over Al Andrews in December 1954, Martinez found himself on the blacklist. It transpired that the Boxing Managers' Guild, of which Daly happened to be treasurer, had imposed sanctions on the boxer. He was both unemployed and unemployable. Martinez had made the unpardonable mistake of ruffling Honest Bill.

'My father and my brother Phil decided we would try to make it on our own, and Phil applied for and got a manager's licence,'

23

Martinez recalled. 'But we ran into a stone wall every place we turned. At first we couldn't understand it. Here I was, a top-ranked contender and not a promoter in the country could give me work. Then we found out. I was blacklisted.'

It took six months before the ban was lifted and only then through the intervention of an angry Julius Helfand, chairman of the New York State Athletic Commission. Helfand told his members, 'I'll clean up boxing or kill it,' but Martinez still had to wait nearly four years before he got his overdue and deserved title shot. Even then, it was too late.

With his best years behind him, Martinez climbed into the ring at the St Louis Arena in June 1958 to fight Virgil Akins, a 2–1 favourite, for the title vacated by Carmen Basilio, who had won the middleweight championship from Sugar Ray Robinson nine months earlier. In the first round, Martinez was battered to the canvas by the hard-hitting Akins no fewer than five times. In the second round, he was down twice more. In the fourth, he was sent crashing to the boards again. On rising, Akins dropped him for the ninth time before referee Harry Kessler, somewhat belatedly, waved his hands wide to indicate that it was all over without starting a count. Vince Martinez's dream had sadly ended.

When Johnny Saxton, who was managed by Palermo, won the world welterweight title from the talented Cuban boxer Kid Gavilan on a 15-rounds points-decision in Philadelphia in October 1954, there was a public outcry over the verdict. Twenty of twenty-two reporters polled at ringside thought Gavilan should have won the dull fifteen-rounder. With Palermo's presence, however, the feeling before the fight was that Gavilan would need a knockout or a stoppage to make sure of victory in what would be his eighth title defence. 'I congratulate you – on your luck,' Frank Weiner, chairman of the Pennsylvania Boxing Commission, told the new champion.

Budd Schulberg, reporting for *Sports Illustrated*, wrote, 'Johnny Saxton may be an orphan, but no one can say he lacks for cousins in Philadelphia. Anyone who can clown his way through 15 listless rounds and still be rewarded with a world championship must have a covey of doting relatives.'

Dan Parker, in the *New York Mirror*, wrote, 'Jack Kearns, the fight manager, told some friends beforehand to send in all they had on Saxton, who, he said, couldn't lose. In New York, many fans who tried to put money on Saxton were told that they could bet only on Gavilan.'

Gavilan had earlier been involved in another questionable decision when he defended his title against Billy Graham, a popular and skilful boxer of Irish ancestry from New York's East Side, in August 1951. The match was scheduled for Madison Square Garden, and it was Gavilan's first defence of the vacant title he had won three months earlier against Johnny Bratton.

A few days before the fight, Irving Cohen, Graham's manager, got a call to visit Frankie Carbo at the bar in the Forest Hotel, a block down from the Garden. 'You want your boy to be the champ,' said Carbo. 'You give me 20 per cent and you got the title.'

Cohen, one of the most honest men in the fight business, told Carbo he could not give him 20 per cent because another manager, Pete Reilly, already had a percentage in Graham. Carbo bent close to Cohen and said softly, 'You go and talk to Graham. He's the one who's got the final say.'

When Cohen told Graham, Billy would not hear of it. 'If I have to turn on my friend Pete Reilly, I'd rather not have the title,' he said. 'I may want to be the champ, but I don't have to be a louse to get it.' Cohen went back to Carbo and told him there was no deal, whereupon the gangster said, 'Does the kid know he's not going to win?' When Cohen said Graham knew, Carbo replied, 'He's got a lot to learn about life.'

The fight went the full 15 rounds, most of them close, though Graham always looked in front. The decision, however, went to Gavilan. Referee Mark Conn scored it seven rounds to each man, with one even, but under New York rules, if both boxers were level on rounds, the points system was brought in, and Conn gave it to Gavilan ten points to seven.

One of the two judges, Frank Forbes, had the same score on rounds but voted for Graham eleven points to ten. The second judge, Artie Schwartz, called it nine rounds for Gavilan, six for Graham, so Gavilan won the split decision and held on to his title.

The verdict caused a near riot. There was uproar and people were shouting abuse all over the famous arena. Graham stood in the centre of the ring, dumbfounded, as his supporters came out of their seats and into the aisles, waving their fists towards the ring and screaming threats at Conn and Schwartz. Police and security men kept the angry crowd from storming the ring.

Ringside reporters agreed that Graham was one of the unluckiest losers in the Garden for many years. Eddie Borden, in *Boxing and Wrestling* magazine, wrote:

> During moments of the battle, Billy used his famous left jab with the precision of a piston rod, and his right-hand punch to the body was a weapon which Gavilan found difficulty in avoiding. He used it steadily throughout the fight, and the Cuban apparently had no method to thwart that particular punch. Billy, too, looked good in landing. He pounded Gavilan's body continually, and it may have been responsible for slowing up Gavilan in the closing rounds.

Garden matchmaker Teddy Brenner, an impartial observer, said he had Graham the winner by ten rounds to five. 'What Graham did was to wait for Gavilan's leads, and if it was a jab, he would pick it off,' he recalled in 1981. 'What he could always do was to turn from the other guy's rights and step inside the long punches. When Johnny Addie announced the decision, a great roar came down from the balconies. The people were angry, and around the ringside, the big spenders were screaming at the officials.'

Many years after the controversial decision that deprived Graham of the fight and the championship, judge Schwartz lay dying in a New York hospital, and he asked his nurse to send a message to Graham's manager to come and see him. When Cohen arrived, Schwartz looked up at him and said, 'You know, Irving, I've got to get this off my mind because you are a very decent fellow. When I voted for Gavilan against Graham, I had to do it. The boys ordered me to do it. I couldn't help myself, and it's bothered me ever since. I'm sorry, Irving, for what I did to you and Graham.'

Cohen took Schwartz's hand and said, 'It's OK, Artie, I understand.'

An interesting and quite amazing sequel to this story is that it took the New York State Athletic Commission thirty-three years – and three years after Schwartz's revelations were made public – to carry out an enquiry into the circumstances surrounding the verdict. The commission, under its chairman José Torres, the former world light-heavyweight champion, announced that despite the passage of time, the decision would be reversed if any evidence of wrongdoing could be substantiated.

However, after due deliberation, the commission was unable to come up with the necessary proof. The case was therefore closed, and unlucky Billy Graham was never able to feel that elusive world-championship belt around his waist.

Gavilan, who seemed to have been involved in a history of disputed decisions, was officially managed by Angel Lopez and Fernando Balido, but it was Frankie Carbo who pulled all the strings in the background, working closely with the IBC.

Carbo and the mobsters effectively controlled the IBC, run by millionaire businessman James Dougan Norris. The organisation had a virtual monopoly on world champions and title fights. The IBC promoted every single heavyweight, light-heavyweight, middleweight and welterweight title fight over a ten-year span. Even when the British promoter Jack Solomons was involved in a world title fight in New York in 1951 – the second Sugar Ray Robinson–Randolph Turpin bout – he had to deal with the IBC.

Whether Norris was a positive or negative force in boxing at the time is open to debate. He made many outstanding matches, but he was too often publicly seen in the company of people like Carbo and Palermo, and the sport's image suffered. 'Norris alone could have starved the boxing mob into submission, on his terms,' wrote Arthur Daley in the *New York Times*. 'The cost would have come high, but he had the resources to do it. Instead, he played ball with the hoods and let the termites eat away the great boxing empire he had built.'

The IBC capitalised on television's infatuation with boxing and would later become known as Octopus International. It would dominate the sport even more completely than Mike Jacobs did with the Twentieth Century Sporting Club in the 1930s and 1940s. Norris's wealth was pervasive. He owned controlling interests in Madison Square Garden, which he used as his boxing headquarters, the Chicago Stadium, the Detroit Olympia and the St Louis Arena. He also held leases on the Indianapolis Coliseum and the Omaha Coliseum.

A smart dresser, suave, tall and good-looking, Norris also owned thoroughbred horses and raced them at tracks throughout the US. He also owned two major hockey teams, the Detroit Red Wings and the Chicago Black Hawks. Norris had previously promoted boxing shows in the Chicago Stadium and knew managers and their charges. For many years, he owned 'pieces' of boxers, including a rugged heavyweight contender in the 1930s named Harry Thomas, a railroad worker when he wasn't swinging punches.

James D. Norris moved into heavyweight boxing promotion in a big way in 1949 at the age of 42 when Joe Louis and his legal adviser, a black Chicago lawyer named Truman Gibson, devised a plan – though some called it a plot – to give up his world title. Gibson would later become a front man for Carbo. The US Government was pressing Louis for back taxes that would eventually burden him with a federal lien in excess of $1,250,000. In simple terms, he was broke. He could risk his title once more, but his skills had deteriorated. Furthermore, his promoter Mike Jacobs was no longer willing to loan Louis money, as he had done in the past in order that Jacobs and his Twentieth Century Sporting Club could maintain a firm hold on the heavyweight championship.

On Gibson's advice, Louis then decided to vacate the title but not before setting up a company called Joe Louis Enterprises and secretly signing up the four leading contenders for his championship – Ezzard Charles, Jersey Joe Walcott, Lee Savold and the former world light-heavyweight champion Gus Lesnevich, now campaigning as a heavyweight – to take part in a tournament to find his successor.

Louis sold the idea to Norris, who promptly set up the IBC. Louis then wrote to Abe Greene, president of the NBA, announcing his retirement. The IBC followed up with an announcement that

Charles and Walcott, the two leading contenders, would fight for the vacant title, and got the NBA to sanction the contest.

The match would be held on 22 June 1949 in the Chicago Stadium, owned by Norris. The promoter could not put the fight on in Madison Square Garden, in which he had shares, because Mike Jacobs's promotional contract with the Garden still had two years to run.

It happened that Jacobs was angered that another promotional organisation was challenging his empire, even though his health was ailing at the time. Effectively, Norris and the IBC were shouldering Jacobs not only out of heavyweight championship fights but out of the business. Without the Garden, the focal point of world boxing at the time, a top New York promoter like Jacobs would be like a fish stranded on the shore.

Charles defeated Walcott on points to assume the role as Louis's successor. The business of Joe Louis Enterprises was transferred to the IBC, with the former champion getting $150,000 as a down payment as director of boxing, although there is no record of Louis ever having acted in that capacity. In any event, he would eventually make a comeback to the ring, and his IBC post was dissolved.

Continuing their plan to extend their boxing activities, and with an eye on New York, Norris and his IBC team 'persuaded' Jacobs to step down as Garden promoter, with Norris handing him a cheque for $150,000. The way was now clear for Norris and the IBC to promote New York matches not only in the Garden but in big outdoor venues like the Yankee Stadium and the Polo Grounds, which were tied in with the Garden.

With the Chicago Stadium, the most important venue outside New York, owned by Norris, the IBC had the whole scenario now pretty well sewn up. It was a fertile ground for Carbo and Palermo to work in as they had the finger on virtually every top boxer and contender. Let Norris and the IBC arrange the fights, Carbo and Palermo would supply the boxers and, in most cases, tell them whether to win, lose or play it straight.

At that stage, Norris found he needed Carbo and Palermo as he had signed a lucrative television contract which stipulated that he

29

put on three shows a week across the country. Effectively, he was forced to work with the two men. There would also be a fee, naturally, for the boxers' television services. The underworld was set to move in on boxing in a big way. Small fight clubs, where young boxers learned their craft, were soon being squeezed out as the mobsters infiltrated all areas of the sport. Not that the IBC introduced boxing to the underworld. They were merely continuing the link.

Two years before the IBC came into being, Palermo's undefeated light-heavyweight 'Blackjack' Billy Fox took part in a blatantly fixed fight, at Madison Square Garden in November 1947, when middleweight Jake LaMotta allowed himself to be punched on the ropes by the light-hitting Fox. The fiasco was stopped in the fourth round, with the angry crowd booing all through and yelling 'fake, fake'. (That particular fight, and the circumstances surrounding it, is covered in chapter seven.)

One world champion who would not play the crooked game was Sugar Ray Robinson. A week before Robinson's challenge to LaMotta for the world middleweight title in February 1951, Carbo personally visited Sugar Ray with a proposition. Saying he was representing LaMotta, the smiling Carbo said, 'Ray, you win the first fight, LaMotta the second, and the third one is on the level. In that way, we'll all make money. What do you say?'

Robinson, who had rejected bribes to throw fights in the past, though he often carried opponents, turned him down. 'No way, Mr Carbo,' he said. 'You got the wrong guy. I've been waiting too long for this big chance, and I'm not going to throw it away now for no money.' Carbo, still smiling, said it was all right, shook hands with the boxer and walked away. Robinson never heard from him again. 'Not many fighters turned down Mr Carbo,' he would say later. 'Maybe he respected me for it.'

In April 1952, shortly before his title defence against former champion Rocky Graziano in Chicago, Robinson was approached to do a deal with the local Mafia, though there was no evidence that Carbo had any involvement, probably because he knew Sugar Ray would not cooperate. A group of businessmen approached Robinson in his training camp with a deal, saying that he would get $3 million if Graziano won the first fight, Robinson the second, and the third match would be on the level.

As he had done with Carbo, Robinson turned them down, whereupon one of the hoodlums patted him on the shoulder and said, 'Fine, Ray, if that's how you feel about it. No hard feelings.' Robinson smiled, the mobsters left, and, as with the Carbo incident, he never heard any more about it. Graziano was knocked out in the third round.

'I don't think anybody could ever question my honesty or integrity in boxing,' Robinson told the author in 1964. 'Of course I received offers to throw fights, and not only against Graziano or LaMotta. Other fights, too, but the mobsters soon got to know that I wouldn't play ball.

'I could have been a much richer man had I listened to these people and had believed in fortune over fame. You must remember, Thomas, that in some fights I was 4–1, 5–1, 6–1 so I could have made a packet by betting on the other guy. The temptation was there, but I never wanted to give in.

'You must stand by your principles in life. It's all you've got. That's why I would have to repeat what I said, that nobody could ever question my honesty in boxing. That's also why I turned down the bribe offers in my title fights with LaMotta and Graziano.'

In the 1940s, Graziano, a street-tough kid born in a decaying tenement on New York's East Side, was at the centre of fixed-fight controversies. On his way to the world middleweight title, he lost two points decisions in 1944 to the slick New York welterweight Harold Green, who had to climb off the canvas in both contests before having his right hand raised as the winner.

In 1945, they met for the third time when Graziano, who was partly managed by the gangster Eddie Coco, came from behind to drop Green with a hard right in round three. A split second after referee Ruby Goldstein counted him out, he leapt to his feet, rushed at Graziano in the corner and had to be restrained from attacking him. Green was subsequently fined $1,000 by the New York State Athletic Commission and suspended for 12 months. Forty-five years

31

later, however, he claimed he took a dive on the advice of 'certain people', and having done so, his anger overtook him.

'I was told to lay down,' he told *Ring* magazine. 'It wasn't easy. When you're doing it, it hurts.' One can only speculate how much it hurt because 12 months later Graziano was given a shot at Tony Zale's world middleweight title, and Green, who would fade into obscurity, was left to wonder what a third victory over Rocky might have meant.

In December 1946, Graziano was training for a fight with Ruben 'Cowboy' Shank in New York when he claimed he hurt his back and his trainer Whitey Bimstein decided to call off the bout. However, in January 1947, Rocky was picked up by the police and taken to the district attorney's office in Manhattan where he was questioned for 18 hours regarding a newspaper story that he had been offered a bribe to lose.

Rocky admitted that an anonymous character had offered him a $100,000 bribe when he took a call in Stillman's Gym, but he had turned it down. 'This sort of thing is common in boxing, and nobody takes any notice of them,' he explained to the DA officers. They suggested, however, that Graziano had in fact accepted the bribe, later thought the better of it and decided not to go through with the Shank fight, the back injury story being just an excuse invented for the occasion.

Graziano was summoned to appear before a grand jury investigating the incident. At the end of the ten-day inquiry he was cleared, but the New York State Athletic Commission, headed by Colonel Eddie Eagan, a former Olympic boxing gold medallist, decided that he was guilty of not reporting a bribe, and his licence to box in the state was revoked.

The following summer, the other boxing states decided to follow New York's lead and banned Graziano, even though by then he was world middleweight champion. Even in Illinois, where he had won the title by stopping Tony Zale in six rounds at the Chicago Stadium, they banned him, ostensibly because he had gone on the run from the US Army during the Second World War and had been court-martialled, dishonourably discharged and sentenced to twelve months' hard labour in the United States Penitentiary, Leavenworth, in Kansas. 'Nobody with a dishonourable discharge can be in boxing,' an Illinois Boxing Commission statement curtly said.

Graziano would claim in later years that a fellow prisoner in Leavenworth sold details of Rocky's army record to a Chicago newspaper columnist for $300. 'It was put in all the papers, coast to coast, how I slugged a corporal, flattened a captain and went over the hill twice, served my sentence and came out in the middle of the war while all the rest of our boys including my own brother were fighting and dying overseas,' Graziano recalled.

Meanwhile, by the middle of the 1950s, time appeared to be running out for Norris and his monopolistic IBC, and the hoodlums were beginning to look over their shoulders a lot more. The New York State Athletic Commission, now under the chairmanship of Robert K. Christenberry, was adopting a much tougher and braver line against the underworld than it had under Eagan's control.

The commission was now more open in confronting the gangster influence. In 1952, Christenberry had written in the American magazine *Life*, 'Below the surface lurks the influence of the underworld. Against this evil we have declared war. The full extent of the invasion of the game by its ringleaders, a clique of hoodlums, racketeers and sure-thing gamblers, is being examined by our own and other investigators.'

Nevertheless, conveniently for the IBC, Al Weill, the unofficial manager of world heavyweight champion Rocky Marciano, was their matchmaker. Consequently, they had control of the heavyweight title, the richest championship. As it happened, however, Rocky's shock retirement in 1956 marked the beginning of the IBC's decline. This was due in large part because Cus D'Amato, the manager of Floyd Patterson, despised Norris and all his organisation stood for and chose to remain fiercely independent. It did not matter one way or the other that the infamous Boxing Managers' Guild had by then lost its power and influence; D'Amato would have remained independent anyway.

The underworld, though, still had considerable influence. There were strong suspicions about the stoppage in two rounds of former world featherweight champion Willie Pep by newcomer Lulu Perez in Madison Square Garden in June 1954. The odds of 6–5 on Perez at the weigh-in on the morning of the fight shifted to 4–1 at ringside, suggesting that something was amiss.

In the language of gamblers, 'late money' is often thought to be 'smart money'. In other words, bets placed before the start of a fight, race or game are presumed to be made by those with inside, or at least up-to-date, information. With the shifting of the odds, did the betters know something? After all, Pep was hardly finished. He was the number-one contender for Sandy Saddler's world featherweight title and one of the all-time greats. And he was still only 31. Perez was 20 and relatively untested.

The fact that Pep's manager Lou Viscusi was a well-known 'yes man' for the mobsters and a close confidant of Carbo did not exactly clear the air either. Though he did not have a police record, nor was he involved in any criminal activities, Viscusi's name would come up frequently in the Senator Estes Kefauver hearings in 1960 into boxing's underworld connections.

The fight justified the late shift in the odds. Perez wobbled Pep in the first round. In the second, he scored three knockdowns which, under the existing New York rules, brought an automatic stoppage. A twist to this incident came 27 years later when, in the July 1981 issue of the American magazine *Inside Sports*, Paul Good wrote a story about a fixed fight involving a boxer known as 'The Champ'. All the details and circumstances were identical to those of the Pep–Perez fight. In the story, The Champ took a dive for $16,000. Three years after the article's publication, Pep filed a $75 million lawsuit, claiming he loved boxing too much 'to do such a thing as throw a fight'. However, in the court case that followed, a six-member jury deliberating for only fifteen minutes ruled against him.

With the net closing in on the IBC, Norris attempted to salvage the situation by offering J. Edgar Hoover, chief of the Federal Bureau of Investigation (FBI), a salary in excess of $100,000 to run the promotional organisation. Not too surprisingly, Hoover declined. In any event, the IBC had by then lost the confidence of the boxing public and the media.

It was left to Senator Kefauver of Tennessee to finally smash the IBC. Kefauver, concerned by the alleged underworld connections of heavyweight contender Sonny Liston, set up the Senate Anti-Trust and Monopoly Sub-Committee to investigate the IBC's illegal practices. They persuaded the Department of Justice and the FBI to act. Kefauver also sponsored a bill calling for the Justice Department to form a national boxing commission, but this was rejected by Attorney General Robert Kennedy, who felt that the responsibility of overseeing boxing and cleaning it up lay elsewhere.

Finally, in March 1957, a federal court handed down a judgment calling for the abandonment of the IBC, which was confirmed by the Supreme Court in January 1958. Norris and Arthur M. Wirtz, president of the Chicago Stadium, were found guilty of monopolistic practices by Judge Sylvester J. Ryan and were ordered to dispose of their stock in Madison Square Garden and dissolve the IBC in New York and Chicago.

Carbo, Palermo and their associates remained free and hoped to become even more powerful if and when the menacing Sonny Liston became world heavyweight champion, an event that seemed almost certain. Liston, an ex-convict, had strong connections with the underworld in St Louis, Missouri, where he spent his teenage years before his parents split up. The St Louis mobster boss John Vitale owned most of Sonny's contract.

The police had found it difficult to track Carbo down. He was in hiding from the long arm of the law, although boxing insiders would have had no trouble in identifying that he was in Florida – Miami to be precise. Later, when the heat was on, he transferred his headquarters to Camden, New Jersey. Finally, early one morning in May 1959, Lieutenant George Salayka and three New York detectives, assisted by New Jersey state troopers, called at Carbo's house. When Salayka announced at the front door that the house was surrounded, Carbo, who was fully dressed, bounded out of a rear window and found himself confronted by two of the detectives with guns drawn. He surrendered meekly, and one of his captors described him as 'mild mannered, polite and soft-spoken'. He had $2,800 cash in a trouser pocket.

Carbo was taken to jail to await trial but was later released on bail. He was subsequently admitted to the Johns Hopkins Hospital in Baltimore to receive treatment for an old kidney ailment. He was already under indictment in New York County for his role as an undercover manager and matchmaker and for conspiracy. Furthermore, he had recently been named by the federal government in a suit aimed at recovering $750,000 of unpaid income taxes.

In December 1960, Carbo and several top associates were called to Washington, along with a number of leading boxers, managers, promoters, matchmakers and mobsters, to testify before the Senate Anti-Trust and Monopoly Sub-Committee chaired by Senator Kefauver. Norris was also called and testified but in a closed hearing because he had a heart condition.

Startling revelations were made public for the first time: about fixed fights, extortion, bribes and the purses which several top boxers did not receive. The stories that came out of the hearings made the Hollywood movies about crooked fights and shady dealings look like *Alice in Wonderland*.

Norris told the committee he was greatly embarrassed to read he had hoodlum connections. He said he had never been to Carbo's home, though Carbo had visited Norris in his apartment in New York. Norris did, however, admit a long-standing friendship with Sam Hunt, a noted Chicago hoodlum who was known as 'Golfbag', because he carried his machine gun as one might carry a set of golf clubs.

Jake LaMotta admitted that he took a dive against Blackjack Billy Fox in November 1947 so he could get a long-deserved world middleweight title shot, while former world lightweight champion Ike Williams claimed that he was blacklisted until he allowed Palermo to manage him. He also said that he did not receive a cent of the $33,400 he had been promised for fighting Beau Jack in a title fight in July 1948, or any of the $33,500 he was due for another championship match two months later, this time against Jesse Flores. Yet he still had to pay tax on both monies.

Williams told the committee that Palermo recommended he leave his purses with the promoters and pick them up the following year to offset taxes. He said that Palermo, however, had collected them, and when Ike went to him about it, Blinky had broken down in tears. Palermo had complained that he was broke, that he feared he would 'get his brains blown out' if he did not pay certain people and that he needed Ike's purses to clear off some old debts. The boxer testified that four offers of bribes, ranging from $32,000 to $100,000, to lose fights were made by Palermo. He also said that Palermo offered him money to lose against top men such as Kid Gavilan, Jimmy Carter and Freddie Dawson. He lost to Carter, twice to Gavilan but beat Dawson.

Ultimately, credit for putting the hoodlums behind bars would go to Attorney General Robert Kennedy, who brought extortion charges against them in a Californian court. Carbo pleaded the Fifth Amendment of the United States Constitution and refused to answer 30 questions by the prosecution. Palermo declined to answer 11 questions.

In December 1961, the sentences were passed down. Carbo got 25 years and a $10,000 fine, and Palermo was given 15 years and a $10,000 fine. Carbo front man Truman Gibson received a five years' suspended sentence and a $10,000 fine, Joe Sica was given twenty-five years and a $10,000 fine and Louis Dragna five years and a $5,000 fine.

Norris was not indicted, but with the IBC disbanded, he withdrew from boxing to devote time to his other business and sporting interests. He died of a heart attack in Chicago in 1966 at the age of 59. The following day, in the *New York Herald Tribune*, Red Smith wrote, 'Jim Norris was the octopus whose stranglehold on the big arenas and network television shows was killing the game. He was the rich ogre, the playboy associate of mobsters, the promoter who did business with the underworld and let boxing fall into the wrong hands.'

Carbo started his sentence in Alcatraz, the old prison in San Francisco Bay, and when it was closed by the government, he was moved to the United States Penitentiary, McNeil Island in Washington where he would die. Palermo was put behind bars at Leavenworth in Kansas. Leavenworth had an earlier connection with boxing going back to the 1920s. It was the prison where Jack Johnson, the first black world heavyweight champion, served nearly a year on a charge of transporting Etta Duryea, a white married woman, across state boundaries from Chicago to Pittsburgh 'for immoral purposes in contravention of the Mann Act of 1910'.

Such was the power of the mobsters, Carbo and Palermo in particular, that even after Carbo had begun his prison sentence and Palermo was out on $100,000 bail, awaiting an appeal that subsequently failed, their powerful influence remained. Several hoodlums remained faithful to their old boss and visited Carbo in prison.

From behind bars, Carbo influenced the career of Sonny Liston before he won the world heavyweight title and continued to do so once the boxer was the champion. Liston never denied his Mob connections. It was no secret in boxing circles that Sonny's career was controlled by John Vitale, king of the St Louis underworld and a close friend of Carbo.

One of the charges against Palermo had been a conspiracy to try and muscle in on the contract of world welterweight champion Don Jordan of the Dominican Republic. Jordan was one of the witnesses questioned by the Kefauver Committee, but he said nothing and refused to name names.

Ten years later, and eight years after his final fight, Jordan would tell all, admitting in an interview that he knew more about the shady side of boxing 'than anyone could print in a lifetime'. He said that the Mafia still controlled the sport, from the four-round fights up. 'Fights I fought were prearranged before I even entered the ring,' he revealed. 'I knew who was going to win and who wouldn't. I fought one top contender twice, and both fights were prearranged.'

Jordan claimed that he threw his world welterweight title fight against challenger Benny 'Kid' Paret, a former sugar-cane cutter from Cuba, in May 1960 after being approached by 'certain people' who were threatening to take his wife as a hostage if he did not cooperate. 'If you remember, I was beating him for 13 rounds and slackened off in the last two rounds,' he revealed. 'The deal was in. He had to win, and I didn't get a rematch because Paret was under Frankie Carbo.'

In 1993, *The Ring Chronicle of Boxing* noted, 'For Jordan, the day was a total disaster. He had lost his title and was paid only $2,000 – for expenses – as he had signed over his $85,000 guarantee in order to end his contract with managers Don Nesseth and Jackie McCoy. So, on the morning of 28 May 1960, the welterweight of the 1960s woke up with no title, no managers and no money.'

Few, if any, boxers shed tears when Carbo and Palermo were put behind bars. One who was glad to see the mobsters locked up was Johnny Saxton, even though he won the world welterweight championship under the management of Palermo, with Carbo making the matches. Saxton claimed that both men had ripped him off financially.

Saxton, from Newark, New Jersey, may well have been good enough to win the title under his own steam at some stage in his career, but with Palermo as his manager and Carbo at work behind the scenes, 'he could hardly miss', as the late *Boxing News* editor and historian Harry Mullan once observed. A skilful boxer, rather than a heavy puncher, Saxton was an accomplished Golden Gloves and Amateur Athletic Union champion before turning professional in 1949. He moved up the ratings in the 1952 to 1953 period and won a bitterly controversial decision over Kid Gavilan in a world title fight in October 1954.

Saxton lost the title on a fourteenth-round stoppage against Tony DeMarco five months later but regained it in March 1956 from DeMarco's successor Carmen Basilio with a points verdict that was even worse than the Gavilan decision. The judges marked it unanimously for Saxton, but the majority of ringside reporters had Basilio in front at the last bell.

Public opinion forced a rematch six months later, and this time Basilio made no mistake by stopping Saxton in nine rounds. Carmen then removed any remaining doubt by knocking him out in two rounds in February 1957. Saxton retired in December 1958, washed up at the age of 27. In March 1959, he went before a judge in New York to face charges of breaking and entering, a crime that had yielded exactly five dollars and twenty cents. The man who had earned more than a quarter of a million dollars in purses was broke and owed $16,000 in taxes. When the judge asked him where his money went, he said, 'I didn't get much of it.' When questioned as to why he gave up boxing, he replied, 'They didn't need me any more.' Later, Saxton attempted suicide and was committed to Ancora State Hospital in New Jersey with mental problems. 'I was supposed to have got the money from boxing on TV, but I never saw it,' he told a reporter who visited him. 'Now I'm here in the hospital. That's what boxing did for me.'

Palermo was paroled in 1971, after serving ten years. In 1978, at the age of 73, he attempted to make a comeback, but after applying for a manager's licence in Pennsylvania, he was turned down. He blamed the media for destroying his chances. 'I think the media is very unfair,' he said. 'I paid my debt to society, so what do they want?' He died in a Philadelphia hospital in May 1996 at the age of 91.

Boxing manager Bill Daly, a friend of Carbo and Palermo, always kept one step ahead of the law and though interviewed by the FBI, was never indicted. It was said that while Honest Bill moved in the company of the mobsters, he was never classed as one of them. At the same time, he was never far from trouble, despite his best intentions. The son of an Irish immigrant who died at an early age from alcoholism, Daly lived in London for some time before the Second World War, having left the US for 'personal reasons', as he once deftly put it, and managed boxers, his best being Maurice Strickland, the New Zealand heavyweight champion.

At Wembley in 1937, when a bad decision went against Strickland in favour of Germany's Walter Neusel, the crowd booed loud and long. Back in Neusel's dressing-room, Daly barged in and attacked the German's manager, Paul Damski. Daly wrongly assumed the verdict had been fixed. The terrified Neusel quickly hid under a table. It was understandable as Daly had a long pair of scissors in his hand.

The British Boxing Board of Control suspended him from British rings, and he returned to the US, surfacing after the war when he was managing Lee Savold, one of the top American heavyweights of the period. Daly took Savold to London in December 1948 for a match with the British hope Bruce Woodcock. The fight, which has always had an air of suspicion about it, ended in the fourth round when

Woodcock sank to the canvas clutching his groin; Savold was disqualified for a low blow.

It was a hugely controversial finish to the fight – promoted by Jack Solomons – as both boxers were wearing protective foul-proof cups. It was also the first time that Savold had been disqualified in 162 fights. He did not have a reputation for low punching, even allowing for the somewhat casual attention to the rules by US boxing authorities.

In 1998, boxing writer Reg Gutteridge, formerly of the *Evening News*, recalled that he had been tipped off after the fight that Daly had arranged the entire business so as to bring about a lucrative return match between the two. Not surprisingly, they met again in June 1950 in a fight which was somewhat jokingly billed as being for the world heavyweight title vacated by Joe Louis, who had retired the previous year.

No surprise either that it turned out to be the big money-spinner of the British boxing year, with over 50,000 fans packing the White City arena in London, Solomons again being the promoter. This time Savold won on a stoppage in the fourth round. Luckily, nobody took the board's or Savold's championship claims seriously, as the two best heavyweights in the world were quite obviously the Americans Ezzard Charles and Jersey Joe Walcott.

Woodcock had previously been involved in an even more controversial affair, recalled by Gutteridge as 'an out and out scandal'. In September 1948, Solomons brought over another American, Lee Oma, to face Woodcock, who was making a comeback after being thrashed the previous year by the rugged Pennsylvanian ex-coal miner Joe Baksi in seven rounds at London's Harringay Arena.

Oma was said to have strong underworld connections through his manager Willie Friedland, who was known in boxing circles as Willie Ketchum and was a confidant of Frankie Carbo. Oma, who had a prison record, did little training for the fight, staying up well into the early hours and doing the rounds of the London nightclub scene with Ketchum and two lady friends. There were rumours and finally allegations that Oma had been offered big money to take a dive.

In the fight, also held at Harringay, Oma was strangely lethargic and hardly threw a worthwhile punch for three rounds, as the cautious Woodcock, whose jaw had been broken by Baksi, probed for an opening with his left hand. In the fourth, with the impatient and bored crowd chanting 'Lie down, lie down', Oma took a right to the chin, hardly more than a tap, clasped his stomach and flopped down to be counted out.

When cornerman Jack Gutteridge, an uncle of boxing writer Reg, rushed over to remove Oma's gumshield, the American opened his eyes, winked and then closed them again. Oma was such a ham actor – he later appeared in the Marlon Brando movie *On the Waterfront* – that there were as many laughs as jeers from the audience as he was led from the ring by his handlers.

The fight, if it could be called that, did absolutely nothing to boost Woodcock's slim hopes as a serious world heavyweight contender. However, it at least provided one London newspaper with one of the classic headlines. Above Peter Wilson's report in the *Sunday Pictorial*, now the *Sunday Mirror*, were just three words: 'Oma? Coma? Aroma!'

Sure enough, Oma subsequently admitted that the fight was crooked. In an interview in later years with the American author and boxing writer Budd Schulberg, who wrote *On the Waterfront* and *The Harder They Fall*, Oma said his purse of $100,000 came with a condition that he was to throw the fight in the sixth round. Oma told Schulberg that try as he might, by sticking out his chin and offering it as a steady target for Woodcock, he could not get in harm's way. After being told by his corner to 'make a fight of it and make it all look good', he shook Woodcock in the third round with a right to the head and then had to hold up the Brit in a clinch in case he lost the $10,000 he had wagered on his opponent. Finally, getting fed up with prolonging the whole business, he went down for the full count in the fourth round.

Although the British Boxing Board of Control withheld Oma's purse, Lee and his manager collected their bets and quickly booked the next flight to France for a short holiday, accompanied to the airport by their two lady friends. When Oma and Ketchum were asked by customs officials how much money they had to declare, they decided it was far better to give than to receive and promptly handed wads of notes to the ladies who said they would use it for a holiday in the US.

Peter Wilson always believed that the Oma fight was crooked and said so in an article he wrote in the *Daily Mirror* in 1955. Wilson recalled that, a few years after the fight, he chanced to meet Oma in New York where he was working as a bartender in a Broadway saloon, and the American revealed that losing to Woodcock was much more difficult than winning many other fights.

Woodcock and Solomons always denied, to their dying days, that the fight was a frame-up, insisting it was all above board from the start and that Oma's claims of a crooked fight were pure fiction. Unfortunately, few, if any, believed them. In any event, in most cases involving a crooked fight, only one of the participants needs to know about any irregularities. In this particular instance, it is quite possible that Woodcock could have been an innocent victim. We will never know for certain.

2

KING OF THE HUSTLERS

In the early 1970s a new kid arrived on the boxing block: the flamboyant Don King, who would become the world's greatest promoter. A huge bulk of a man, who stood 6 ft 3 in. and weighed over 21 st., he had served time for beating a man to death because of a debt. Although he did not yet sport the shock of candyfloss-like hair which would become his trademark, King's involvement in boxing began when he met up with Muhammad Ali.

After a friendly chat, he persuaded Ali, then the leading contender for his old title, the world heavyweight championship, to box an exhibition to raise funds for a hospital that looked after black people in Cleveland, Ohio, which was in danger of closing. 'It drew $80,000, the most money ever made at an exhibition,' King would later boast. 'Whatever I did, and whatever I do, it has to be the first, the biggest and the best.' What King did not say was that the hospital allegedly got only $17,000, the balance being swallowed up for 'expenses'.

Two years later, King pulled off an even bigger coup by talking George Foreman into defending his world heavyweight title against Ali in Zaire – now the Democratic Republic of Congo – in what would become known as the 'Rumble in the Jungle'. King persuaded President Mobutu to provide financial backing for the fight on the grounds that it would create publicity and trade for the country.

It is now history that Ali sensationally won back his title by knocking out Foreman in the eighth round in October 1974 with his 'rope-a-dope' tactics. From that day on, King would be the dominant force in world boxing, whether people liked it or not – and many didn't because of the Don's criminal background. The US fight fraternity thought that the bad old days of undesirable elements blackening the sport had gone forever. Not so.

In his promotional career, King would face fraud charges and accusations of tax evasion and would seem to be constantly engaged in some form of litigation, either against rival promoters or by boxers who claimed he had ripped them off. Former world heavyweight champion Mike Tyson claimed King cheated him out of $100 million over a ten-year period. Tim Witherspoon, another former heavyweight champion, successfully sued King for back purses owed him and ultimately settled for a sizeable out-of-court figure.

Larry Holmes, another ex-heavyweight champion, admitted he received only about 45 per cent of his purses over the course of his career with King as his manager and promoter. Holmes did concede, however, that without King, he might have been a nobody. Earnie Shavers, a top contender also managed and promoted by King, said that in some of his fights he got only a few thousand dollars of his promised earnings.

In 1977, scandal reared its ugly head like some serpent coming out of the sea when King teamed up with the ABC television network and the prestigious *Ring* magazine, known as the 'Bible of Boxing', to launch the United States Boxing Championships. Native titles had been dormant for years. Besides the heavyweight title held by Ali, all the world championships at the time were held by boxers from either South or Central America. The US was being pushed off the world boxing map, and Don King promised that these new championships would change all that.

Ring magazine, founded in 1922 by Nat Fleischer, former New York sports editor and boxing buff, would give the tournament instant credibility. More importantly, King would use its monthly boxing ratings as a gateway for boxers to qualify for the tournament, which would be spread over several months.

From the outside, it seemed like a wonderful enterprise when explained by King at a packed media conference, and there was unanimous approval by the press and television that the championships were something that were very badly needed. The participants in eight weight classes would get national television exposure, receive unprecedented pay cheques provided by the network and get the kind of publicity afforded champions and contenders of other countries where national titles were – and still are – seriously regarded. 'This kind of publicity will help American boxers get world title bouts,' declared King.

He would later acknowledge that, 'Ring magazine was the heart of the tournament. I needed their reputation, their ratings and their sanction to give validity and authority to the tournament.' King also agreed to pay $20,000 each to boxing managers Al Braverman and Paddy Flood to serve as consultants in the organisation and administration of the tournament.

Nine months before the tournament began, King gave Johnny Ort, an assistant editor of Ring and the man who controlled the ratings, £2,000 in cash. Later in the year, he handed him an extra $3,000 and sent an initial $10,000 cheque to the magazine 'to alleviate expenses incurred in preparing the ratings of the many boxers that will participate in the tournament'.

It later transpired that Ring was paid $70,000 for their ratings services. At that time, the magazine was under the editorship of Nat Loubet, formerly an assistant editor who had succeeded Fleischer when he died in 1972. Ort compiled records for the magazine from a mass of information that he received from all over the world and was considered the leading statistician in his particular field. He was meticulous in his record-keeping operation, and Ring's monthly ratings were long regarded as the most authentic in the boxing world.

King also approached James A. Farley, jun., chairman of the New York State Athletic Commission and son of James A. Farley, who was campaign manager for President Roosevelt in the 1930s and himself a former NYSAC commissioner. Farley, jun., had an annual salary of $82,950 plus generous expenses. King got his agreement to be supervisor of the tournament in exchange for expenses and travel reimbursements. As it happened, none of the cards took place in New York, the only state where Farley had any jurisdiction.

US fight fans expected to see the country's best boxers battling it out for supremacy, but it did not work out quite like that. It soon became apparent that only King-connected boxers were winning decisions and that records supplied by some managers for the purpose of making matches were false.

One particular manager, Henry Groom, later admitted that he added four victories to his featherweight Richard Rozelle's record to make him twelve wins and no losses, three wins to lightweight Greg Coverson giving him another 12–0 record, three to light-heavy Marvin Johnson to make it 16–0 and five to lightweight Len Mayweather for a 16–0 tally.

Instead of seeing top names like Muhammad Ali, George Foreman and Earnie Shavers, who all had to keep out because of their stature, television viewers were watching unheard-of boxers and hopeful wannabes. And that was only in the heavyweight division. In the other weights, just about anybody was eligible. It seemed that if you could push your fists into boxing gloves, you were a contender.

There were good fights and bad fights, but the general impression among knowledgeable boxing fans was that the television people were wasting the precious time of boxers who hardly even merited main-event status at small New York fight clubs like Sunnyside Garden. At the same time, many ordinary boxers, who were usually getting $300 to $1,000 in their previous bouts, were suddenly laughing all the way to their banks with fat cheques.

A rival tournament soon got in on the act, sponsored by World Television Champions Incorporated and headed by businessman Hank A. Schwartz and matchmaker Don Elbaum. The World Television Championships came up with its own roster of American talent, although some boxers, as happened with the King tournament, opted out because they were too big for the money and honours being offered. It became obvious that chaos would soon come about.

As it was, viewers were becoming tired, disgusted and suspicious by the standard of fights, which were a plethora of mismatches and bouts between unknown novices. They wondered how the boxers were getting in on the act, who was hiring them and how some of them managed to find their way into the US ratings.

They came to the conclusion that the network people were being conned by boxing hustlers who reckoned that anything goes when it came to the fight business, especially as there was no federal commission around to regulate policies, punish violators or settle grievances. Even many top US boxing writers and columnists admitted they were finding it embarrassing to write about some of the alleged fights perpetrated by the two networks, with most of the criticism levelled at the so-called United States Boxing Championships. 'The stench gets stronger by the week,' wrote Gary Deeb in the *Chicago Tribune*. 'The outraged cries of injustice grow louder. And yet ABC, the undisputed worldwide champion of television sports, seems oblivious to the cruel standard being perpetrated. As things now stand, the United States Boxing Championships may well set boxing back 20 years – to the days when the government stepped in and uncovered a series of scandals that nearly killed boxing.'

According to Deeb, most of the $2 million in ABC prize money was going to King, his pals and boxers under their control. Some boxers who said they wanted to get into the championships, which meant good paydays and television exposure, were told they would have to give back a part of their purses or else get rid of their existing managers and turn their careers over to King.

George Kanter, a representative of foreign boxers for many years, admitted later that when he got Texas featherweight Kenny Weldon into the tournament and secured him a fight for $7,500, he had to deduct $2,300 from the purse money to get him sanctioned. Kanter subsequently returned the money to the boxer.

Texan middleweight Ike Fluellen, who also doubled as a police officer in Houston, got a call from Chris Cline, a Maryland promoter and a friend of the ratings editor Johnny Ort, to know if he wanted to be in the championships. According to the *Washington Post*, Fluellen said he did not see how he could because he had not boxed for nearly two years, he was ring rusty and basically retired. Cline, however, told him he could get him rated in *Ring* magazine's top ten rankings but only if he agreed that Cline could manage him and paid the manager a booking fee.

'What had I got to lose?' Fluellen later said. 'Cline said getting into the tournament meant big money. I was a middleweight, but I managed to get down to junior middleweight, and I found myself rated number three in the US and twelfth in the world by *Ring* magazine, despite my long inactivity. Almost immediately I got a call from Don King inviting me into the tournament.'

As it happened, Fluellen never got that far. Amid unconfirmed rumours that the boxer was claiming he was being short-changed, he suddenly found he was out of the tournament. The reason given by King was that 'he had been idle for over a year and a half', even though *Ring* had him rated in their top ten.

An angry Fluellen, who had been training for months, then went to Jeff Ruhe, assistant to ABC president Roone Arledge, and told him the whole story of his involvement with Cline and Ort. Fluellen signed an affidavit which was subsequently turned over to the federal grand jury in Baltimore.

Among the top men excluded from the championships was Marvelous Marvin Hagler, at the time the uncrowned middleweight champion of the world. His co-manager, Goody Petronelli, wrote to King and ABC to plead his boxer's case, but Petronelli was told he would have to sign over Hagler's contract to King. Petronelli refused, preferring to go his own way. Hagler won the title in September 1980, and Petronelli never allowed King to promote even one of the champion's 13 defences.

It was a 27-year-old New York City boxing nut named Malcolm Gordon who first exposed the championships as a fraud and sham. Malcolm, known as 'Flash Gordon' after the comic-strip hero, was a recluse who lived in a cramped apartment in the Queens district and ran his own newsletter which he sold to subscribers for 35 cents.

Flash kept accurate records of boxers and had lots of contacts in the city's gyms. He soon discovered, however, that many of the records of the boxers in Don King's tournaments were invented and a lot of the names pure fiction. Others had long losing streaks and many were not even listed in the *Ring Record Book*. He referred to certain people involved in the tournament as conmen, extortionists, crooks and wheeler-dealers.

Nevertheless, King pressed on, with the support of ABC, though some of their executives became concerned about the bad publicity the event was attracting. The first card, in January 1977, was held on the deck of the battleship USS *Lexington* in Pensacola, Florida, against a colourful visual backdrop of sailors and the blue sea. Unfortunately, the action in the ring was less impressive, the fights being undistinguished.

The second tournament, a month later, was staged at the US Naval Academy in Annapolis, Maryland. Like the first card, it was on federal property, outside the reach of any local boxing commission, with King picking the judges and referees.

That tournament ended in controversy and chaos when, in a heavyweight fight, Scott LeDoux clearly outfought Johnny Boudreaux, a member of the King stable, but did not get the decision. LeDoux lost control of his emotions and tried to kick his opponent but instead kicked the toupee off ringside-commentator Howard Cosell's head on live TV. When the embarrassed Cosell retrieved his hairpiece, he put it on backwards.

When he got it right, he did a very professional interview with the still angry LeDoux, who told the national audience that the whole tournament was fixed to favour boxers tied up with King. Cosell then interviewed King, who said LeDoux's views were 'absurd' and that 'every precaution was taken to make sure the tournament was open, honest competition'. It was, however, LeDoux's sincere anguish on live television that brought the tournament's shady background out into the open. A much bigger public now knew all about the allegations of rigged results and conflicts of interest. National boxing writers and TV were spotlighting the situation.

Still the championships went on. The third card was staged in

March 1977 at Marion prison in Ohio, which was, ironically, where King had served his time. The audience consisted of 1,300 armed robbers, rapists and murderers. It was another fiasco with dull fights. Mike Jacobson described the programme in the New York newspaper the *Village Voice* as 'a bunch of smelly mismatches and slow waltzes, causing one guy to yell, "Hurry up, I've only got 20 years."'

The tournament continued in Texas at the Randolph Air Force Base near San Antonio later in March, and throughout April at other venues in San Antonio and Miami Beach. Pressure on ABC to pull out was now mounting day by day, including the screening of an investigative programme on the rival CBS network which exposed the phony fights, padded records and rigged admissions of the tournament.

New York Governor Hugh Carey finally ordered an investigation into the whole bizarre affair, requesting an explanation. There were persistent rumours that State Athletic Commissioner Farley would be shafted to another post and replaced by the retired former world light-heavyweight champion José Torres, but Farley got there first and handed in his resignation.

With further resignations and sackings being undertaken, as well as official probes being instigated, ABC suspended the tournament three hours before a Miami card was to feature a heavyweight bout between contender Larry Holmes, one of the few good boxers in the championships, and Stan Ward, both of whom were managed by King. The network said that they had official proof that a number of boxers had doctored records.

Later, ABC officially confirmed that they were terminating the telecasts of the tournament because 'some of the records were inaccurate and contain many fights which apparently never took place'. The public now had conclusive evidence of blatant favouritism, proof of kickbacks, doctored records and indiscriminate matchmaking with top names placed against stiffs. Around the same time, King announced the end of the championships after just six cards.

Ring magazine editor Nat Loubet admitted he had published inaccurate records but claimed the magazine was the unknowing victim of false reports by various boxing managers. Alex Wallau, an

ABC executive, and Flash Gordon, who ran the newsletter, had earlier compared the records supplied to ABC with those in the 1977 *Ring Record Book* and found a great many discrepancies. They got hold of the 1975 *Ring Record Book*, compared it with the 1977 edition and uncovered fictitious fights listed as taking place in 1975: ones that were not in the 1976 book but were in the 1977 edition. The 1977 book contained five fake one-round knockouts in Biff Cline's record, four fictional wins for Richard Rozelle, two phony victories for Pat Dolan, four fake knockouts for Anthony House and two imaginary wins in Mexico for the retired Ike Fluellen. Johnny Baldwin had one fake win in Mexico, and Hilbert Stevenson had four fictional victories.

Soon after the championships collapsed like a house of cards, ABC announced they were launching an independent investigation into the scandal conducted by the law firm of Barrett, Smith, Shapiro and Armstrong. The Armstrong Investigation, as the enquiry became known, was conducted under the guidance of Michael Armstrong, the firm's chief litigator. Armstrong, who had earned his reputation a few years earlier when he was chief counsel to the Knapp Commission investigating police corruption, said he found 'no criminal conduct' but did find 'a good deal of unethical behaviour by individuals involved in the administration of the tournament'.

Eighty-three irregularities were probed. More than 200 people were interviewed by the investigators, not excluding telephone interviews with several state boxing commission officials and local writers in an attempt to verify boxers' records.

The investigators – comprising three of the firm's partners, seven associates, five law students, one paralegal and a detective – acknowledged that they were hampered by a lack of subpoena power and the inability to compel testimony under oath. They persevered and eventually submitted their findings to the network in the form of a voluminous internal document consisting of a 133-page statement of facts, a 327-page report and 119 exhibits.

Armstrong conceded that several key people refused to talk to them or produce relevant records. Some baulked at supplying specific information because they felt that making allegations against King,

Ring magazine and others would affect their ability to make a living from boxing. The investigators found that ABC was not guilty of any wrongdoing and could not be characterised as being grossly negligent in any way.

As for King, the report stated that his $5,000 cash payment to *Ring* ratings editor Johnny Ort 'seriously compromised the integrity of the selection process'. The report also made it clear that Ort admitted receiving money from managers whose boxers got into the tournament. The report did not hold King responsible for any of the documented kickbacks paid to get boxers into the championships, or the bribing of *Ring* magazine, or the blacklisting of boxers who wanted to remain free agents. Essentially, the report said that everything went wrong but nobody violated any laws.

Not for the first time, and certainly not the last, King managed to get off the hook. The scandal sent out the warning, nevertheless, that the promoter was not a man to be trusted. But inside a few months he bounced back with seemingly greater enthusiasm than ever.

King started doing business once more with ABC, the same network that had vowed never to have anything to do with him again. He also put on shows for Home Box Office (HBO) and the hotel casinos of Las Vegas and Atlantic City, looking none the worse for wear from the bad publicity he had received from the disastrous and best forgotten United States Boxing Championships. No wonder people in the fight game today call him boxing's Houdini.

Meanwhile, the furore and adverse publicity created by the championships not unnaturally had a detrimental effect on the World Television Championships, which were running at the same time on the WNEW network. Not that the WTC tournament was free of controversy itself. It transpired that president Hank Schwartz and matchmaker Don Elbaum had five state commissioners on their payroll as advisors. Bill Brennan, Emile Brunea, David Ott, Van Nixon and Bobby Lee received expenses and $250 fees for meeting to 'coordinate the tournament with local commission rules', a statement that did not make much sense to boxing writers when they read it in a press release.

Not surprisingly, WNEW pulled the plug after three shows

because the derogatory media attention given to the United States Boxing Championships had scared off potential advertising sponsors. Many people felt that there were other reasons, too. The shows were certainly poor draws, with weak talent on display generally, and the only advertisement on their three cards was one of Muhammad Ali demonstrating his rope-a-dope act with a skipping rope.

In 1981, only four years after the boxing championships scandal, the American fight scene was rocked by more shame, this time involving one Harold J. Smith, chairman of Muhammad Ali Professional Sports, known as MAPS. Smith, described by one boxing man as 'a likeable rascal', promoted rock concerts as well as boxing shows, but he once explained that while music gave him a buzz, the fight game generated more excitement for him.

A flamboyant character – the kind that the American boxing scene always seems to throw up – Smith lived in a plush home in the expensive Bel Air neighbourhood of Los Angeles. He owned a block of apartments, an $80,000 powerboat and two luxury cars, one a stretch limo. Money, or the lack of it, never seemed to be a problem for him.

He had set up MAPS with the intention of enticing Muhammad Ali out of retirement after 'The Greatest' had won the world heavyweight title for an unprecedented third time by outpointing Leon Spinks in September 1978 and announced he was hanging up his gloves. After that, Ali was honoured at a series of retirement dinners and public celebrations, with his weight ballooning up to 19 st. 4 lb, but it was reported that he was restless to get back into the ring. An egotist, he was said to have missed the thrill and excitement of the sport. Several promoters, including Smith, Don King, Murad Muhammad and the government of Egypt, were dangling big offers in front of him to meet unbeaten Larry Holmes, who had proven himself the best of the heavyweights around and was holder of the World Boxing Council title. Smith attempted to promote an Ali–Holmes fight under the MAPS banner, and although the organisation carried Ali's name, the former champion was only paid a fee for the lease of it. He was not part of MAPS and was under no obligation to fight for them.

Smith arrived in downtown Easton, Pennsylvania, where Holmes had property, and met with the boxer and his lawyer Charles Spaziani in Holmes's office. Smith placed two cheques on the desk, each for $500,000, drawn on the Wells Fargo Bank of California. 'If they don't clear, we don't have a deal,' he said. 'What have you got to lose?' Before Holmes could give him an answer, Smith brought out an old leather case and showed the boxer what he said was $1 million in cash. The case was full of old bills – 100s, 50s and 20s. Holmes and Spaziani just kept staring at the money and were speechless. 'The million is yours if you agree to the fight,' said Smith.

A few minutes later, Don King's limo screeched to a halt outside. King had heard about the Smith deal and was not going to be out-hustled by his rival. King walked in and the two promoters started talking. Soon they were issuing threats, then cursing each other, with King screaming that Smith's was 'drug money'. Smith said that he had investors who were oil millionaires in the Middle East.

They argued and argued, but in the end, Holmes refused the million in cash and the million in Wells Fargo cheques. He was nervous about the origins of the funds and did not like the way Smith seemed to be throwing money around. Besides, Holmes was a friend of King, who had promoted some of his important fights. He felt obligated to the Don, a situation that would change drastically and dramatically within three years when Holmes would charge King with short-changing him after two big fights. King would go on to promote the Holmes v. Ali title fight in October 1980, won easily by Holmes in 11 rounds.

A disappointed Smith left the meeting saying, 'The money is still good, and it's always out there for you, Larry.' Neither would prove to be the case, as things turned out. Smith was philosophical about losing the Ali–Holmes fight. After all, there were others out there. He had signed up many top boxers and outstanding prospects by offering them astronomical purses, and he was responsible for securing world title fights for Thomas 'Hit Man' Hearns, Aaron Pryor, Jeff Chandler, Holmer Kenty and Leo Randolph. He was indeed a major player in the fight game.

Towards the end of 1980, word got around that Smith was planning a spectacular show at Madison Square Garden in the new year. Sure enough, the big tournament was scheduled for 23 February and would feature no fewer than three world title fights: Thomas Hearns against Wilfred Benitez at welter, Saad Muhammad v. Eddie Mustafa Muhammad at light-heavy and Wilfredo Gomez meeting Mike Ayala at bantamweight. They would be supported by a heavyweight bout between top contenders Ken Norton and Gerry Cooney, with the winner going in against World Boxing Council champion Larry Holmes.

All said, it was a truly spectacular bill, labelled 'This Is It'. MAPS' co-promoter would be Tiffany Promotions, a New York-based organisation run by businessman Sam Glass. Boxing insiders agreed that MAPS was opening up a new era for boxing, with plenty of world title action, lots of new faces and plenty of money going around for the boxers.

For over a year, MAPS had been doling out a seemingly endless supply of money to co-promoters and boxers. Purses skyrocketed to astronomical levels, and champions would not lace on the gloves for less than $1 million. Nevertheless, there were unconfirmed reports that MAPS shows were losing hundreds of thousands of dollars, and rumours were rampant as to the source of the money supply.

Plans for the This Is It promotion, however, were running smoothly, until two weeks before the scheduled date when it was announced that the Los Angeles branch of the FBI was probing an alleged scam. It was investigating the transfer of large amounts of money – estimates put it 'in the millions' – between accounts at two branches of the Wells Fargo National Bank in Beverly Hills and Santa Monica. At the centre of the probe was Harold J. Smith.

The FBI seized records from MAPS offices and discovered that funds from an organisation known as the Muhammad Ali Youth Athletic Association, which was part of the MAPS operation, was transferred into a business account that cheques were then drawn on. Little by little, the story of how Smith embezzled the money emerged. He had accomplices: a couple of assistant managers in Wells Fargo branches who made the scam work. Originally, Smith had used his connection with Ali and had introduced him to the accomplices to get them to trust him and to eventually cover a few of his cheques. These bank officials obviously knew how the Wells Fargo central computer system worked. It turned out that there was about a week's delay before cheques bounced, and they set up new accounts for Smith. This went on for more than a year. Smith had planned to catch up on his 'borrowed' funds with a big payoff from his promotions and return the money before it was missed. He was caught out when a small cheque was misdated and caused the bank to check on the account. Suspicious, they alerted the FBI, but nobody knew at that stage exactly how much money was involved. 'Talks with law enforcement officials, former Wells Fargo officers and rival bankers led to the conclusion,' the *Wall Street Journal* reported, 'that the fraud couldn't have continued as long as it did had it not been for flaws in the bank's internal auditing and operating controls.'

Not surprisingly, Smith was not at the MAPS office when the FBI officers called, nor did anyone know of his whereabouts. Madison Square Garden officials said they could not get in touch with him, although they were reluctant to rush into cancelling the show as MAPS was committed to paying out a total of $8 million in purses to the main event boxers.

With the promoter still missing, one report stated that Smith was 'armed and dangerous', but this proved to be erroneous and was promptly corrected. He was simply a man on the run. Then one day, a man claiming to be Smith telephoned a Los Angeles radio talk show to say he was just a 'pigeon' in a massive fraud scheme involving Wells Fargo officers. The caller said he had gone to Switzerland and was now back in Los Angeles because his wife and son 'were not in a safe place'. He went on to say, 'I had to do it this way. We're not talking about $21 million. There's over $200–300 million involved, and we were used as stool pigeons.' The caller claimed he had learned that thirty-five bank officials and twenty Wells Fargo branches were involved in an embezzlement scheme that had been going on for eight or nine years. 'The bank,' he said, 'put $21,305,105.18 to the very penny in our account.' He also claimed that MAPS had been under the impression that this was to serve as a line of credit.

Meanwhile, Smith's promoting partner Sam Glass was making a determined effort to salvage the Garden show and was trying to get the boxers and their managers to agree on purse reductions. Some did agree, but Glass said that 'a happy medium' could not be reached in view of the extravagance of the original purses. There was no choice but to cancel.

Garden officials made refunds of ticket sales which totalled over $700,000, though John Condon, their director of boxing, pointed out that the Garden was to have merely been the site, and it was not connected with the running of the promotion.

Ali issued a statement through his lawyers that he was withdrawing permission for MAPS to use his name. It was not a hasty decision. He said that his legal team had become concerned when the organisation got bigger and bigger, despite losing money on promotions. 'We wondered how things were happening,' he recalled later. 'We could never get the books to audit the figures.'

When the scandal broke, Garden matchmaker Gil Clancy said, 'It's all been unrealistic, the money they have been paying. The Garden just couldn't compete. No one could compete. Now we will all have to go back to basics.' Angelo Dundee, Ali's long-time trainer, commented, 'It was great while it lasted, and I'm just glad the kids were able to get the money while it was going.'

Smith was convicted of embezzling $21.3 million from Wells Fargo and sentenced to ten years in federal prison, with a $30,000 fine and three thousand hours of community service. He served five years. However, there were more twists to the story. For a start, Harold J. Smith was not Harold J. Smith at all. His real name was Ross Fields, and it was as Fields that he had been a member of a university mile relay team in the 1960s, winning an indoor title. Soon after, he dropped out of college and somehow persuaded the entertainer Sammy Davis Jr., a member of the Rat Pack, to allow him to use his name in conjunction with a disco that Smith, or Fields, ran in Washington, DC. It was there that he began writing bad cheques, enough of them so that by 1976 he and the woman living with him as his wife were on an FBI wanted poster charged with using 'interstate fraudulent cheques'. Authorities later claimed that he left a trail of around 100 bogus cheques through 30 different states. By growing a beard, putting on over 3 st. in weight and changing his name to Harold J. Smith, Fields adopted a new life in Los Angeles.

Many boxers benefited from being handsomely paid for their fights, but the spin-off clearly hurt the sport and added more ammunition to the charges by boxing's critics that the game was littered with crooks and undercover men. '[The] MAPS scandal puts US boxing on the floor,' said a top-of-the-page headline in the British weekly *Boxing News*.

Smith, or Fields, made a lot of enemies but one of them was not Larry Holmes. 'Funny thing, his heart was in the right place,' recalled the former world heavyweight champion. 'He wanted to unify the titles in each weight class and kill the governing bodies with their corrupt ratings and political skulduggery. He wanted a panel of forthright boxing people to rank the boxers so that they got title shots on merit and not the usual backroom manoeuvres. It wasn't to be.' The jail term did not sever Smith's connection with boxing. He would gain more headlines in 1993 by taking Ali and around 120 guests to Beijing for the first ever professional boxing tournament in China.

Hardly had the stench of the MAPS crime and the shame of the United States Boxing Championships – both of which did the sport almost irreparable damage – died away than boxing was rocked by yet another scandal. This one became known as 'The Mysterious Case of the Cut Gloves', a title which could well have been used for a thriller by the likes of John Grisham, Sidney Sheldon, Patricia Cornwell or any other crime novelist. Only this one, sadly, happened to be a true story.

The fight was at Madison Square Garden on 16 June 1983. It was in the light-middleweight division – or junior middle as it is sometimes referred to – between Billy Collins Jr., a promising prospect from Nashville, Tennessee, and unbeaten in 14 fights, and Luis Resto, a rugged Puerto Rican boxing out of New York. A scheduled ten-rounder, it was chief support to Davey Moore's defence of his World Boxing Association light-middleweight title against Roberto Duran, the talented Panamanian. Duran, billed as 'Hands of Stone', was favoured to win and become the seventh man in history to take world titles at three different weights. There was no surprise in store for the capacity crowd of 20,061 as they watched Duran pound his way to victory in the eighth round, the New York boxer stumbling around the ring in a defenceless state before referee Ernesto Magana threw his arms around Moore and took him to the sanctuary of his corner.

The Collins–Resto fight was equally one-sided, although the result did not go according to plan, or at least not the plan of Collins's handlers and promoter Bob Arum. They envisaged Collins, 21, being promoted to national television overnight. Resto was merely an 'opponent' brought along to give Collins, who had Irish lineage, a good test and nothing more. Resto, however, shattered those dreams by soundly beating the favourite. Normally a light hitter, he was always the aggressor in the fight, warding off or blocking the hard punches Collins threw and retaliating with blurring flurries and combination punching from start to finish.

Resto staggered the Tennessee boxer over and over again and inflicted severe facial damage, with ugly cuts and swellings under and over both eyes, which became mere slits. His left cheekbone was also gashed. 'Every time he hits me, it feels like he's throwing rocks,' Collins said to his father Billy Collins, sen., who was in his corner.

Collins, sen., a top welterweight in the 1950s who both managed and trained his son, winced every time Billy suffered another sickening blow. At one time he turned to a cornerman and remarked, 'There's something fishy about all this. Resto is not that hard a puncher.'

The decision was unanimous, and when Resto crossed the ring to console the loser in an ironic gesture of good sportsmanship, he extended his gloves to Collins, sen., who was within reach. Suddenly, the elder Collins grabbed hold of the gloves and said, 'Hey, just as I thought. No wonder my boy is so busted up.' He held on to Resto's gloved hands and shouted for the New York State Athletic Commission inspectors. 'All I feel are knuckles and fingers,' he barked to John Squeri, the chief inspector, who had hurriedly climbed into the ring. 'No padding at all. Don't let those gloves get out of your sight.'

Squeri made sure the Puerto Rican did not remove his gloves in the ring and he accompanied Resto, with Collins, sen., alongside, back to Resto's dressing-room. To make sure there would not be any trouble, Squeri told Carlos 'Panama' Lewis, Resto's manager and chief second, 'There's nothing wrong, but I've got to have those gloves.'

The inspector turned the gloves over to commission chairman Jack Prenderville, who had been at ringside. Prenderville discovered that the gloves had been cut and much of the padding removed and, in one of his last decisions before being replaced, ordered a full investigation, over the loud protests of Lewis and his cornerman Pedro Alvardo. 'All I do is train fighters,' said Lewis, protesting his innocence. 'When you have the best fighter in the world and you have to lose him, it's impossible. Especially when you didn't do anything wrong. I've got to fight this.' Resto became branded for the rest of his life as 'Rockfist Resto'.

'My son could have gotten killed,' said Collins, sen. 'This was worse than a mugger getting you on the street with a baseball bat.' The gloves were sent to the manufacturers Everlast and then to the New York State Police Laboratory, and both of their verdicts were that they had been tampered with.

Thirteen days after the fight, the commission met with all the relevant people involved. Everlast vice-president John Towns said a considerable amount of stuffing, about half the regulation quantity, had been removed from the gloves, and a microscopic examination showed that two slits had been made by a sharp instrument. The gloves had weighed the regulation eight ounces when they left the company, and then after being dried out after the fight, were two ounces lighter.

All the principals gave evidence, but Resto's people denied any wrongdoing, with Lewis and cornerman Alvardo both claiming that the hearing was 'a witchhunt'. Two commission inspectors who were supposed to have supervised Resto putting on the gloves in his dressing-room were not present at the hearing. In the murkiness of conflicting testimony, only one fact was established: the gloves arrived at the Garden in mint condition and were found to be tampered with at the end of the fight. The evidence of what happened in between was less clear.

The commission looked at all the circumstantial evidence and ruled that Lewis 'failed to fulfil his responsibilities' as Resto's chief second. They suspended Lewis for life and the boxer for a year. Lewis's lawyer Charles Simpson, of the prestigious Manhattan firm of Shea and Gould, agreed it was a serious charge. 'If he's guilty, he shouldn't be allowed in anyone's corner,' he pointed out. 'But if he's not guilty, and there appears to be insufficient evidence here, this is a harsh punishment.' Criminal charges were also made, and both Lewis and Resto were convicted in the New York Supreme Court in 1986 and sentenced to a term of imprisonment of three to six years. Both served over two years, and Resto, disgusted with the fight game, never fought again.

'As long as a fighter's hands are taped,' wrote Michael Katz in *Ring* magazine, 'removing padding from gloves is about the same as adding, well, horseshoes. Some other tricks might be called sly. This was slimy.' Katz also criticised the New York Commission for being too lax in not only checking the gloves before the fight but in their whole operation. He also cited a card in Ridgewood Grove, New York, shortly before the Resto–Collins fight when one boxer wore 16-oz training gloves while his opponent wore regulation 8-oz gloves.

When veteran trainer and legendary boxing figure Ray Arcel, who had given Lewis some cornerwork in the past, heard about the Resto scandal, he said, 'I am astounded but the padding didn't come out by itself. I'm sorry for the guy. I never dreamed he could do something like this. Otherwise I'd never have let him in the corner. He never gave me any indication he was an individual who could do something like that.

'I've been in boxing a long time, and I can't think back to any incident where somebody would have taken horsehair out of a glove. It's the lowest form of anything I can think of. Wait, there was another time when I was working a corner in Jersey City right after the First World War. I went over to the opposite corner and asked to feel the gloves. The guy stuck out his left hand and I said, "No, let me see the other one." He had a rivet in there. I said to the guy, "Are you crazy? This is a felonious assault.'" Arcel was surprised that there was nobody in Collins's camp present when Resto put on the gloves in the dressing-room. 'You holler before, not after,' he said. 'Some of these guys go haywire. I was around guys who taught me. You can't trust anybody because everybody's out to win.'

Lewis returned to boxing on his release and resumed as a trainer, still insisting he was innocent of any wrongdoing. 'I don't know where the tampering was done or who did it,' he said. 'I just know that I didn't do it.'

The biggest loser in the whole shabby affair was Collins, sen. Collins Jr. was killed in Nashville less than a year later when the truck he was driving left the road and landed in a creek. The official verdict was accidental death, but Collins, sen., was convinced it was suicide. He said that his son had been depressed and had turned to drink, his promising career having ended on the night of shame against Resto. He had also been suffering from permanently impaired vision since the fight.

The New York State Athletic Commission, to their credit, later changed the verdict to a no-decision, but the stench remained. The sordid affair brought boxing back to the gutter once again.

Before the Resto scandal, Lewis had earned a good reputation as a trainer when he worked with Roberto Duran. His reputation suffered, however, and he became known as one of boxing's craftiest operators when undefeated Aaron Pryor, known as 'The Hawk', defended his World Boxing Association light-welterweight title against the Nicaraguan contender Alexis Arguello in Miami in November 1982.

Pryor, from Cincinnati, Ohio, won in the 14th round of a thriller, considered by many as the fight of the decade. However, between the 13th and 14th rounds, the TV microphone picked up Lewis saying, 'Give me that bottle, the one I mixed.' Pryor went on to stop Arguello in the 14th and left people wondering forever what Lewis had put in that water bottle.

Officials of the local commission, who forgot to bring a bell to the Orange Bowl arena that night, did not take any urine tests afterwards. Lewis said it was Perrier water mixed with tap water, but nobody could be certain. Artie Curley, one of the most respected cut men in the business, worked with Lewis that night. Shortly after the fight, when the bottle incident became an issue, Curley reported that Lewis had merely added some peppermint schnapps to help settle Pryor's stomach. One official said he heard Pryor belch during the fight. There was an enquiry but nothing happened, and the incident quickly passed away because there was no victim. Cheating perhaps, but no victim. Yet it was enough for people in boxing to remember Lewis and to point an accusing finger at him, recalling the Collins–Resto debacle.

Sadly, within two years of the bottle incident, Pryor tragically hit the downward path. After knocking out Arguello in ten rounds in a 1983 rematch, another thriller, he became a drug addict. Although he continued his boxing career at the top level, he was in a drug hell by 1984 and during an altercation in Miami he was shot by a Jamaican cocaine dealer.

Pryor fought on and off before retiring from the ring with a detached retina in 1990, the year his third marriage broke up after less than 12 months. The man once tipped for greatness was jailed for drug abuse in 1991, though he managed to kick his addiction and became a respected trainer and church deacon in his home town of Cincinnati.

His fans remembered him, too. With the help of boxing writers, they were instrumental in getting him inducted into the International Boxing Hall of Fame in Canastota, New York, in 1996. In an interview in 1997, he lamented on his once-promising career: 'I lost everything but the most important thing – my life.'

3

GENTLEMAN JIM AND THE SAILOR

Bribery and corruption have always been the bane of boxing, and despite stricter and tighter control today, illegal practices, including fight fixing, continue to seep in from time to time. However, the sport has come a long way from the dark days of the past, though the very nature of boxing will always ensure, unfortunately, that its shady side will never be completely eliminated.

Fixed fights, even if they are rare today, have nevertheless been an integral part of boxing since the old bare-knuckle days, particularly in the latter part of the eighteenth century when the sport was in decline and the reward for 'straight' fights had practically disappeared. Given the amounts which were put up, or staked to use the term of the period, it was always worthwhile for a boxer to oblige a gambler in return for a slice of his winnings.

Crookedness was rife in that period, most notably following the retirement of Jack Broughton, a clean-living English pugilist who stood for honesty in the sport. Broughton was recognised as the 'Father of the English School of Boxing' and his rules formed the groundwork of fair play. Adopted in August 1743, Broughton's rules barred gouging and striking a fallen opponent, although wide latitude was left for wrestling and rough-and-tumble fighting. He also had a boxing school in London and introduced gloves, or mufflers as they were called, which added to the sport's popularity. More importantly, however, the mufflers, padded with lamb's wool and horsehair and weighing around 10 oz, lessened the risk of serious facial injury to his pupils, many coming from aristocratic families.

Once Broughton departed from the scene, however, the sport fell into disrepute, with crooked fights quite common. One of the most notorious fixers was Jack Slack, 'The Norwich Butcher', who held the championship of England from 1750 to 1760. A sleazy character who not only threw fights but arranged fakes for other pugilists, Slack was also credited with introducing the 'chopper', the equivalent of today's rabbit punch, an illegal blow caused by chopping the hand onto the back of the neck.

Slack lost the championship to Bill Stephens in June 1760 in dubious circumstances. Stephens, son of a female blacksmith and consequently known as 'The Nailer', lost the title a year later to George Meggs, a relatively unknown fighter and a coal miner by trade, in a blatantly pre-arranged affair.

When approached by a supporter who had lost a large bet, Stephens exclaimed in great humour, 'Why, Lord bless you, I got 50 guineas more than I should otherwise have done by letting George beat me, and, damn it, ain't I the same man still?' The result so angered the Duke of Cumberland, who had been a keen supporter of prizefighting, that he became an enemy of the sport and its participants.

After a series of undistinguished champions and dubious fights which put the championship and the sport into further decline and shame, Peter Corcoran became the first Irishman to win the title. Yet he was no better than the rest as far as dishonesty was concerned.

Corcoran, from County Kildare, had fled Ireland after a row in which he killed a man who shared his enthusiasm for a village girl. He worked as a coalman, then went to sea and eventually settled down in London where he bought a pub. He had a reputation as a man who would fight anybody, anywhere, having once disposed of a whole gang of ruffians in a brawl. He was encouraged to try pugilism and made quick progress to enable him to challenge for the title, then held by a bar owner named Bill Darts.

They met in May 1771 in a ring pitched on Epsom racecourse in Surrey but the fight was crooked. Darts had agreed to lose in return for £100 from Corcoran's patron, Colonel O'Kelly. A notorious rogue who had risen from poverty and illiteracy in Ireland, O'Kelly had been in prison after running up gambling bills and bought himself an army commission, calling himself Colonel, sometimes Captain. He also became a successful gambler, racehorse owner and associate of the nobility by sheer cheek. O'Kelly knew no bounds in ensuring his man always won the fight and took the championship.

After about a minute of tame sparring around by both men, Corcoran landed a blow to the champion's face. Darts, with O'Kelly's money safely in his pocket, promptly surrendered, just as Corcoran knocked his opponent's head against a ring post in a moment of unnecessary violence. Cries of 'fix' and 'shame' rang around the racecourse but the result stayed. A smiling O'Kelly also picked up a small fortune in bets from disgruntled patrons.

Darts was ostracised from the sporting world. Customers no longer wanted to be seen in his tavern and he died a pauper in 1781, the year O'Kelly's horse Young Eclipse won the Derby at odds of 10–1. He would make more than £1 million from the horse.

Corcoran lost the title to Harry Sellers in Middlesex in October 1776 without putting up much of a battle, which led to suggestions that he threw the fight. Corcoran was backed at 4–1 by his many supporters, and it was said he put a considerable amount of money on Sellers, despite Harry's somewhat dubious reputation of often losing if things were going against him.

The claim that Corcoran made a fair bit of money on the result was strengthened when, within days of the fight, he had his bar premises, The Blakeney Arms in London, stacked out with every brand of liquor and had the whole premises painted inside and out. Yet only a week earlier he had been threatened with eviction because of his inability to pay the rent. Despite these improvements,

Corcoran's trade slumped, and he fell heavily into debt. He was reduced to begging on the streets and when he died in 1784, a public subscription had to be raised to meet the cost of his burial.

The sport went into decline in the early 1800s, an era which became known as the 'Dark Age of Pugilism'. Prizefighting was very much frowned upon by the authorities. Disqualifications were common as men toiled for hours, often manipulating the rules by dropping when tapped or cuffed simply to get out of tough situations or when they wanted a rest.

In the US, which lagged behind in the development of the sport, those who were handy with their fists were likely to take the boat to England where a market for their special wares was known to exist, despite the slump in the sport's popularity. In ports like Boston, New York and Philadelphia, pugnacious British sailors were not unknown, and international brawling along the waterfront was common enough. There was practically no organised prizefighting as such. In any event, such combat was illegal, and the infrequent matches were hidden from the authorities in the back rooms of drinking places or private clubs, with only a handful of spectators present. Even then, they often had to look over their shoulders in case of raids, which were frequent.

Back in England, with bare-knuckle fighting declining rapidly, things were about to change dramatically. In April 1866, John Sholto Douglas, 8th Marquess of Queensberry, sponsored an amateur tournament and decreed that the contestants wear padded gloves. Within a year, the practice had spread to the professional side of the sport, now governed by what was to be termed the Queensberry Rules.

Old habits die hard, however, and for some time the old bare-knuckle and gloved codes existed side by side. It was not until the arrival on the scene of a handsome San Franciscan bank clerk named James J. Corbett that the real revolution came about. In September 1892, Corbett became the first world heavyweight champion of the gloved era when he knocked out the brawling John L. Sullivan in 21 rounds at the Olympic Club in New Orleans. A dashing, handsome man, Corbett enjoyed showing himself in full evening dress, complete with top hat, tails and silver-topped cane. He was known as 'Gentleman Jim' and attracted high society to the ringside for the first time.

Nevertheless, the advent of Corbett and the gloved age did not eliminate the skulduggery. Around the turn of the century, three major scandals within two years of each other pushed the sport back to what it had experienced in the 1700s and early 1800s. Ironically, the first two involved Corbett himself, the man who was credited with bringing respectability and credibility to the sport.

Corbett was the son of Irish emigrants who sailed for the 'New World' following the ravages of the 'Great Famine' of the 1840s when potato blight caused more than a million people to die of starvation or disease. Because of the famine and mass emigration – mainly to the US and Australia – the Irish population dramatically declined by almost two million in the ten-year period up to 1851.

Pat Corbett from County Mayo and Catherine McDonald from Dublin met in San Francisco and were married in 1858. James J. would be the sixth of their twelve children. Like most Irish families of the period, Pat and Catherine – or Kate as she was known – had visions of their son becoming a priest but it was not to be.

James J. gave up a respectable job as a bank clerk because he had one ambition – to be a boxer. Nothing else would satisfy him. As it turned out, his natural talent and unshakeable belief in himself proved he had made the right choice. He made fast progress. Stylish and upright, possessing a fast left-hand as well as fancy footwork, Corbett brought scientific boxing to a peak, and legend has it that throughout his career he never had a black eye or a bloody nose.

When James J. knocked out Sullivan he would hold the title for five years, apart from a brief period when he retired and later changed his mind. He lost the championship to England's Bob Fitzsimmons, an ex-blacksmith who had learned his boxing in Australia and New Zealand, on a knockout in 14 rounds in March 1897. Corbett demanded a return fight, but Fitzsimmons was not interested and instead toured in a two-act play specially written for him called *The Honest Blacksmith*.

Corbett returned to baseball, one of his early loves, and played for the Paterson club from New Jersey in the Atlantic League. While still waiting for Fitzsimmons to make up his mind, he accepted a fight with the tough Irish heavyweight Tom Sharkey at the Lenox Club, New York, on 22 November 1898. They had met over two years earlier in San Francisco when Sharkey gave the San Franciscan an uncomfortable evening, wrestling Corbett, who was the world champion at that time, to the floor in the third and fourth rounds. In that fight, James J. seemed unable to cope with the Irishman's bull-like rushes. The fourth round was nearly over when the chief of police, fearing the brawl would incite a rough section of the crowd, jumped into the ring and stopped the fight. The referee then declared it a draw, much to the disgust of the spectators who felt the Irishman was getting the better of it and was unlucky. A furious Sharkey, claiming he was robbed, vowed to make no mistake if he got a return fight.

Sharkey was a remarkable pugilist. He stood only 5 ft 11 in. and usually weighed no more than 12 st. 12 lb, a few pounds over the light-heavyweight limit by today's standards. However, he packed enormous strength in his powerful arms and shoulders and took the best wallops from the top heavyweights of his day without even blinking. He was known as 'Sailor Tom' because he had started his boxing career while in the US Navy. His massive chest was decorated with tattoos of a sailing ship and a large star, while his rugged face was adorned by a cauliflower left ear of which he was very proud. In his retirement years, he offered $5,000 to anyone who could restore the ear to normality. A well-known specialist agreed to do the job, but Sharkey changed his mind on the way to the surgery. 'So what?' he mused as he looked at his reflection in a shop window. 'I was a fighter, wasn't I? Why should I be ashamed of my personal souvenir?' So the misshapen ear stayed with him for the rest of his days.

Sharkey was a fearless fighter who would take on anybody, but he too was involved in his share of controversies, most notably when he fought Bob Fitzsimmons in San Francisco in 1896 in an unofficial eliminator to find a challenger for Corbett. Much to the violent objections of the Fitzsimmons camp, Sharkey and his manager Tom O'Rourke brought along their own referee, the notorious gunslinger

Wyatt Earp, who happened to be in town with some of his horses for a race meeting. Earp had been a deputy marshal in such boisterous 'Wild West' towns as Dodge City in Kansas and Tombstone in Arizona and was alleged to have shot dead ten men including his brother-in-law. It was in Tombstone that he had joined up with another gunfighter, Doc Holliday, in the famous 'Gunfight at the OK Corral'.

What his qualifications were as a boxing referee was hard to understand, but the Sharkey camp insisted it was 'Earp or nobody'. As Fitzsimmons felt he had the beating of both Sharkey and Corbett, his manager Martin Julian agreed. To nobody's surprise, the fight ended in a farce. In the eighth round, referee Earp disqualified Fitzsimmons for an alleged low blow, even though he was comfortably beating the rugged Irishman. The English camp howled 'robbery' and claimed that Sharkey and his manager had paid the gunfighter to make sure the Irishman won. The decision, nevertheless, stood. Fitzsimmons obtained a court order holding up Sharkey's end of the purse pending an investigation, but the court later decided in Sharkey's favour. Public sympathy, however, was so strong for Fitzsimmons that it was he who got the title shot with Corbett and won the championship.

Nearly two years after the Earp fiasco, Sharkey and Corbett had their long-awaited return match, and like the first fight, it would end in controversy, with allegations of crookedness and shady deals flying around like confetti at a wedding. A week before the contest, the manager of the former world middleweight champion Kid McCoy told the *New York World* that the fight was pre-arranged. W.B. Gray said he had inside information that the contest, scheduled for 20 rounds, would not last more than 12 and that Sharkey would get the decision.

When the New York fight was first announced, the odds were originally 2–1 on Corbett, but Sharkey money appeared in such large amounts as the contest approached that the odds were cut on Gentleman Jim to 10–7, 10–8, 10–9 and eventually to even money. An anonymous bet of $20,000 on Sharkey came from Chicago.

The Lenox Club was packed to capacity, and when referee

'Honest' John Kelly called the two principals to the centre of the ring for their instructions, Corbett's extra 4 in. in height and 11 lb in weight were very obvious. From the bell, Sharkey was the aggressor, rushing at Corbett and trying to force matters. Corbett, 'smiling his devilish smile at him' as the *New York World* reported, seemed content to feint his man and take things easy, conserving his energy.

In round two, Sharkey was becoming wild with his punches and after missing with a roundhouse left to the head, caught Corbett on the jaw with a right that sent the former world champion to the canvas in a sitting position. Gentleman Jim had a wide grin across his face and held on to Sharkey's leg with his left hand.

From then on, Corbett made a big improvement. In the third and fourth rounds he took the lead and attempted to wear the Irishman down by darting in and out with fast punches from both gloves. Sharkey, however, was still fighting strongly, although he looked as tired as an amateur mountain climber as he walked back to his corner at the end of the fourth.

The interval rest must have done him good, because he appeared surprisingly fresh when he answered the bell for round five. By now Corbett seemed fatigued, and the Irishman landed a stinging right that hurt. Sharkey had tremendous stamina, and he just ploughed forward with swinging punches.

Corbett led to the head at the start of the sixth, but Sharkey brushed aside any attempts by the heavier man to gain advantage, and by the seventh, Corbett seemed unable to withstand the sailor's rushes. Sharkey scored with a terrific left hook to the body and followed with a right smack on the jaw which made Corbett back away.

Sharkey was first to lead in the eighth, landing a left chop on the neck. They clinched frequently, and referee Kelly was kept busy separating them. Sharkey shook Corbett with a right to the face, but Gentleman Jim quickly replied with a left hook which grazed Sharkey's right ear. Both men were hammering away when the bell went.

There were further clinches as the ninth round opened, and Kelly had trouble parting them. Corbett landed a very low left hook, and

Sharkey complained to the referee, but Corbett said, 'Oh, go away,' to the official. The Irishman's manager, knowing the strength of his boxer, yelled, 'Pay no attention to Corbett's fouls, just get him.' Seconds later, Corbett's chief second Con McVey suddenly rushed into the ring protesting, as he would say later, at Sharkey's wild style of fighting. It was a strange claim as Corbett was the real culprit as far as the low blow was concerned. The crowd started shouting 'Foul, foul' as nobody apart from the boxers and the referee are allowed in the ring during a contest. With the angry fans demanding that Corbett be disqualified for contravention of the rules, the referee ordered both men to their corners. He told announcer Charlie Harvey to inform the crowd that Corbett had been disqualified and that all bets were off.

Allegations of the fix which had been rumoured before the fight were now rampant. The next day, Bill McLaughlin, one of America's leading sportswriters, led the claims, and his report that appeared on the front page of all Hearst newspapers maintained that a gambling clique, which stood to gain heavily from a Sharkey win, was foiled by the referee's decision to call off bets. He wrote that while Corbett knew nothing of the deal, his chief second McVey was 'in on it'.

The *Chicago Tribune*, under headlines on page one which read 'Big Fight Ends in a Scandal, Evidence of Crookedness', wrote:

> Sharkey had clearly outfought his famous opponent, and McVey's entrance into the ring had a decidedly queer appearance. The result of the fight did not surprise those who were in a position to know the inside facts. From the day the match was made, there has been talk about a deal. The rumours have been flying thick and fast. At the ringside there was a vast amount of Sharkey money which was offered freely.

The reigning world champion Bob Fitzsimmons was in Chicago when he picked up a paper. 'What did I tell you?' he laughed to his companion. 'I knew all along it would be a fake fight.' Kid McCoy, whose manager had forecast a week earlier it was all pre-arranged, said, 'We told you so, didn't we?'

Corbett claimed he would have won the fight had it gone on. 'I did not want to win on a foul,' he said. 'Sharkey hit me low twice. I did not see McVey jump into the ring as my back was turned to him.' Later, Corbett would tell a meeting chaired by Senator Tim Sullivan – who drew up the Horton Law permitting boxing in New York – that he knew nothing of the fix allegations.

The hot-headed Sharkey told Corbett at the meeting, 'You were whipped, and you didn't have a Chinaman's chance of winning. That's why McVey came to your rescue. You needed him badly. I am not a dirty fighter. I have never lost a fight on a foul. I fought fair.'

Referee Honest John Kelly was also at the meeting, and he confirmed what he had said to pressmen after the fight: 'I stopped it because McVey jumped into the ring in violation of all the rules. I called all bets off because I believe the action of McVey was paid for by somebody who had a bet on Sharkey, and I did not propose to decide public money on a fake. I would not be party to any such fraud. Nobody can tell me McVey lost his head. He has been behind fighters for years, and there was some fraudulent deal behind his movement.'

McVey, in a letter to the *New York World*, explained his actions by saying he saw Sharkey fouling his man. 'I called out to the referee time after time in the ninth round and then I could not stand it any longer and got into the ring,' he wrote. 'I guess I lost my head, but I could not stand Jim getting fouled without making a protest.'

Hardly had the stench of the fiasco died down when Corbett was involved in another equally controversial fight, this time against Kid McCoy, arguably the most notorious conman in boxing history. McCoy was not even his real name. He was born Norman Selby in Rush County, Indiana, in October 1873 and ran away from home at the age of 18 'to seek adventure in the great big world', as he once put it.

He picked up odd jobs and travelled throughout the US under freight cars, 'riding the rods' being a popular and cheap method of getting from state to state. He wandered into boxing after reading about the big money that top boxers were earning. When he stopped off in Louisville, Kentucky, one day, he joined the local Young Men's

Christian Association, a recreational club known as the YMCA. It was there that he learned the rudiments of the noble art. He also changed his identity, borrowing the name Kid McCoy from a burglar character he had read about in a popular novel. He showed a natural aptitude for the sport, boxed all over the world and is credited with popularising boxing in England, France and South Africa.

McCoy is also acknowledged to have introduced a new blow in boxing: the corkscrew punch, a looping left which finished with the turning of the wrist on impact. This was subsequently developed into what we now know as the left hook. But he would resort to any trick, fair or otherwise, to attain victory, which was surprising as he was a very talented ringman who could win on his own abilities. He was also known to take dives at regular intervals, betting on his opponents and collecting big pay outs afterwards.

He often changed his name, too, masquerading as a third-rate fighter to hide his true identity and so give himself an advantage over the man he was facing. This cunning device prompted sportswriters of the day to wonder whether or not they were seeing 'the real McCoy', a possible origin for the well-known phrase used to indicate whether something or somebody is the genuine article. 'Let the suckers have the glory,' he used to say with a smirk creasing his face. 'I'll take the dough.' Another popular ploy of McCoy's would be to divert an opponent's attention for a split second during a fight with one of his tricks and then take full advantage.

His most famous, or infamous, ruse was when he conned world welterweight champion Tommy Ryan into a fight in Long Island, New York, in March 1896. The fight was effectively for the world middleweight title, vacant following the decision of champion Bob Fitzsimmons to move up and campaign as a heavyweight. The light-heavyweight division would not be created until 1903. Ryan was having trouble making the welterweight limit anyway, although he continued to hold on to the title, and he agreed to meet McCoy in a fight to be recognised as being for the world middleweight championship.

McCoy turned up at Ryan's training camp one day, his powdered face as white as snow, his back stooped and with a wheezing cough preventing him from talking for any length of time. He told Ryan in hushed tones and in between coughs that he was suffering from consumption and that he desperately needed the money for medical bills. Ryan took pity on him and agreed to the match. 'I'll take it easy on you, Kid,' he said. 'You've nothing to worry about.' It turned out to be the greatest mistake of his boxing life.

When McCoy climbed into the ring on the night of the fight, Ryan's jaw dropped in horror. The Kid looked to be the fittest man he had ever seen. No pale face, no bent back, no cough. Too late, Ryan knew he had been conned – and he had barely trained, thinking he was going in against a soft touch. He took a systematic beating before being knocked out in the 15th round.

Corbett was coming to the end of his career when he agreed to meet McCoy, who had relinquished the middleweight title to campaign against the heavyweights where there was more money to be made. There was no love lost between the pair. They had met by chance in a New York bar in September 1898 and had become embroiled in a heated row. McCoy called Corbett a 'monkey' because he went around dressed in fashionable tails, also known as a 'monkey suit'. 'You're a fine looking man to be calling somebody else a monkey,' retorted Corbett. McCoy replied that the Gentleman Jim tag was a misnomer and reminded Corbett of his bad manners in several of his fights. The verbal battle ended with blows being struck and Corbett being kicked in the groin. He was laid up in bed for several days as a result.

It was never ascertained whether or not the incident was a publicity stunt, knowing McCoy's tricks and ruses to needle an opponent. However, rumours were circulating days before the two men entered the ring that the fight was fixed: that McCoy had accepted a bribe offer to take a dive.

The fight was set for 30 August 1900 at Madison Square Garden, and it would be the last contest staged in New York under the Horton Law, which had governed boxing in the state since 1896. This law allowed fights with an unlimited number of rounds, decisions by referees and the posting of forfeits and side bets. There was such an outcry, however, about the levels of corruption and trickery in the sport, with regular accusations and claims about fixed fights to facilitate gambling interests, that reform was called for. As it happened, the Horton Law was replaced by the Lewis Law, which restricted contests to clubs that had a 'members only' clause and where proceedings would be more supervised, but there were still too many loopholes.

In 1911, the Frawley Law was introduced, which limited contests in New York to ten rounds and stated that referees were not permitted to give decisions. The only way a champion could lose his title was by knockout or stoppage. This proved generally unsatisfactory, too, and finally, in 1920, the Walker Law was brought in, specifying 15-round fights concluding with a decision. It was supervised by the New York State Athletic Commission. This turned out to be acceptable and the rest of the United States introduced the system which would serve as a pattern for boxing authorities across the world until 15-rounders were cut to 12 by a decision in the 1980s and adopted worldwide.

The Corbett–McCoy fight, however, produced the type of scandal that led to the reform of the old Horton Law. The early betting favoured Corbett, and to win $60, you had to put down $100. Both men agreed to 60 per cent of the gross gate receipts, with each to receive 30 per cent, but with the persistent rumours of a fix, the attendance of 8,500 fell short of the expected crowd to watch two top drawing cards. The $35 box seats were not full, and the total takings reached a disappointing $56,000, with both boxers' share coming to a total of $33,810.

The fix rumours were fanned by George Siler, who had refereed Corbett's title fight with Bob Fitzsimmons three years earlier. Writing in the *Chicago Tribune* on the day of the fight, he said he had proof that it was not going to be on the level. Under five headings at the top of the page, including 'Rumoured in New York that Tonight's Battle is Fixed For Corbett to Win' and 'Well Known Pugilistic Manager Declares All Has Been Arranged By the Principals', Siler wrote that he had met a fight manager whom he would not name but who had told him that there was no way McCoy could win. 'It's all fixed for McCoy to get knocked out,' Siler claimed the manager had said. 'I do not know what round, but I got it pretty straight and was told to get a good bet down.' He continued, 'Corbett, so I was informed, has not been taking the best care of himself in the last two days. In fact, it was given to me confidentially that he imbibed too freely last night and retired at a late hour a little under the influence.'

The preview in the *New York World* the same day made no reference to rumours of a fix, though stories around town that something was amiss had been gaining momentum. The paper's correspondent W.O. Inglis gave a straightforward summing up, saying that while McCoy had the harder punch, Corbett was the more skilful boxer. 'Who has the greater endurance? Of the two, Corbett comes nearer the rugged husky type than his opponent,' he wrote. 'While the facts seem to point to Corbett as the winner, I think the contest should not be only the prettiest ever seen in the ring but one of the most exciting. On paper it looks rather like Corbett's fight. In the ring it will be even money and take your pick.'

By the time the two climbed into the ring, the odds on a Corbett victory were in fact 2–1. Corbett, at 6 ft 1 in., was only an inch taller but at 13 st. 1 lb he was 11 lb heavier. In McCoy's favour was that James J. at thirty-four was the older man by seven years.

McCoy was first into the attack, but Corbett danced away, waiting for an opening. Kid landed twice on Corbett's shoulder, and while the heavier man swung in return, the tame round ended even. The crowd were getting impatient with the lack of action. The sparring tactics continued in the second round, McCoy doing the leading and Corbett continuing to back away. Corbett was using his reach advantage to score with long-range blows, and he hurt McCoy with a solid right to the body. Corbett also had the better of the third round as McCoy clinched and tried to prevent the ex-heavyweight champion's greater strength from prevailing. Corbett crowded his man in the fourth, swinging lefts and rights, and hurt McCoy with jolting uppercuts. James J. now looked well in front and seemed to be mastering the style of the former middleweight king, coming in and catching him with sharp punches.

In the fifth round, Corbett was encouraged by advice from his cornermen and shouts from his supporters to move in and attempt to knock out his man. McCoy livened up and caught Corbett with blows to the mid-section, but James J. now had victory in his sights and trapped his rival in a corner where he rained blows on him. McCoy managed to extricate himself and fell into a clinch. After both men were parted by referee Charlie White, Corbett rushed in and with a barrage of lefts and rights sent McCoy staggering across the ring. Corbett gave him no respite, and after a series of blows, McCoy slumped to the canvas. He tried to rise and managed to get to his knees, but it was in that position he was counted out.

Many spectators, though, were not convinced that the knockout was genuine and felt that McCoy, had he wished, could have risen to his feet before White reached ten. Supporting this theory was the fact that McCoy made a very quick recovery and was able to walk unassisted to his dressing-room.

The *New York Times* was satisfied that the fight was genuine and that the punches which finished McCoy were 'merciless'. World heavyweight champion James J. Jeffries supported this view in his report in the *New York World* when he wrote that Corbett 'completely outclassed McCoy in cleverness, strength and speed'.

However, George Siler in the *Chicago Tribune* wrote, in effect, 'I told you so.' Backing up his story from the day before about an unnamed manager telling him the contest was pre-arranged, Siler wrote, 'It was hard to believe the men were not acting. At the end, one had the same feeling as a person coming away from a decadent play – he wants to take several long breaths of good, fresh air and a drink of cool, clear water to take the taste out of his mouth.'

The controversy may well have died away and been forgotten in time had it not been for a sensational front-page story in the *New York World* nearly two weeks later under the headline 'Corbett Runs Away McCoy Fight Fixed'. The previous day, it was reported, Corbett had disappeared from his New York home and sailed on the Cunard liner *Campania* for England. He was accompanied by his manager George Consodine and singer Marguerite Corneille, whose friendship with the boxer was no secret. He also left a message to be delivered to his wife Vera after he set sail. When she got the note, intimating that he would never return, she angrily rushed into her husband's Broadway saloon, demanding to know what was going on. She got no satisfaction from the barmen and waiters, and not even from John Consodine, brother of Corbett's manager. Vera then rushed home and contacted her lawyer, asking him to draw up papers for a divorce on the grounds of cruelty and desertion.

Interviewed the next day by the *New York World*, Vera claimed that Corbett had run away because he feared new disclosures about the McCoy fight. 'The true facts of the fight were coming out, and he was afraid to stay here and face them,' she said. 'The fight was a fake and every sporting man in town knows. It was fixed up in this very room in which we are sitting. Corbett was to lie down. McCoy did not train, knowing Corbett was to lose. But half an hour before the fight, Corbett refused to lie down and gave McCoy the double cross.'

McCoy was furious when he read her story. Interviewed in his Broadway bar, he strongly denied the charges. 'They are ridiculous, and the best way to treat them is to ignore them,' he said. 'There was no agreement before the fight. That fight was on the square, and the best man won.'

Corbett said little about the controversial fight when questioned by reporters as soon as the liner docked in Cork on the Irish coast, except to confirm that it was on the level. Twenty-five years later, in his autobiography *The Roar of the Crowd*, he elaborated on the incident:

> The accusations hurt me more than anything that had ever been said about me or done to me in my life. I certainly saw no evidence of McCoy's reported efforts to lie down, and he fought very hard in the fight. I had bluffed my opponents sometimes, but it was beyond me ever to descend to fixing a fight.

Two years after the fight, the author William Naughton wrote in his book *Kings of the Queensberry Realm* that while it might have been true that McCoy had sold himself to some bookmaker 'there is no gainsaying the fact that the punch that finally sent McCoy to the floor was a wicked one'.

It was a view shared by Charlie White, the referee in the fight.

Some years later, White told Nat Fleischer, of *Ring* magazine, that he felt there was nothing crooked about it. He said the left to the stomach which put McCoy down 'was hard enough to take the fight out of any man'. White, who was no more than two feet away from both men when McCoy went down, added, 'If there was anything phoney about the fight, McCoy alone was accountable for it. I'll stake my last dollar that Jim Corbett, who got an undeservedly raw deal from the press, was not to blame in any respect.' One person who dismissed reports that the fight was genuine was Tad Dorgan, respected boxing writer with the *New York Journal*. 'This was the finest piece of play-acting I ever saw,' he wrote.

The controversy refused to go away. Twenty-seven years later, the boxing historian and author Alexander Johnston, in his book *Ten and Out! The Complete Story of the Prize Ring in America*, wrote that, 'McCoy dropped to the floor and gave an excellent imitation of a man in distress.'

As late as 1958, Samuel Hopkins Adams, a novelist and historian who was at the fight, recalled the incident in an article in *Sports Illustrated* entitled 'There's No Fraud Like an Old Fraud'. In it he wrote:

> While the house shrieked and McCoy writhed on the floor in a touching representation of 'The Dying Gladiator', the referee tolled ten with his arms, and it was all over. Eight-thousand-odd happy suckers, including world champion Jeffries and my humble self, departed in the fond illusion that we had witnessed one of the great events in ring history. So we had, but what we had been watching was not a supreme fight. It was a supreme fake.

Was it a sham or the real McCoy? An honest fight or a hoax? The truth will never be known, but one clear fact remained. Coming so soon after the Corbett–Sharkey debacle, irreparable damage had been done to the sport at the beginning of the new century.

4

THE GREAT STENCH

The affair known as 'The Great Stench' that took place in Chicago was a devastating blow for boxing at the turn of the twentieth century. The intensely controversial fights involving James J. Corbett, Tom Sharkey and Kid McCoy were bad enough without another scandal occurring, especially with the widespread furore and condemnation of boxing causing the public to treat the sport with scepticism and cynicism at that time.

The events in Chicago transpired on 13 December 1900. The principals on that occasion were two of boxing's all-time greats: Terry McGovern – the reigning world featherweight champion and former bantamweight title-holder – and Joe Gans, a future world lightweight champion. The fight was such a blatant fix that it led to boxing being banned in the 'Windy City' and later the state of Illinois as a whole.

McGovern had been featherweight champion for almost a year, with three successful title defences, when he climbed into the ring at Tattersall's arena to face Gans in an overweight match. It was scheduled for six rounds and was easily the boxing event of the year in Chicago, some said for decades. The big attraction was McGovern, boxing's best draw outside the heavyweight division, but the fact that he was going in with Gans, one of the world's crack lightweights, was enough to pull in the fans from all quarters. The *Chicago Tribune* reported, 'There is no doubt that the battle is arousing more general interest than anything of the kind that has occurred in the Middle West for years.'

If McGovern was the darling of the fight crowds, it was not too surprising. A little tearaway of Irish extraction, he was known variously as 'Terrible Terry' and the 'Brooklyn Terror', nicknames that well suited him. He was a powerful hitter with both gloves and knew no fear. He would take on anyone, anywhere, any place, irrespective of their reputation and weight.

McGovern had little if any time for the skilful side of the sport and just wanted to get in there from the first bell, finish off his opponent in the shortest possible time, hurry back to the dressing-room, get dressed quickly and leave the scene of the battle. 'I just wanted to get it over with and get out of there,' he used to say. 'My job was finished.'

Nat Fleischer, regarded as the most knowledgeable boxing writer and historian of his day, had the highest opinion of McGovern. 'No bantamweight or featherweight ever packed a more dangerous punch than did Terry,' he wrote. Up until his death in 1972, Fleischer always rated McGovern as the number one featherweight of all time, ahead of great nine-stoners like Willie Pep and Sandy Saddler. 'One of McGovern's greatest distinctions was the fact that in a period embracing only two years, he defeated the champions in three divisions,' Fleischer recorded. 'No fighter of his weight piled up such a consistent record for tearing pell-mell into his adversaries and smothering them with wicked jolts, hooks, uppercuts and vicious swings. In every sense of the phrase, he was a pugilistic marvel.'

Steve Farhood, a later editor of *Ring*, felt that more recent champions like Carlos Zarate, Wilfredo Gomez and Ruben Olivares owed McGovern a debt of gratitude: 'The destructive Pennsylvanian was the first lighter-weights champion to prove that small fighters can punch too.'

Gilbert Odd, a boxing historian and author who knew the fight game like few others, wrote in his 1974 book *Boxing: The Great Champions*, 'There have been many strong punchers among the little men but none fought fiercer or hit harder than McGovern. He just waded in, determined to batter the opposition into pulp as quickly as possible.'

Terry was inducted into the International Boxing Hall of Fame in New York in 1990. 'In his prime McGovern was a fearless, powerful puncher who recorded 38 knockouts in his first 62 fights,' said Edward Brophy, executive director. 'Not much for fancy manoeuvres, McGovern simply went after his opponents with a ferocious will to win.' That was Terry McGovern, idol of the fight crowds and whose popularity knew no bounds. He was born in Johnstown, Pennsylvania, on 9 March 1880, and his family moved to New York City when Terry was six, settling in Brooklyn, which would remain his home for the rest of his life. 'Brooklyn was and is my home town. Always was and always will be,' he once said.

South Brooklyn was a tough neighbourhood where the Irish labouring class predominated, and the boys Terry hung around with were pretty rough. Street battles, with bricks as the chief ammunition, were common, everyday occurrences, so aggression and fighting were second nature to him. Soon little Terry was the top street fighter in the area.

He was 14 when his father died, which meant that he and Hughie, his next elder brother, had to find a way to provide for their mother, sister Mary and younger brothers Patsy, Jimmy and Phil. The breadwinners sold vegetables from a cart, and Terry also managed to sell newspapers, though he more often than not had to fight to keep his pitch.

A friend of Terry's named Charley Mayhood, who was foreman at a local timber yard, told him that there was a job going. He applied for it and was successful. He soon became captain of a baseball team he assembled among the workers, arranging games in the neighbourhood. It was something for them to do when their work was finished, and they were delighted to participate. On one occasion, there was a heated dispute with the opposing captain over a particular decision, and it soon developed into a fight. There were also skirmishes in the timber yard itself over demands by truck drivers, and McGovern often found himself coming to the aid of Mayhood.

One day Charley suggested to Terry that he had the makings of a good boxer and offered to train him for a professional career. 'You'll go places,' he told the youngster. McGovern wavered and said to Mayhood that he would think about it. However, he did join the Jackson Athletic Club of Brooklyn and, for the very first time, pushed his hands into boxing gloves, much to Mayhood's delight. A few weeks later, he entered an amateur tournament in the 7 st. 7 lb class, today's strawweight limit. After eliminating eleven opponents over the three nights, all inside the scheduled distance, he won the championship and was awarded a gold watch.

It was at that stage Terry decided he wanted to box for a living. 'It's terrific, this boxing,' he told Mayhood. 'A great feeling. You're right. Someday I'll be champion of the world.' Mayhood linked up with Harry Fisher, one of the top New York lightweights of the day who knew his way around the fight business. Between them, they got the promising boxer started in the paid ranks, Mayhood doing the managing and Fisher looking after the training.

McGovern had his first professional fight in April 1897 at the age of 17 and made fast progress with his powerful punching, developing a large and loyal following. In his second year, he attracted the notice of boxing manager Sam Harris, a slender Jewish youth who was destined to become one of America's most prominent theatrical producers. In an agreement with McGovern and Mayhood, Harris took over the boxer's management, with Mayhood as trainer. It was a wise and sensible agreement because under the astute arrangement with Harris, who had several important contacts, Terry would become internationally famous in the ring.

Harris secured him a world bantamweight title fight with the British champion Tom 'Pedlar' Palmer in the open air at Tuckahoe, New York, in September 1899. Palmer, because of his cleverness, was also known as the 'Box O' Tricks' and took a large contingent of fans with him from England who backed him heavily.

Palmer's manager, A.F. 'Peggy' Bettinson, told reporters when the party arrived in New York that his man would easily outbox

McGovern. 'With all due respect, McGovern is just a slugger,' said Bettinson, an astute boxing man and one of the founding members of the famous National Sporting Club eight years later. 'Palmer will hold on to his title for the fifth time and you can bank on it.'

There was a record crowd of over 10,000 spectators in attendance, and the ringside celebrities included former world heavyweight champions James J. Corbett, looking very handsome and fashionably attired in evening dress, and his predecessor John L. Sullivan, hearty and husky, and easily distinguishable with his heavy, curling, iron-grey moustache.

It was all over in precisely two minutes and thirty-two seconds of the first round, with all the fighting coming from the American whirlwind. McGovern dropped the shocked Palmer with a sweeping left hook to the jaw, and the Englishman was so dazed he only took a count of six. After groggily getting to his feet and shuffling along the ropes to escape the human tornado, McGovern dropped him again, this time with a stiff left hook to the body and a hard overhand right to the head. Palmer was well and truly out before referee George Siler shouted, 'Ten.'

Terrible Terry McGovern, the Brooklyn Terror, was champion of the world at the age of nineteen years and six months. The fight, if it could be called that, is still one of the shortest world bantamweight title bouts on record, even in the present era of multi-championships and belts being handed out like promotional leaflets in the street.

McGovern relinquished the title within three months, because of increasing weight, and won the world featherweight championship in January 1900 by stopping George 'Little Chocolate' Dixon in eight rounds at New York's Broadway Club. Dixon started well and outboxed the younger man, but as the rounds progressed, the fiery McGovern's non-stop aggression and harder punching were too much for his opponent. Dixon went down eight times in the eighth round before his manager, Tom O'Rourke, threw the sponge into the ring, signalling it was all over. Terry made three successful defences of the title within a year, keeping to his promise that he would be a fighting champion. He ended 1900 with the non-title fight against Joe Gans which would cause so much controversy.

Gans was one of the world's leading lightweights and would win the title inside two years to become one of the true greats of all time – though he always had to 'remember that he was black' and was therefore expected to 'behave himself' when dealing with his 'white masters'. Born in Baltimore, Maryland, on 25 November 1874, Gans came from a very poor family who eked out a living by selling oysters and fish on the waterfront.

Young Joe enjoyed the minimum of schooling and found he could earn extra money for the family in so-called 'battle royals'. In an age of despicable racial prejudice, up to a dozen black men would be thrown blindfolded into a ring and left to eliminate themselves one by one to the amusement of the white spectators who would throw nickels and dimes into the ring, some of which were red hot. Gans learned his boxing this way and decided that the sport would lift him and his family out of the poverty trap.

To achieve this aim, he skipped an amateur career and went straight into the professional game at the age of 17 in 1891. Gans turned out to be a natural boxer–fighter and, in time, developed wonderful coordination and fluidity of movement. He also acquired the ability to punch hard without being hit in return. Before long, he would become known as the 'Old Master'. Gene Tunney, world heavyweight champion in the late 1920s, would describe him as 'one of the all-time great ringmen' and 'one who glided on perfectly coordinated feet'.

Gans' earnings soon enabled his family to eat such luxuries as bacon now and again. When he became established as a boxer and was regularly fighting away from home, he would let his mother know he had won a contest by sending her a telegram that always read, 'Hello, Mom. I'm bringing home the bacon.'

Joe lost only three of his first seventy fights and two of them were questionable, allowing unscrupulous backers to clean up on the results. His points defeat by Dal Hawkins in October 1896 was marred by boos and shouts from the gathering as it was obvious he was not doing his best. Not surprisingly, he knocked out Hawkins in a return match just over three years later.

Then, in March 1900, Gans retired in controversial circumstances with a cut eye in a world lightweight title challenge against Frank Erne, and, surprise, surprise, in a return fight two years later, he knocked Erne out cold in the first round to win the championship. The fight, staged in Fort Erie, Ontario, was all over in 40 seconds, including the count. Erne did not get an opportunity to land a single punch. After sizing up his man, Gans pierced the champion's defence with a strong left jab and followed it immediately with a cracking right that landed squarely on Erne's chin, leaving him with no chance to beat referee Johnny White's count. It was the fastest world lightweight title fight up to that point, a record that would stand for 28 years.

In between the fights with Erne, Gans accepted the challenge from McGovern. Terry was ambitious and anxious to move up to the lightweights, and a good win over Gans would strengthen his claims as well as give him some credibility in the heavier division. Anyhow, McGovern dominated the featherweights. Why not go for the 9 st. 9 lb crown, too, by first beating the formidable Gans? The match was set.

An agreement was made by McGovern's manager Sam Harris before the fight, set for a distance of six rounds, that Gans would have to weigh no more than 9 st. 7 lb against McGovern's 8 st. 12 lb. Failing to make that weight would mean that Gans would have to forfeit half his purse. The second agreement reached was that Gans would have to knock out Terry to win.

McGovern made the required weight at the afternoon weigh-in but Gans was one and a quarter pounds over the agreed poundage. Harris waived the forfeit, providing McGovern won. If Terry lost, the Gans camp would have to pay up. Gans' manager Al Herford nodded in agreement. Both boxers wished each other good luck and went back to their respective hotels. Arrangements were also made to film the fight, a process then still in its infancy.

Before the fight, there were reports that the police would serve arrest warrants on Gans and McGovern, along with everybody else involved with the event, because, technically speaking, prizefighting was illegal in Illinois. However, there were always ways and means around these things, and nobody paid any attention to the threats. Oddly enough, Mayor Carter Harrison did not go along with the proposed action by the police and said he saw nothing wrong with the whole thing, although he did not plan to attend himself.

Almost from the day the fight was announced, there were strong rumours that it would be a fake. There were also stories published in Chicago newspapers warning of possible race riots not only in the city and state but all over the US if a white man lost to a black man.

Malachy Hogan, sports columnist with the *Chicago Times-Herald*, summed up the prevailing sentiment when he wrote, 'If Terry should go down before the Baltimore lightweight, I make a guess that there will be a scene at Tattersall's. Not that I predict a disorderly time, but McGovern's defeat would cause a big howl of disappointment from the thousands who have reached the conclusion that he is invincible.'

In the end, after the threats of race riots, rumours of the fight being a fake and the warnings of arrests, the atmosphere was anything but tranquil as the two contestants entered the ring. A crowd of 10,000 was on hand, and no sooner had the signal gone for the fight to start and the movie camera begun to roll than McGovern went straight into action. He tossed a left hook, which Gans neatly parried, before rushing the heavier man to the ropes where he landed lefts and rights. As Gans broke away, McGovern followed him but missed with rights and lefts. Gans was looking decidedly worried, and Terry caught him with a strong left hook that sent Gans' head snapping back. The fans were now standing on their seats and pandemonium reigned.

Gans already looked a beaten man, his defence being as fragile as a piece of antique furniture, as McGovern came in again and hurt him with powerful left and right smashes to the ribs. The man from Baltimore finally landed his first blow of any consequence, a right uppercut under the heart, but it made no impression on Terrible Terry, who allowed Joe to connect with a further left and right to the face to bring Gans within range.

McGovern stormed back with a combination left–right to the jaw that sent Gans staggering back to the ropes. Terry followed him like a jungle beast after its prey and landed blows from every angle. McGovern kept up the incessant attacks and hurt his opponent with a terrific left hook to the face, but it landed a little too high to be effective. Seeing that he had his man going, McGovern measured

92

Gans with a left jab and followed through with a stunning right to the jaw that sent him to the floor.

The future lightweight champion took a count of seven from referee George Siler. As he arose, the bell went, but McGovern had already started a powerful left hook that landed squarely on Gans' jaw and dropped him for the second time. Joe's cornermen quickly climbed into the ring, picked up their groggy boxer and took him to the corner. Many onlookers were surprised that Gans' manager did not claim a foul. There was not even a mild protest. Strange?

Gans looked as frightened as a deer as he came out for the second round. Straight away, McGovern was after him like a terrier and knocked Joe down for the third time. Gans was up quickly, only to be caught with a cracking right to the ear followed by a stunning left to the mouth and went down for his fourth count. McGovern, realising that he was not putting enough power into his blows against an already beaten opponent, moved in and sent Gans to the floor for the fifth time with a powerful right to the jaw.

On arising, Gans was floored for his sixth count with a fast left–right and on rising, was sent down for count number seven. It was getting monotonous. When the lightweight got to his feet, McGovern rushed in and shot over a smashing right to the jaw that had every ounce of his power behind it. Gans went down and landed on his back. At Siler's count of six, he rolled over on his face. At eight, he arose to one knee where he stayed as the referee reached ten. Tapping Gans on the shoulder, Siler said, 'The fight's over, Joe. You can get dressed.'

Gans left the ring through a shower of crumpled newspapers and cigar butts as the crowd booed loud and long. They had been cheated. McGovern had won too easily, and it was obvious that Gans had not done his best. 'I fought as well as I could,' he told reporters in his dressing-room, 'but McGovern was too fast for me.' In his quarters, the winner said, 'I'm naturally delighted I won. He hit me once: a left to the mouth; that was all. He is a clever and game fellow and can stand a world of punishment.'

The newspapers the next day predictably denounced the fight as being crooked. Typical headlines included the ones in the *Chicago*

Tribune, which read, 'McGovern Wins Fake Fight' and 'Spectators Call it Fraud'. The *Philadelphia Evening Item* said in its report, 'There is no manner of doubt that last night's fight between Terry McGovern and Joe Gans was an absolute fake. It outdid the most barefaced ring fraud that ever played in New York.' The *Tribune*'s report said, 'The fight looked like a bald fake, and the betting previous to the fight changed hands so quickly and queerly as to indicate clearly that something was wrong.' The paper also claimed that Gans made more money – $8,000 – by losing than he would have done by winning.

'There were some who knew the result in advance,' said the report. 'The black man only offered feeble resistance, and it gradually dawned on the crowd that something was wrong. Ringsiders were shouting "Fraud", and last night's affair will go a long way towards killing pugilistic contests in Chicago.'

In the same paper, George Siler, who both refereed and reported the fight, wrote:

> I do not wish to accuse any fighter of faking, but if Gans was trying last night, I don't know much about the game. The few blows he delivered were the weakest ever seen from a man of his known hitting abilities.
>
> His left-hand leads, one of his strongest points, were sent out in a faint-hearted manner, and his right jolts, which have laid many a good man away, were conspicuous by their absence. Gans will never be seen here in a fight again, and the probability is that he will find it difficult to secure a match elsewhere. The public can be fooled once, and probably twice, but not all the time.

Denials by Gans' manager Herford and promoter Lou Houseman only seemed to infuriate public opinion. It was known that many politicians in Chicago had lost large bets on the fight – and it was the politicians who carried the public's outrage against the sport into legislative action when Mayor Harrison introduced a resolution calling for boxing to be officially banned in the city. 'If the game is too bad for the council, it is too bad for me,' he said. The final outcome was that all permits for boxing matches to be held in the city were revoked. By 1906, six years after the McGovern–Gans debacle, the sport was banned not only in Chicago but throughout the state of Illinois and would remain so for twenty years. One of the first major fights to take place on boxing's return to Chicago was the world heavyweight championship bout between Jack Dempsey and Gene Tunney in 1927.

In *'Terrible Terry': The Brooklyn Terror*, a biography of McGovern published in 1943, Nat Fleischer stressed that the fight was very definitely a phoney, as if any further proof was needed. He wrote:

> The bout was recorded as a fake, and as such, it has been accepted by fistic historians. Whether McGovern was aware that Gans intended to lie down was never proved. The chances are that he was just told to go in and fight, without knowing anything about the conspiracy.

After the McGovern fiasco, Gans was back in action within two months with a win in six rounds over Jack Daly in Baltimore. In 1902, he won the world lightweight title from Frank Erne and retained it six times. In 1904, he even managed to hold world welterweight champion Joe Walcott, the 'Barbados Demon', to a draw over 20 rounds, an indication of his immense talent with the gloves.

Even up until the end of his life, however, Gans was short-changed. His biggest purse – $34,000 – was for his third last fight, an unsuccessful lightweight defence in San Francisco against iron-jawed Battling Nelson in July 1908. Already a sick man suffering from tuberculosis, Gans only received $11,000, having agreed under contract to give Nelson the balance of $23,000, win, lose or draw. Nelson won with a knockout in the seventeenth round and repeated the win two months later, this time in twenty-one rounds in Colma, California.

Gans' final ring appearance was in March 1909 when he boxed a ten-round no-decision contest with Jabez White in New York. No official verdict could be given under law, but the newspapermen around the ringside, as per custom, named Joe the winner.

The Old Master never talked at any great length about the controversial McGovern fight, before his death from the illness in August 1910 in his home town of Baltimore. He was three months short of his thirty-sixth birthday. Gans is still remembered today and is generally regarded by boxing historians as one of the truly great lightweights of all time, alongside Benny Leonard and modern legend Roberto Duran.

McGovern lost his world featherweight title when he was knocked out in two rounds by Young Corbett in 1901. He would never really regain his old form, and Terrible Terry finally hung up the gloves after an unimpressive performance in a no-decision match with Spike Robson in New York in 1908. He turned to refereeing, but his health was not always good, and he died of pneumonia in his beloved Brooklyn in February 1918. He was 38 years old. Like Gans, McGovern never wanted to talk about the events concerning that mysterious fight back in Chicago in 1900.

Many years after both McGovern and Gans were dead, Joe Humphries, the announcer at the fight, admitted in an interview, 'They got to Gans, but Terry never knew it. Joe was in bad financial shape, and he got what was left of his roll down on McGovern when the price was high.'

Nevertheless, the controversy of The Great Stench refused to go away. In 1955, in an article about fixed fights in *Boxing and Wrestling* magazine, Wally McManus wrote that the McGovern–Gans fight 'proved [to be] one of the most amateurish jobs ever perpetrated on the public. Gans had the "cuffs" on, that was obvious. But if Gans had been allowed to fight his way, McGovern wouldn't have been around for very long.'

In 1967, the controversy surfaced again when Daniel M. Daniel of *Ring* magazine came across a long-lost film of the fight. After watching it, he came to the conclusion that the movie was far more revealing than any newspaper reports of the period. Daniel, assuming the role of what he described as the 'Ring Detective', said that after studying the film, he became convinced, more than ever, that Gans had gone 'into the tank', a boxing description for somebody taking a dive.

'Gans rarely, if ever, showed excitement or emotion, but on this occasion he was downright pathetic,' said Daniel, who published photographs from the film. 'The decision of the Ring Detective is that Gans was guilty of the most aggravated case of non-performance in the history of boxing, especially in a fight involving a world champion and a world champion to be.'

5

MISADVENTURES OF THE AMBLING ALP

They called him 'Man Mountain', 'Old Satchel Feet', the 'Gorgonzola Tower', 'Da Preem' and the 'Noblest Roman'. However, it was Damon Runyon, the celebrated boxing columnist of the *New York American* and short-story writer, who tagged him with the name that stuck: the 'Ambling Alp'.

Others were less kind to Primo Carnera. They called him a freak and a fraud for the way he was promoted and finally exploited by mobsters, cheated of most of his purses, and then sacrificed and abandoned in poverty. Perhaps his only lasting claim to fame is that he is the only Italian to win universal recognition as heavyweight champion of the world, boxing's most prestigious honour. One of his countrymen, Francesco Damiani, held the title during 1989–91 but received recognition from only the World Boxing Organisation.

Carnera, the gentle giant who stood 6 ft 7 in. and weighed over 18 st., saw only the good in people. Yet he is one of boxing history's most tragic figures. His sad and shameful manipulation by unscrupulous people is a stain on the sport that can never be erased or forgotten.

'No prizefighter of note was ever treated with less decency, ever shorn more completely of dignity,' wrote John McCallum, the American boxing writer and historian. Gilbert Odd, the British author of several bestselling books, expanded on more or less the same theme when he observed, 'There was something quite pathetic about the boxing career of Carnera. Simple and amiable, he had a fighting career thrust upon him and was easy prey for those who managed his affairs in America, where he was exploited, robbed and finally ditched.'

The son of a poor stonecutter, Carnera was born in the little village of Sequals in the north-east of Italy on 26 October 1906, the eldest of six children. His parents were normal-sized people, and none of his brothers was over 6 ft. By the time he was 21, he would fill out to over 17 st.

Primo grew up during the First World War. The area in which he lived was occupied by Austro-German forces, so there was very little food about. The youngster had to help out and search the fields for anything edible to supplement the family larder. Things improved after the war, but with hardly any education, young Primo could barely read or write. He got a job as an apprentice to his uncle who was a carpenter, but there was still not enough food to satisfy his 6 ft 7 in. frame, let alone the remainder of his family. Therefore Primo left home at the age of 14 and travelled around northern Italy, leading something of a hobo existence, picking up whatever work he could get – labourer, bricklayer and, occasionally, stonecutter.

Carnera eventually made it to France and arrived in Le Mans wearing one of his father's suits, his feet encased in old rope sandals and carrying all his worldly goods in a cardboard box. He stayed with an aunt and got a job in a circus where his size and strength were useful in setting up and dismantling the big top.

Primo eventually became part of the show, working as a strong man, weightlifter and boxer, even undergoing a nationality change by the circus proprietor who billed him variously as 'Juan the Unbeatable Spaniard' and 'Terrible Giovanni, Champion of Spain'. His speciality in the strong-man act was a tug-of-war in which he outpulled a heavy motor vehicle.

When the circus reached Bordeaux, he was spotted by former French heavyweight champion Paul Journee, who suggested that Primo take up boxing seriously, because the Italian's size and strength meant he could well go places. A contract was duly signed. Journee put him up and trained him for three months before turning him over to his own former mentor, the diminutive Leon See, who was France's most successful manager and had a training camp outside Paris.

See was a former amateur bantamweight who boxed in England as a 17 year old by virtue of his father having a home and business interests in Birmingham. At the time, *la boxe anglaise* was little known in France, where a form of kickboxing, or *savate*, was more popular. Later, See did much to introduce the Queensberry style in France and subsequently formed the French Boxing Federation, before going into management and training.

See said he would take 35 per cent of Carnera's earnings but promised he would move him ahead. Primo agreed. What had the big fellow to lose? At least he would eat regularly. See got some local boxers to coach him in the rudiments of the sport and arranged with Jeff Dickson, an American promoter domiciled in France, for some fights. Dickson matched Primo with veteran puncher Leon Sebillo for a purse of 1,000 francs at the Salle Wagram, Paris, in September 1928. Carnera knocked him out in the second round. See would later reveal in a book he wrote that he gave Sebillo 500 francs out of his own pocket to throw the fight and that Sebillo agreed to leave his guard open so that Carnera could land a right which would lay him out for the full count. The shrewd See clearly did not want to take any unnecessary risks with his new meal ticket.

This would set the trend in Carnera's career. See revealed that at least 28 of Primo's fights up to the end of 1930 were fixed as the naïve boxer 'knocked out' opponent after opponent – and all this before Carnera got into the big time and American mobsters moved in and took over his management. In those early fights, Primo did not know what he was being paid. See oversaw each contract.

For Carnera's second fight, against Joe Thomas, See took half of Primo's 3,000 francs and gave it to Thomas 'to take it easy and go

101

down in the third round'. Thomas duly obliged. And so it went, See coming to financial arrangements with Carnera's opponents – many times the money coming out of Carnera's own purse. Primo was still none the wiser. Those who were not paid to fall down were either faded veterans or no-hopers who would lose anyway.

Ironically, in his first honest fight, against Germany's Franz Diener in Leipzig in April 1929, Carnera was beaten when he was caught by a vicious left hook to the groin in the opening round. Primo went down groaning, and for some unaccountable reason, the referee, instead of immediately disqualifying Diener, ordered Carnera to continue after a five-minute rest. When Primo, still groaning, refused to leave his corner after a further five-minute rest, the German was awarded the fight on a disqualification. In addition, Carnera's purse was held up.

As the giant Italian moved back into his 'winning streak' with the help of See and some willing opponents, promoter Dickson decided to move into the London scene. He matched Primo, with See's approval, with the talented American Young Stribling at the Royal Albert Hall in November 1929. The arrangement was that Stribling would hit Carnera below the belt in the fourth round and be disqualified. This would leave the way clear for a lucrative return, and certain sellout, in the Vélodrome d'Hiver in Paris a few weeks later – again, of course, promoted by Dickson. Stribling would win the second fight, again on disqualification, with the exact finish to be worked out later. Then there would be a demand for a money-spinning third fight either in London or Paris.

The first one went according to plan, with Stribling landing a right well below the belt in the fourth round 'with all the force of a dessert spoon dipping into a rice pudding', according to Carnera's biographer, Frederic Mullally. Carnera slithered down and rolled over from side to side, whereupon Stribling was disqualified.

The second fight also followed the script, with Carnera punching Stribling after the bell ending the seventh round, even backhanding the referee to make certain of being ruled out. Sure enough, he was promptly disqualified. Plans for a third fight somehow fell through, because See now had his eyes on the more financially secure American market and a world title fight.

To ensure that Carnera's interests were well looked after in the tougher US scene, See was 'persuaded' to hand over his claim on Primo to a syndicate comprised of a New York manager/talent scout named Walter 'Good Time Charlie' Friedman and two of his friends, Bill Duffy and Owney Madden, both well-known hoodlums but with the right connections. Also in the syndicate were 'Big Frenchy' de Mange and Frank Churchill, two gangsters with an interest in the fight game, including close and convenient friendships with referees, judges, officials and boxing commissioners. Christmas cards would be sent to the boxing people every year without fail.

At first, See was reluctant to part with Carnera, but when it later came out in the newspapers that he had agreed, the supposition was that some additional incentive was offered to the little Frenchman by the hoodlums, such as 'insurance against accidents detrimental to his health'. In any event, under US rules, Carnera had to have a licensed manager.

Duffy, a shady New Yorker known as 'Big Bill', owned several speakeasies and had served prison terms for an assortment of crimes including armed robbery. Madden was a bootlegger, club owner, hotelier and numbers racketeer with interests in slot machines and lottery games. Dubbed by the FBI as 'Public Enemy No. 1', he was known in the underworld as 'Owney the Killer'. He too had a long prison record, with seven murders and a manslaughter to his name.

The syndicate, after some consideration, allowed See to act as Carnera's manager in Europe and said he could also come on Primo's American tour as an adviser. After all, they did not want Carnera to feel lonely or isolated from the man who had been with him from the start. Dickson would stay behind as Primo's European promoter, but both See and Dickson would be on a small percentage of Carnera's American earnings.

Also on the Carnera payroll was Luigi Soresi, an Italian with banking interests in New York. Soresi would be the front man and look after Primo's financial affairs when his pals Duffy and Madden, who both had the major share of Carnera's purses, were 'otherwise engaged'. Is it any wonder that big Primo himself usually received less than 10 per cent of the money earned from his fights?

Carnera was introduced to American fight fans by means of a cross-country tour featuring quick knockouts. 'Primo's opponents either came into the ring leaning on, or were more than normally sensitive to, strong drafts,' recalled the historian and author John McCallum. 'Primo only had to swish his great glove through the air and – crash! – down they would fall.'

As was the case in Europe, Carnera was not aware that many of his opponents were taking dives, and when he was told, it caused him much embarrassment. On one occasion, when a rival fell down from a light punch and was later fined by the boxing commission for not giving of his best, Primo insisted on reimbursing him.

On his US debut at Madison Square Garden in January 1930, Carnera knocked out the Canadian 'Big Boy' Peterson in 70 seconds. What the spectators were not aware of was that Peterson had agreed to take a right to the chin and go down for the count. Owney Madden was unavoidably absent from ringside. He was back behind bars in Sing Sing, on a first-degree manslaughter rap.

A week later in Chicago, another Canadian, Elzear Rioux, fell to the canvas for no particular reason after 47 seconds of the first round. When Carnera yelled at Rioux to 'get up', he did so, only to be immediately put down again with a light right cross to the head for the full count. The Illinois Athletic Commission confiscated Rioux's end of the purse and fined him $1,000 for 'playacting unbecoming to a fighter'.

In Philadelphia in March 1930, rugged Roy 'Ace' Clark, all 6 ft 8 in. of him, chose to ignore his corner's instructions and was giving Carnera all kinds of problems for five rounds. As he sat on his stool awaiting the bell for the sixth, a gruff voice shouted up at him, 'Look down here, Ace.' He did so, and his jaw dropped, because sitting at ringside was a mobster pal of Duffy's, with a long, glistening knife in his hand. Clark got the message and took the full count after thirty seconds of the sixth.

There was the occasional mishap. In Oakland in April, a tough individual named Leon 'Bombo' Chevalier refused to be bribed. He bombed Carnera with heavy rights for a few rounds, splitting the big Italian's left eyebrow and bruising his self-confidence. The hoods who controlled Carnera, however, were prepared for such an emergency. Between the fifth and sixth round, one of Chevalier's handlers rubbed resin into their man's eyes. The half-blinded Chevalier still managed to put Carnera on the canvas in the sixth for a count of five, but on instructions from Primo's corner, Chevalier's second, Bob Perry, threw in the towel, even though Bombo was capable of continuing the fight. The arena erupted in protest, and Bombo was beaten up when he climbed down from the ring by a group of spectators angry at his quitting. Both men's purses were withheld by the California State Athletic Commission, which also suspended the state licences of Carnera as well as those of Duffy, Friedman, Soresi and See.

New York followed the lead of California and also suspended their licences, as well as ordering a full investigation into all of Carnera's fights, but the syndicate simply moved elsewhere – Portland, Detroit, Philadelphia, Omaha, Cleveland, Atlantic City, Newark, Chicago and Boston.

One opponent, Riccardo Bertazzolo, a proud and gutsy boxer, refused to take a dive against Carnera in Atlantic City in August despite a guaranteed percentage of the gate on top of his purse, which would have netted him $10,000 overall against Primo's $6,000. Bertazzolo, however, was double-crossed by his own manager Aldo Linz, who slit Riccardo's eyebrow with a razor between the second and third rounds, covering up the cut with Vaseline. With the first blow that landed on Bertazzolo's eyebrow, the blood spurted, and the referee stopped the fight, awarding Carnera a technical knockout.

Carnera had three more fights in the US before heading back to Europe in November for a few months' rest. Pat McCarthy took the easy way out in the second round in Newark, going out to meet Primo with the enthusiasm of a man facing a walk to the electric chair. Jack Gross did likewise in the fourth round in Chicago, both bouts taking place in September. Jim Maloney – a seasoned campaigner, although past his best – refused to be bribed in their match in Boston in October, and in one of the few genuine fights in Carnera's pre-championship career, Primo lost the decision. Most people, though, felt Carnera should have won. He would get a close decision over Maloney in a return match five months later in Miami, though Maloney's corner disputed the verdict on that occasion.

Primo was back in the US in March 1931 on a campaign which the syndicate hoped would lead their man to a world title fight with Germany's Max Schmeling. More quick victories followed, most of them against either washed-up boxers or ones who were bribed to stay down. By the spring of 1933, Carnera had attracted enough attention, and built up a record of wins, with only the occasional loss, to warrant a shot at the title which Schmeling had since lost on a hotly disputed points decision to Boston's Jack Sharkey.

Like many of the top American boxing writers, Paul Gallico of the *New York Daily News* could not quite come to terms with Carnera. He wrote:

> He steps unchanged out of the limbo of things that used to frighten or excite us. Had he but one eye in the centre of his forehead, he might pass for Cyclops. Indeed, as he climbed into the ring he might have stepped from some nursery frieze or from between the covers of an imaginatively illustrated copy of *Jack the Giant Killer*. It is from this tribe that Carnera springs.

To earn the title fight, Carnera had to take on and beat the tough Ernie Schaaf, a former US Navy champion. They met in New York in February 1933. After a dismal fight, with both men punching half-heartedly for round after round and Carnera taking a points lead, Schaaf suddenly collapsed from three punches to the head in the thirteenth as spectators rose in their seats and cried, 'Fake, fake.' Soon there were boos all over Madison Square Garden.

Schaaf was removed unconscious from the ring on a stretcher to the Stuyvesant Polyclinic Hospital across the street, but he failed to regain consciousness and died five days later. Carnera, who was distraught, was charged with manslaughter but acquitted when it was found that Schaaf had entered the ring with a blood clot on his brain as a result of a hammering from contender Max Baer the previous summer. He had lapsed into a coma after that fight and should never have been allowed into the ring again.

Carnera's syndicate, led by Duffy, shamefully played up the death and called Primo 'The Man Killer', much to the genial Italian's embarrassment. The New York State Athletic Commission then announced they were banning Carnera from fighting not only Sharkey but any other average heavyweight because he was 'too big'. In future, he would be allowed to box only in a 'dreadnought' class, defined as a boxer weighing over 17 st. and of a height not less than 6 ft 2 in.

Carnera could have fought outside the jurisdiction of New York, but he wanted a title fight, and champion Sharkey was under contract to Madison Square Garden, which worked in association with the State Athletic Commission. Commission chairman William Muldoon had no choice but to lift the ban on Primo, and the title fight was set for 19 June 1933 at New York's Long Island Bowl, a part of the Garden organisation and somewhere that they often leased for big fights.

The day before the match, Sharkey was a 6–5 favourite to hold on to his title on the basis that he had outpointed Carnera on Primo's second American tour nearly two years earlier. By the time the champion and challenger entered the ring, though, the odds on Carnera mysteriously shifted to make him the 7–5 favourite.

Sharkey was a good technical boxer, fast on his feet, had a useful punch in both hands and he had 36 wins in 47 fights, but he was totally unpredictable, given to emotional outbursts and prone to weeping tears of frustration and rage. *New York Times* sports columnist Arthur Daley once described him as 'one of the most unstable characters ever to step into a ring'.

Born in New York of Lithuanian parents on 6 October 1902, his real name was Joseph Paul Zukauskas. Growing up in the Depression years he became restless and ran away to sea at the age of 18, joining the US Navy and seeing service on the USS *South Carolina*. It was on board the *South Carolina* that he got interested in boxing, watching his shipmates spar on deck and eventually taking part himself. After four years at sea, he made up his mind to try his luck as a professional boxer, adopting the surname of the old fighting sailor from Ireland, Tom Sharkey, and the Christian name of his ring idol, Jack Dempsey.

Sharkey made good progress but with some controversies along the way. In July 1927, in a world heavyweight title elimination fight against Dempsey in New York, he was hit low with a left hook in the seventh round. When he turned to referee Jack O'Sullivan to protest, he was promptly struck by another Dempsey left hook, this time to his unprotected jaw, and was counted out despite protests from his corner.

In February 1930, in another world title eliminator, he floored the erratic British champion 'Phainting Phil' Scott with a low left hook in the third round of their Miami fight, then burst into tears, fearing he would be disqualified. Scott was dragged to his corner, his handlers yelling, 'Foul.' However, instead of disqualifying the still weeping Sharkey, referee Lou Magnolia ordered Scott to continue. The Brit, still in pain, limped to the centre of the ring, Sharkey hammered him to the body and Scott held up his hands in surrender.

Sharkey got his world title chance in June 1930 in New York when he was matched with Max Schmeling for the vacant crown, but his temperament got in the way. In the fourth round, he fired a low left hook to the body, similar to the blow that felled Scott. The German, his face a mask of pain, sank to the canvas, clutching his groin. Schmeling was urged to take a three-minute rest by referee Jim Crowley, who felt that while the blow was definitely low, it was not the occasion for a fight, particularly one for the heavyweight championship of the world, to be decided on a foul. However, as Schmeling's seconds carried the stricken boxer to his corner, his Jewish manager, Joe Jacobs, screamed that Sharkey should be disqualified.

There was total confusion at ringside – chaos might be a better description – with one of the judges, Harold Barnes, signalling to the referee that he had seen the foul blow. When the bell rang for the fifth round, Schmeling was still being administered to in his corner. With no official ruling having been made, it was announced that Crowley had disqualified Sharkey and that Schmeling was the new heavyweight champion of the world.

Controversy continued to follow Sharkey like a tracker dog on a scent. In a return bout in New York two years later, he was awarded what most people regarded as an atrociously bad decision when he was adjudged to have won on points after fifteen rounds. 'We wuz robbed,' Schmeling's furious manager Jacobs famously yelled. 'We shouda stood in bed.'

Now here was Sharkey back in New York in June 1933 against Carnera in his first defence and against a challenger with a considerable weight advantage. Carnera had scaled 18 st. 8½ lb against Sharkey's 14 st. 5 lb. Sharkey, at 6 ft, was also conceding 7 in. in height.

Joe Williams, boxing writer for the *New York World-Telegram*, had voiced his scepticism a week before the fight when he said it was a peculiar match between an unpredictable ex-sailor with an almost uncontrollable habit of tossing blows below the belt and a former circus strong man owned by hoodlums. Sharkey's manager 'Fat' John Buckley also had underworld connections. 'Put on the hot seat,' Williams wrote, 'I would have to admit I would not trust either one of these guys as far as I could throw the Empire State Building with my left hand. Which is another way of saying that in this fight, you can make your own choice. I don't want any part of it.'

Boxing scribes who visited both camps were not slow to notice that mobsters and undercover characters seemed to be everywhere. In Carnera's quarters in Pompton Lakes, New Jersey, as well as Duffy and Madden, there were other known racketeers present. In Sharkey's camp in Orangeburg, New York, a group from Detroit's infamous 'Purple Gang' hung out every day with the intention of muscling in on the motion picture receipts. Pete Reilly, a noted New York mobster figure who was banned at the local race tracks, was also seen playing baseball with youngsters at the camp.

With the fight only a week or so away, Sharkey raced from his camp to his home in Newton, Massachusetts, after reports that someone had threatened to kidnap his three children. In fact, three threats were issued before he took the warnings seriously, and he made the four-hundred-mile round trip to put them under police protection, missing two days of training.

On fight night, which was a very sultry evening, there was a crowd of over 40,000 in attendance, and among the celebrities around the ringside were former world heavyweight champions such as Jack Dempsey, Gene Tunney and Tommy Burns, ex-world light-heavyweight title-holder Tommy Loughran and top heavyweight contender Max Baer, who was expected to challenge the winner. The referee was Arthur Donovan, who would become a prominent 'third man' in heavyweight championship fights, most notably involving Joe Louis.

From the opening bell, Carnera was surprisingly agile. Moving around Sharkey, he speared the champion with his long, left jab and covered up to prevent counterpunches. Sharkey would later liken Carnera's defence to 'the limbs of a tree you would need an axe to cut through'.

Sharkey began to come into the fight from the second round, using an effective right to stop the big Italian in his tracks. He was starting to counter Carnera's long lefts with overarm rights to the head and body, and there were worried looks from Primo's corner. 'Go after him,' yelled his man Duffy. 'Wear him out.'

Carnera was still behind on points after the third round, as Sharkey continued to attack, keeping his chin guarded and moving back from the Italian's strength-sapping blows. Close-quarter work against the stronger Carnera had to be avoided, his corner had warned, but Sharkey never stopped coming forward like a tank.

In the fourth, Carnera used his extra weight to try and tire Sharkey by leaning on him. The world champion from Boston just missed Carnera with a hooking left as both men stepped up their attacks. Jack Dempsey remarked to a ringsider, 'Sharkey is having his work cut to handle this big Italian. Anything can happen.'

By the fifth, Carnera looked to have a narrow lead. He was rushing his man to the ropes and attempting to pin him there, although Sharkey was slippery and managed to connect with a smashing left to the jaw that shook the challenger. Carnera was short with a long left near the bell and took a stiff left hook to the jaw in return.

At the outset of the sixth, neither man seemed to be punching his weight. Primo missed with a hooking left before Sharkey slipped to the boards but was up almost at once. Jack fired a right, but Primo's counter-punch was a harder left to the body that drove Sharkey back.

Carnera followed through, with Sharkey still on the defensive, and in the last minute of the round, the Italian missed with a big right but then connected with a lunging right uppercut to the chin that sent Sharkey face down for the full count. He didn't move a muscle as he lay on the canvas. Thirty-three seconds of the round remained.

Following the sensational finish to what had been a somewhat routine fight – a finish which had taken the crowd by complete surprise – 'Fat' John Buckley demanded that the officials examine Carnera's gloves to see if Primo had anything concealed in them, but the charge was ignored by commission member Bill Brown.

Was it a genuine knockout, or a fake? A film of the fight – shot from one angle, as was the custom at the time – shows Carnera landing a right uppercut and Sharkey slithering to the floor. Was it hard enough to knock out the world champion? Or was it a punch packed with real power?

Sharkey's first words to his manager in his corner were, 'Now that he has the championship, he can have the headaches.' Back in his dressing-room, he repeated Jack Dempsey's famous reply to his wife after his first defeat by Gene Tunney: 'I forgot to duck.' Carnera said he thought Sharkey fought better than he did in their first fight two years earlier, which the 'Boston Gob' had won on points. 'But he didn't reach me as often this time, and when I discovered that, I knew I would win,' he said.

Surprisingly, no boxing writer at ringside immediately brought up any suggestions of a fix to either man, given Carnera's past history of crooked fights. Perhaps they thought otherwise in the presence of the shady people associated with the new champion and the former one. They would give their opinions in the safe haven of their reports the next day, though even then, views were divided.

Murray Lewin of the *New York Mirror* wrote, 'I didn't see the punch but sure smelled it.' Offering his reasons for suspicion, Lewin reported: 'Sharkey, after failing to exert himself to any great extent during the first five rounds, suddenly folded up in the sixth and made little if any real effort to keep Carnera off, as he did in the preceding rounds.' Paul Gallico of the *New York Daily News* said, 'Nothing will convince me that it was an honest prizefight, contested on its merits.'

Westbrook Pegler in the *Chicago Tribune* wrote, 'The punch didn't seem sufficient to cause the damage it was purported to cause.'

However, James P. Dawson of the *New York Times* described the finishing blow as a 'terrific right uppercut'. And *Ring* magazine's Nat Fleischer saw it as 'a right-hand blow to the chin that dropped Sharkey in his tracks', although he recalled in his 1949 book *The Heavyweight Championship* that many at the gathering insisted 'an invisible punch' was responsible for the knockout. The historian and author Bert Sugar, recalling the fight, said, 'If boxing had been a wake, it would have been an insult to the deceased.'

Carnera didn't say too much about the fight in later years, rarely elaborating on it, though he always maintained that he put every ounce of power into the punch that put Sharkey on the canvas and emphatically denied the bout was not on the level, despite the allegations. 'I had too much power for Sharkey,' he would say in his fractured English.

Sharkey was much more forthcoming about the fight and the controversial knockout. 'I'll never live it down,' he said in an interview in 1982 when he was 80. 'People don't remember me for being the heavyweight champion. They think of me as being the champion who took a dive. I didn't. I'll swear on my grave I didn't. I saw a vision of Ernie Schaaf, the guy who died after a Carnera fight, in front of me. The next thing Carnera hit me, and that's the end of the story, but I could never convince anybody. I couldn't even convince my manager. He wanted to know if I bet my purse on Carnera.'

Primo's purse from the fight was $12,000, but after all the deductions had been made to the syndicate, he received only a few hundred dollars. A simple man, he was seen the next day on a street off Broadway with writer Damon Runyon's wife Patrice, buying size 16 shoes with a carrier bag containing dollar bills.

Carnera successfully defended his title twice, with points decisions over the rugged if unskilled Spaniard Paolino Uzcudun and the Philadelphian stylist Tommy Loughran, who was outweighed by a record 6 st. 2 lb. Loughran, a former world light-heavyweight champion, later complained that he could not box his usual fight because Carnera's big feet were constantly stepping on his toes. He revealed that the big toe on his right foot was fractured. 'A bigger factor was the Italian dinner Primo had before the fight,' he recalled. 'When he leaned over my face and let me have that garlic at full blast, I was almost helpless.'

In his third defence, Carnera was hammered to defeat in eleven rounds by Max Baer in 1934 after being on the canvas ten times. From then on it was mainly downhill: he was butchered by the promising Joe Louis in six rounds in 1935 and, the following year, was twice smashed to defeat by young Leroy Haynes, 'The Black Shadow'. In the first fight, Haynes stopped him in three rounds and in the second, less than two months later, in nine. In that second fight, an unnecessary rematch in which Carnera took another terrible beating, he climbed out of the ring with a damaged kidney.

Benito Mussolini, the Fascist dictator who had supported and befriended Primo as champion, now had nothing to do with him. Duffy and Madden walked out on him, their former meal ticket of no further use to them. Promoter Jeff Dickson refused to book Carnera on the basis that he was no longer a big draw. Everyone was deserting the gentle giant, like vultures abandoning their prey after picking the last ragged piece of flesh from the bones.

The big Italian announced his retirement in 1937 but made an abortive comeback after the war, finally quitting in May 1946, after losing three fights inside the distance against the same man, Luigi Musina. Carnera's luck changed remarkably in retirement. A surprise letter from an all-in wrestling promoter in Los Angeles named Harold Harris suggested the ex-champion should try the sport, saying he could earn some big money. Carnera thought, 'Why not?' After all, he had started out as a circus strong man, and if he could be a success in the grunt-and-groan racket, why not give it his best shot? Anyway, what had he to lose?

Primo wired his acceptance to Harris and, in July 1946, left for California. He began his new career a month later, winning convincingly against Tommy O'Toole. Soon, invitations flowed in from all over the US, and this time he was not being fleeced by crooked managers and agents. He made enough money – usually between $1,000 and $2,000 a week or the equivalent of between

$8,000 and $16,000 today – to be able to bring his wife and family to California and purchase a house in Hollywood for $30,000.

During breaks from the all-in wrestling circuit, Carnera had parts in several major movies before he fell foul of the movie capital when he sued Columbia Pictures in 1956 over *The Harder They Fall*. The film, in which the main character was depicted as little more than a simpleton, was transparently based on his own life. It seemed an open and shut case for an award of punitive damages, as the identification between Carnera and the character in the movie, Toro Moreno, as well as the similarities to the storyline of Primo's own life, were so obvious. However, in a Californian court and with a major, powerful Hollywood studio as defendant, Carnera had little chance, even though he had some top lawyers. In the Santa Monica courtroom, Judge Stanley Mosk threw out the former champion's $1.5 million claim, saying, 'One who becomes a celebrity waives the right to privacy and does not regain it by changing his profession from boxer to wrestler.'

With Hollywood slamming the door on him, Carnera managed to get a few small parts in European movies, but his main income was from all-in wrestling. He took part in matches all over the world and from the proceeds bought a restaurant and liquor store in Los Angeles, though it was said that he drank more than he sold.

Primo became ill, and, at his own request, his wife Pina took him home to Sequals where he died of cirrhosis of the liver in June 1967 at the age of 60. By an extraordinary coincidence, his death came 34 years to the very day he had won the world heavyweight championship so controversially from Jack Sharkey.

Even up to the end, Carnera was philosophical about his unhappy life in the boxing ring. 'Life has a way of evening things up,' he said from the wheelchair to which he had become confined in the closing months of his life. 'Where are those greedy vultures now? They were either killed by their own kind or put in jail. Some of them became little better than beggars and panhandlers. All that money. What good did it do any of them?'

6

MADISON MADNESS
AND MAYHEM

In the spring of 1996, the respected referee Mills Lane considered Riddick Bowe the best heavyweight around, at a time when the world title was fragmented. He likened the big Brooklyn boxer to modern greats like Muhammad Ali, Sugar Ray Leonard and Marvin Hagler. 'On the whole, Ali, Leonard and Hagler were true warriors who maximised their talents and unflinchingly charged head-long toward their goal,' recalled Lane, whose famous catchphrase was 'Let's get it on', the title of his 1998 autobiography. 'Nothing was going to stand in their way. They fought through the daily aches and pains, through the traumas of disappointment and failure of life, and eventually succeeded, no matter what the obstacle. That spring of 1996, I honestly believed Bowe was in this category. I had seen all three of his fights with Evander Holyfield, the first two of which were as good as any in recent years, and I considered Bowe to be the best of the heavyweights. His tools were far better than Holyfield's, and at least one notch above Mike Tyson's.

'Bowe had it all – size, strength, an impressive chin and devastating punching ability. Although he couldn't knock you dead, he did have a good left jab, a better than average right-hand, a decent hook and he knew how to handle himself on the inside. Despite these impressive credentials, though, Riddick Bowe did not maximise his capabilities. He would not pay the price to be the best. Although I liked the guy, he was, in my mind, a failure because he didn't go as far as he could.'

Bowe was undisputed world heavyweight champion in the early 1990s and the dominant figure in the division during Mike Tyson's period in jail on a rape charge. On the way up, he proclaimed, 'When I'm world champion and one of the most famous athletes on the planet, I plan to use my name to make the world a better place for people of all colours. I'll be an example. You can count on me.'

The trouble was that Bowe was never an example and nobody could count on him. His former trainer, the legendary Eddie Futch, said of Bowe: 'The guy had the agility of Muhammad Ali and a left jab like Larry Holmes, but he could never handle success. He had inconsistent performances, an intense dislike for training, and a passion for eating junk food and not listening to advice from his corner. Bowe was one of boxing's great enigmas. He was a man who had it all but threw it away.'

Bowe was also the man involved in the infamous riot at Madison Square Garden on 11 July 1996 following his brawl with the rugged Pole, Andrew Golota. Ignited by Bowe's rowdy entourage, it was the worst riot in the 117-year history of boxing at the New York venue, with a spate of injuries and arrests. The beleaguered fight game had suffered yet another savage blow below the belt.

A New Yorker, Bowe was born in the teeming ghettos of Brooklyn on 10 August 1967. His childhood wasn't easy as he came from a family of 13 children, all raised by his mother Dorothy after his parents split up. Like many kids in his tough neighbourhood, he used to hang around local gyms watching the pros in training and soon developed an interest in boxing.

Bowe joined an amateur club and seemed to be a natural. He made fast progress and in a career in which he won four New York Golden Gloves titles, he achieved his greatest successes abroad. In 1985, he

116

won the light-heavyweight gold medal at the World Junior Championships in Bucharest. Three years later, he won a silver medal as a super-heavy at the 1988 Olympics in Seoul, losing out in the final to Lennox Lewis, who was the Canadian representative.

Riddick won the first round with his harder and more accurate punching, but Lewis opened up in the second and forced a standing count after a burst of five punches sent Bowe leaning back over the ropes and gasping for air like a beached whale. The end came after forty-three seconds of the round when a looping right and a fast left rocked Bowe again for a second count of eight before the referee intervened.

Bowe protested that he was fit to continue, waving his hands at the referee. 'The decision to stop the fight was premature,' he complained later. 'I was trying to indicate I was OK.' But his pleas were to no avail and the gold medal went to Lewis. Not surprisingly, Lewis saw the fight differently. 'I really tagged him,' he would say. 'His eyes were glazed and he was gone. I wish I'd knocked him out because he kept complaining he was robbed. He was walking around trying to waste time so that he could get his senses back. His eyes weren't there.'

Riddick's Olympic effort was also marred by emotional turmoil. His brother was dying of cancer, and his sister was murdered when she tried to stop a drug addict stealing her welfare cheque. However, out of all this chaos and his Olympic final defeat, he became a more positive person. On his return home, he re-evaluated his life and boxing career and decided to turn professional, making his heavyweight debut in Reno, Nevada, in March 1989 with an impressive win in two rounds over Lionel Butler.

With Eddie Futch in his corner, the future looked rosy. The veteran trainer was a former Golden Gloves champion out of Detroit and had worked in the same gym as Joe Louis when the Brown Bomber was on the way up in the early 1930s. He had been training boxers since middleweight contender Holman Williams approached him in 1938, and he would go on to guide 21 boxers to world titles including Joe Frazier, Larry Holmes, Ken Norton, Michael Spinks, Alexis Arguello and Bowe.

From the outset, Futch's instructions to Bowe were that he would have to train, train, train. 'If you consent to do what I say, you can be the best heavyweight in the world,' said Futch, who was in his late 70s at the time and considered Bowe to have tremendous potential. 'The minute you slouch off on me, though, I'm gone. At my age I'm not going to let Riddick Bowe or anybody else waste my time.'

Bowe assured the wise old trainer, 'I'll do anything you ask me to.' He kept to his word and trained hard — and diligently. He finished the year with thirteen wins, all but one inside the scheduled distance, and eleven before the third round. Boxing writers and the public were impressed by his punching power and his ability to take a good belt on the jaw and stay upright. In a division where size can matter, his solid physique provided him with the power to destroy. The Brooklynite was 6 ft 5 in. and weighed 17 st. 2 lb. He would be known as 'Big Daddy', not because of his considerable bulk but because of his large family. The boxer and his wife Judith had seven children.

Riddick moved up the ratings with victories over Pinklon Thomas, Tyrell Biggs, Tony Tubbs, Bruce Seldon and Pierre Coetzer, which led to a shot at the undisputed world heavyweight title against Evander Holyfield in Las Vegas in November 1992. Along the way, however, he would be dogged by controversial incidents.

The first sign of things to come was in October 1991 when he was taunted at the end of the first round of a fight with Elijah Tillery in Washington, DC. At the conclusion of the round, Bowe swung a punch at his opponent who retaliated by kicking the Brooklyn boxer on the backside and then on the shin. Bowe replied by punching Tillery and then pushing him through the ropes. Rock Newman, Bowe's volatile manager, then grabbed Elijah around the neck and yanked him out of the ring as a number of other skirmishes broke out. Tillery was disqualified for 'flagrantly kicking', fined $2,000 and suspended for a year. For their part in the fracas, Newman and Bowe were fined $2,500 and $500 respectively. It would not be the last time that Bowe and Newman would run foul of the boxing authorities.

In the Holyfield fight, however, both were good boys. In a thriller, Bowe put Evander, older by five years, on the boards in the eleventh round of their twelve-rounder for the first time in twenty-nine fights and won the decision and the unified heavyweight championship. *Ring* magazine voted it 'Fight of the Year'. The sport had a new Golden Boy: a big, powerful hitter with a strong chin, good infighting ability and a solid jab. At 25 and with $7 million in prize money in his bank account, Bowe's adventures, or sometimes misadventures, had just begun.

'When I'm world champion . . . I plan to use my name to make the world a better place,' he had said – and now he was the king. This was his chance to stand by his words. He embarked on a world tour, stopping off to shake hands with Pope John Paul II, meet Nelson Mandela and offer support for his African National Congress party, visit a Somalia torn by famine and civil war, and continue his support for America's President Clinton.

Futch, though, could see trouble ahead, and he took Bowe aside one day. 'Look,' he said, 'you're doing too much travelling, too much running around, Riddick. Remember, you're the champion now, the best, and you'll have to put boxing number one to stay that way. I've seen too many good fighters in my time fall by the wayside.'

The World Boxing Council were putting pressure on Bowe to defend the title against their leading contender Lennox Lewis, but neither Riddick nor his manager were anxious to accommodate the man who had ruined Bowe's Olympic gold-medal dreams. 'Not just yet,' said Newman. They were also at war with promoter Don King and his control and monopoly of the WBC.

The Council threatened to strip Bowe of the title, but when the Bowe entourage were in London for the BBC's Sports Personality of the Year Awards in December 1992, Riddick and Newman beat the WBC to the punch by announcing they were giving up the title. With that, Riddick walked out of the hotel by a back entrance, and with photographers and reporters in hot pursuit, dumped his belt into a rubbish bin. Embarrassed WBC officials quickly retrieved the belt and promptly announced they were withdrawing recognition of Bowe.

A few weeks later, they proclaimed Lewis as the new champion. Meanwhile, Bowe, remembering Futch's warning about not devoting enough time to competitive boxing, quickly got into action early in

1993 by twice defending his World Boxing Association and International Boxing Federation championships, knocking out Michael Doakes in the first round and stopping Jesse Ferguson in the second.

Bowe and Newman agreed to a return fight with Holyfield in Las Vegas for 6 November, but, much to Futch's worst fears, Riddick was beginning to lose the plot. His training efforts were desultory, whereas Holyfield worked diligently to build up his body and strength. Bowe's weight ballooned up to 17 st. 10 lb with nearly a stone of unwanted flab.

A capacity crowd of 14,242 filed into the open-air arena at Caesars Palace expecting a war, and it was the aggressive Bowe who provided it in an explosive first round. He hurt Holyfield with a barrage of blows, and it almost looked like Evander was heading for the door marked 'exit', but he was able to recover. By the second round, he seemed to be in charge with sharp combinations.

By the third, the fitter Holyfield had stepped up the pace and forced the champion backwards with long lefts and smashing overhand rights. By the sixth, the halfway stage, Bowe was already a forlorn figure, blood seeping from cuts over his left eyebrow and on the bridge of his nose. He was breathing deeply, his lack of training clearly showing. On the other hand, Holyfield still looked fresh.

It appeared that Holyfield was ready to blitz his way to a sensational win and regain the titles when, after one minute and two seconds of round seven, one of the most bizarre incidents in boxing history occurred. Holyfield suddenly broke away from a clinch and walked away, staring incredulously up into the darkened sky. Bowe's gaze followed, and neither could quite believe what they were seeing.

Hurtling out of the night sky towards the ring was a paraglider who crash-landed seconds later, hitting the apron of the ring near Bowe's corner and falling backwards into the crowd, the parachute becoming entangled in the overhead lights. Chaos reigned, and the reaction from the shocked crowd was that the 'invader' might be a suicide bomber or a crank who planned to kill the boxers. The lights above the ring were popping, leading many to believe it was gunfire. Bowe's pregnant wife fainted when she thought somebody was trying to shoot her husband and was rushed to hospital, as was trainer Futch, who experienced heart palpitations. Several spectators also needed hospital treatment suffering from minor injuries and shock.

During the mayhem, the lunatic paraglider, who turned out to be a 33-year-old publicity seeker named James Miller, was beaten up by Bowe's by now infamous security men. Meanwhile, the remnants of the yellow, blue and pink parachute were untangled from the ring canopy by an athletic individual who hauled himself overhand, to thunderous applause, up the 30-foot ring support and then crawled along the canopy. Miller was eventually released from the straps of his parachute and hustled away to a police cell. The next day he was given a derisory fine for 'dangerous flying' and warned about any more eccentric exploits.

After a 21-minute delay, order was eventually restored. The two boxers had both been wrapped in dressing gowns and blankets to keep their bodies as warm as possible in the cold winter air and were anxious to resume the official action. However, there was no question that the enforced rest had been of more help to Bowe and had allowed him to gain a second wind.

It was Holyfield, nevertheless, who dominated the seventh and eighth rounds, picking up his rhythm immediately, stifling Bowe's own attacks and peppering the champion with hard, accurate counters. Sensing the titles were slipping away from him, Bowe summoned the willpower to launch a despairing late challenge and rocked Holyfield, particularly in a sensational final round when Bowe charged at him like an enraged bull.

Holyfield withstood the blazing attack until the bell and though it was close, he got the verdict of two judges, with a third scoring the contest a draw. Bowe had been champion just seven days short of a full year, though he would reign again sixteen months later by knocking out Britain's Herbie Hide in the sixth round of a match also held in Las Vegas. The Hide fight was only recognised by the World Boxing Organisation as being for the title, but all that mattered to Bowe was that he could call himself champion for the second time. He visited Mike Tyson in prison and told him, 'You can have a title shot, Mike, when you get out. The chance is yours.'

Tyson thanked him and said, 'It's a deal, man.'

In between the Holyfield return and the Hide fights, Bowe was involved in two further controversial incidents. In August 1994, he floored the unbeaten Buster Mathis Jr. in the fourth round in Atlantic City, and while Mathis was on one knee, landed a powerful right on his already dazed opponent. It seemed disqualification was inevitable yet referee Arthur Mercante, sen., called the punch 'an unintentional foul' and the New Jersey commission ruled the fight as a no-contest.

Four months later in Las Vegas, Bowe struck his opponent Larry Donald at the pre-fight conference with a cracking left–right combination after Donald made some uncomplimentary remarks. Bowe won their dull 12-rounder convincingly on points, but mayhem erupted again at the post-fight conference when a court official attempted to serve Riddick with a lawsuit, charging him with assault and battery. Unsurprisingly, he refused to sign the papers, and in the mêlée that followed, both camps traded insults, with Bowe having to be pulled out the door by the police.

There was yet another contentious incident at a pre-fight conference involving Bowe. This time it happened before his fight with Jorge Gonzalez in Las Vegas in June 1995 when he threw a glass at the big Cuban, and Gonzalez attempted to attack Bowe before order was restored. As a result, both men were given a restraining order by the Nevada State Athletic Commission which forbade them appearing together at any press conference in the lead-up to the fight. This rule even extended to the weigh-in.

The fight passed without incident and Bowe won with a knockout in the sixth round. *KO* magazine ranked him the world's number one heavyweight, with an impressive thirty-seven wins in thirty-nine fights, one loss and one no-contest. Thirty-two of his victories had ended inside the scheduled distance.

'I really want Tyson,' he said in an interview. 'I want there to be no doubt who is the greatest heavyweight out there today, and the best way to do that is to give Tyson the whupping of a lifetime. We don't know what kind of fighter Tyson will be after his layoff, but we can be sure he will be prepared and motivated. But he is a one-dimensional fighter. Going forward, he's setting the pace and firing big punches but get him to back up, like "Buster" Douglas did, and he's an easy target.'

Bowe also gave his assessment of the other heavyweights around at that time. On George Foreman he said, 'Everybody has the lowdown on him. He's old, slow and immobile, but he still packs a punch, though I don't think I would have any trouble with him.' On Lennox Lewis he said, 'For a guy who has been a pro for a while now, he still looks like an amateur in the ring. Take away his left jab and he doesn't know what to do.' On Evander Holyfield he commented, 'Evander likes to throw punches in bunches, and the best way to prevent him from doing that is to keep him off balance. I'm ready for him.'

Holyfield and Bowe had now been in the ring together on two occasions, with a win each. Two years after their second fight – now known as 'The Parachute Affair' – they met for a third time in Las Vegas in November 1995. Holyfield was no longer champion, but most people nevertheless considered him and Bowe the two best active heavyweights in the world.

Like the first two clashes, the third fight was also a thriller. Bowe won by a knockout in the eighth round, but he had to climb off the canvas in a dramatic sixth session to achieve victory. A terrific left hook sent him sprawling for an eight count, the first knockdown of his career, but fortune smiled on him like it would a helpless swimmer confronted by an alligator without an appetite. Bowe managed to get through the round and in the seventh he was back on top. Then, after putting Holyfield down twice in the eighth, referee Joe Cortez intervened as a beaming, if battered, Riddick did a war dance around the ring.

Tyson was now back on the rampage, hungry to reclaim his place at the top of the heavyweight division. He had served only three of his six years on the rape charge and had already won his comeback fight, dismissing Peter McNeeley in eighty-eight seconds in August 1995. The outclassed McNeeley was disqualified when his manager Vinnie Vecchione, a former mobster with a .22 bullet still lodged in his shoulder, climbed into the ring to force referee Mills Lane to stop the fight. Obviously he reckoned that a disqualification would look much better on McNeeley's record than a straight knockout, and he got his wish.

Now only one fight really mattered: Bowe v. Tyson. They were clearly the two best heavyweights in the world irrespective of the fragmented world titles that were being tossed about like scandal stories at a movie party. Both were anxious for the match, although Tyson did say he wanted a few more fights under his belt before taking on any of the top contenders.

Meanwhile, what the Americans like to call 'a foreigner' was making noises, this time a Pole, not exactly a common nationality to figure in the world heavyweight shake-up. Based in Chicago, Andrew Golota had been an outstanding amateur with a record anyone would be proud of – a silver medal at the World Junior Championships in Bucharest, a gold at the 1986 European Juniors in Copenhagen and a bronze at both the 1988 Seoul Olympics and the 1989 European Senior Championships in Athens. He was also a four-time Polish champion.

A poor kid from the streets of Warsaw, Golota grew up with a foster mother after his parents went their separate ways. A street fighter by nature, he fled Poland in 1990, after being involved in a pub brawl, and settled in Chicago. An all-round sportsman, he told reporters in interviews that his favourite sporting stars included Pelé, Monica Seles, Andre Agassi and Michael Jordan, with Muhammad Ali his all-time number one.

At 6 ft 4 in. and weighing around 17 st., he knew he had the power and the strength to be as good, if not better, as a professional than he had been as an amateur. All he wanted was the chance, and his veteran trainer Lou Duva of the promotional group Main Events, Inc., would provide that. Duva was convinced that the burly Pole had what it would take to go all the way to the top, always providing he learned to curb his natural impetuousness, which included butting, low punching, using his elbows and shoulders in clinches, and the occasional bite on the blindside of the referee. 'Besides all that,' said Duva in all seriousness, 'he's as clean as a whistle.'

Golota got his big opportunity in New York, at Madison Square

Garden no less, against Riddick Bowe on 11 July 1996. Undefeated in 27 fights which were mostly brawls, 25 by the short route, Golota was given little chance against a man rated as one of the best heavyweights in the world. Bowe was no longer champion – Tyson held the honour at that time – but he was still a formidable contender with thirty-nine wins, one loss and a draw, and he climbed into the ring a solid 10–1 favourite. Consequently, Riddick did not take the rugged Pole seriously and paid scant attention to his training despite Eddie Futch's protestations: 'Don't underestimate this guy. He could be dangerous.'

It all came very close to being cancelled. On the afternoon of the fight, a controversy erupted over the scheduled distance. Golota shared the general impression that it was to be a ten-rounder but was informed the contest was to be over twelve rounds. He had never gone 12 before. The wording of the contract gave Bowe's contentious manager Rock Newman the option to make it a 12-round match, which he had chosen to do that morning without informing Golota or his team.

Golota was furious when he heard that he would have to box two extra rounds. He stormed around his room as his promotional group Main Events, Inc., tried to calm him, but he refused to back down and started to pack his bags. He was going straight home to Chicago, fight or no fight, despite the fact that an extra six minutes of action would presumably benefit him as he was in better condition than Bowe for the longer haul.

When Newman was hastily summoned to his room, Golota told Bowe's manager that Main Events, Inc., had agreed to the shorter distance for which he had trained accordingly and that was it. Newman, part of Spencer Promotions, who were putting on the fight, insisted that Golota would have to go through with it as per his contract. Eventually, Main Events, Inc., solved the problem by agreeing to add on an extra $50,000 to the Pole's $600,000 purse. All was saved, though doubts were still expressed among boxing writers that the angry and confused Golota would climb through the ropes at all.

There was a crowd of 11,252 in attendance and as referee Wayne

Kelly called the two to the centre of the ring, the tension was heavy in the air. This could be a war. Bowe, aged 28, had weighed a career high of 18 st. ¼ lb, and Golota, also 28, was 17 st. 5 lb. Golota was expected to come out brawling but instead showed good boxing ability, outspeeding and outjabbing Bowe. Whereas the 6 ft 5 in. Bowe fought flat-footed and showed no head movement, Golota, only an inch shorter, was effectively able to duck under the blows or nimbly dance away.

Bowe did get through with a few sharp jabs and a couple of strong rights, but the Pole clearly won the round, which had been a rough one. Golota had landed three punches, each borderline, and when he got back to his corner, he was told by his seconds, 'Watch those body shots, Andrew, or you [will] find yourself disqualified.'

Referee Kelly had been concerned before the fight about the Pole's reputation for dirty fighting, including biting. 'If this guy bites Bowe, I've got a plan on what to do,' he said without any elaborations, although it was clear he had disqualification in mind. The fight never reached the biting stage, but Golota was soon in trouble for other misdemeanours.

In the second round, Golota continued with his jabbing and was making the former world champion miss with counter-shots by moving his head back. Bowe was simply marching after his man, looking for that big shot which never seemed to come. Even when Bowe did land, Golota took the blows well and did not seem to be in any danger. With about fifty seconds remaining in the round, Bowe finally got through with two good left hooks to the jaw, and the stunned Pole backed off. Riddick moved in, but Golota unleashed a fast two-handed flurry that had Bowe holding on. Bowe punched back wildly and at the bell just missed hitting the referee who danced swiftly out of the way.

Bowe's left eye was starting to swell as the bell rang for the start of round three, and he began the session determined to take control, stiff jabs pushing Golota back a few paces. The Warsaw warrior, however, quickly got the upper hand and landed a smashing left hook to Bowe's head five seconds before the bell. In the fourth, Bowe seemed as if he was tiring, leading to suggestions by boxing writers that he was not as fit as he should have been. His punches were becoming wild and sloppy, and Golota was showing superior hand speed.

A solid right staggered Bowe, and he fell into the ropes in some distress. Suddenly, like a bomb going off, the fight exploded into action. Golota delivered a vicious left hook to the groin, and Bowe sank to the canvas, his face a mask of pain. Kelly immediately yelled 'Stop' and deducted a point from the Pole. He also informed Bowe that he would be given five minutes to recover or he would be disqualified. Riddick took close to two minutes before resuming the fight. There was a little less than 30 seconds remaining in the round, and the action was uneventful.

Things began to go further downhill for Bowe in the fifth. He had a promising start, but then Golota hurt him against the ropes and raked him with punches. Bowe, looking in bad shape by now, punched back wildly, but the Pole saw them coming and was able to land more hard, accurate blows. At the bell, a frustrated Bowe pushed his opponent who replied with a scowl. It was now a hate fight.

The pace had been hectic over the first five rounds, and in the sixth, both were content to take things a little easier. Golota, however, landed another low blow and again had a point deducted. Although the punch did not land in the groin area, it was clearly below the belt. Bowe doubled over, grimacing in pain, and took an additional minute to recuperate.

In the seventh, Golota really took control. He punched hard and accurately with hardly a reply from the tired and dispirited Bowe but then got his third point deducted when he landed a very low right uppercut. Riddick grimaced but did not ask for a rest. While Bowe was the victim of low blows, he was not blameless either. He used rabbit punches throughout, though Golota was by far the worse offender.

The Pole moved in and hammered Bowe with both hands, and the Brooklynite was in real trouble. He was shaken, tired and mentally discouraged, and looked like he was only a few punches away from a stoppage defeat. Golota, having had three points deducted and on the brink of disqualification himself, needed only to bide his time and watch his punches to pull off a win. Then, quite inexplicably, he unleashed a powerful left hook which landed smack in Bowe's groin. The American went down on his back like a sack of potatoes dropped off a truck, and Kelly immediately moved in to signal he was disqualifying the Pole, resulting in his first defeat as a professional. Twenty-seven seconds remained in the round.

As Bowe writhed on the canvas, his entourage – consisting of manager/promoter Newman, Jason Harris and Bernard Brooks, sen., two of Bowe's associates, plus Stephen Bowe, Riddick's cousin – climbed through the ropes and rushed towards Golota's corner. After Brooks shoved Golota, the Pole retaliated with a left hook that put him on the canvas.

Bernard Brooks Jr. had followed them into the ring and struck Golota on the back of the head with a mobile phone – and they were considerably bigger and heavier then than they are today. It opened up a gash in the big Pole's crew-cut head, which later required 13 stitches. Brooks Jr. would later say, 'I went in to make sure Rock was all right. I tried to hold Golota away, but he swung at me with a left. At that stage I struck him with the phone.'

By now, the whole scene was one of sheer chaos and turmoil. Several fans who had been waving Polish flags and had come to support the Warsaw boxer also tried to storm the ring but were beaten back by stern police officers yielding batons. From then on, the trouble escalated. Heavy folding chairs, drink cans and any other objects the crowd could find were thrown, and the ring was filled with people punching, kicking and shouting. The scene resembled a battlefield.

After Golota was struck by the mobile phone, Lou Duva entered the ring to 'pull my fighter out of there', as he explained later. Earlier in the day, the Pole's 74-year-old trainer had relinquished his role as chief cornerman after his implanted cardiac stimulator had failed him. Once in the ring, Duva was pushed to the canvas, where he lay flat on his back before being removed to New York University Medical Center for observation, due to fears that he had suffered a heart attack.

Golota, the back of his head covered in blood, had meanwhile

Billy Graham shakes Kid Gavilan with a right, but it was the Cuban who won a highly unpopular decision. (Author's private collection.)

Promoter James D. Norris (left), and mobsters Frank 'Blinky' Palermo (centre) and Frankie Carbo. (Author's private collection.)

Bruce Woodcock sends Lee Oma's head back with a long left hook. With the crowd chanting 'Lie down, lie down', Oma obliged by taking the full count in the fourth. (Courtesy of the *Boxing News* library.)

Flamboyant promoter Don King with a cardboard cut-out of Mike Tyson. King got his start in boxing by persuading Muhammad Ali to appear in a charity exhibition. (Author's private collection.)

Kid McCoy (left) and James J. Corbett square off for a publicity shot before their fight. McCoy was knocked out in the fifth and claimed he deliberately lost. (Author's private collection.)

Terry McGovern lands a right to the body of his brother Hugh, also a boxer, in a sparring session. McGovern and Joe Gans were famously involved in a fight scandal in Chicago. (Author's private collection.)

One of boxing's biggest shocks: Jack Sharkey is counted out by referee Arthur Donovan in the sixth round as new champion Primo Carnera comes forward. (Author's private collection.)

Andrew Golota fires a left hook against Riddick Bowe, shortly before Golota was disqualified in the seventh round. (Courtesy of the *Boxing News* library)

The riot in Madison Square Garden following Riddick Bowe's disqualification win over Andrew Golota. (Author's private collection.)

Jake LaMotta takes a left hook to the head from Billy Fox but later confessed that he threw the fight to get a world middleweight title shot against Marcel Cerdan. (Courtesy of the *Boxing News* library.)

An enraged Mike Tyson bites Evander Holyfield's ear in the third round of their return fight, shortly before Tyson was disqualified for a second bite. (Author's private collection.)

Evander Holyfield with a chunk out of his right ear. (Author's private collection.)

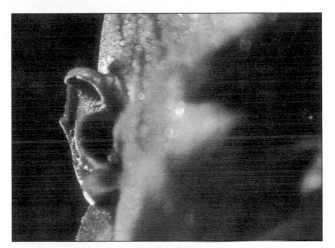

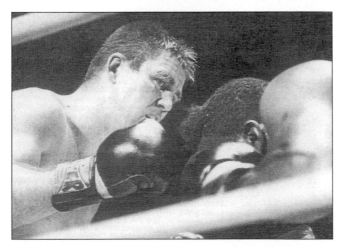

Jerry Quarry (left), too brave for his own good, at close quarters in his drawn fight with Floyd Patterson. (Courtesy of the *Boxing News* library.)

Referee Jersey Joe Walcott attempts to get Muhammad Ali to a neutral corner as Sonny Liston lies face down on the canvas. (Courtesy of the *Irish Independent*.)

'You be careful what you write about me, you hear,' warns Muhammad Ali as the author takes notes, and Billy Conn, another boxing great, looks on. In the background, partially obscured, is Ali's trainer Angelo Dundee. (Courtesy of the *Irish Independent*.)

Sandy Saddler gets Willie Pep in a wrestling headlock in their fourth fight, which was marred by fouls from both men. Each boxer claimed the other started the illegal tactics. Pep retired in the ninth. (Author's private collection.)

Sugar Ray Leonard taunts Roberto Duran in their second fight, which ended when Duran sensationally quit in the eight round, exclaiming, '*No más, no más*.' (Courtesy of the Lonsdale International Sporting Club library.)

The author meets movie star George Raft (centre) and former world heavyweight champion Rocky Marciano when all three were in London for the Muhammad Ali v. Henry Cooper title fight. (Courtesy of the *Irish Independent*.)

Rocky Marciano sends challenger Don Cockell floundering into the ropes before winning on a stoppage in the ninth round, but Marciano broke every rule in the book. (Author's private collection.)

Referee Douglas moves in to warn Jack Doyle to keep his punches up against Jack Petersen or risk disqualification, which was what happened in the second round. (Courtesy of the *Irish Independent*.)

The author feels Jack Doyle's big right hand when the 'Gorgeous Gael' was in Ireland for a singing tour long after his retirement from the ring. (Courtesy of the *Irish Independent*.)

managed to climb out onto the apron of the ring, jump to the floor, stare down a young spectator who had confronted him and hurry through the crowded aisle to his dressing-room. By this stage, the ring was filled with police officers, security guards and spectators punching, pushing, stomping, shoving and yelling, with much of it covered by Home Box Office, which televised the fight live. As the mêlée spread into the arena, some spectators tossed more folding chairs towards the ring, with many ringside fans hastily retreating to the relative safety of the upper seats.

Several minutes passed, however, before the announcement, 'All security to ringside,' by Michael Buffer blared over the public address system. Moments later, it was followed by, 'All New York City police report to ringside.' This left the rest of the arena unsupervised, and the thugs took advantage of the chaotic situation, with more fights breaking out. A standard staff of 76 uniformed security men had been assigned to work the fight, and 18 New York City police officers were marked for duty outside the Garden. However, this number was obviously inadequate to handle what had now become a full-scale riot, the likes of which had never been experienced at a boxing match before, in New York or anywhere else. An extra 150 police officers were rushed to the scene as was the city's chief citizen, Mayor Rudolph Giuliani. Five years later, Giuliani's dust-streaked face would be seen on television screens and newspapers all around the world, memorably embodying the grief of New Yorkers and their determination not to be beaten down by the terrorist attacks on the Twin Towers.

Police wearing riot helmets set up flares on 33rd Street and 7th Avenue, directing traffic away from the Garden's entrance as hundreds of onlookers continued to mill about, many visibly shaken. In the previous Garden – there have been four in all – three riots occurred in the mid-1960s, each involving spectators throwing bottles and cartons at the ring following an unpopular decision but nothing on such a massive scale as this.

The mayhem continued inside the arena, with fist fights breaking out all over and people shouting and screaming. Because of the ethnic differences between the two boxers – one a black man who had clawed his way up from poor beginnings in Brooklyn and the other an equally impoverished white man from a Warsaw ghetto, although both were considerably richer at that point – much of the mêlée was fought along racial lines.

The ringside reporters had long hurried to the safety of the dressing-rooms, pulling Mayor Giuliani along with them. Moments later, when it seemed that things were getting better, it all erupted again, with pockets of fights breaking out between Polish Americans and African Americans.

Waving batons, the police, reputedly the toughest in the world, eventually got the situation under some semblance of control, although it took over half an hour, as Garden officials ordered everybody to vacate the building. Twenty-two people, including eight police officers, were taken to St Vincent's Hospital for treatment. Remarkably, nobody was killed. There were 16 arrests. 'This was the product of a few people who acted like criminals,' said Mayor Giuliani.

Ironically, Madison Square Garden, the traditional home of US boxing for over a century and an independent sports promotion outfit in its own right, had closed its doors to boxing three years earlier when it was taken over by the giant Paramount Communications. The new owners had apparently been scared off by yet another US Senate investigation into the fight game and wanted to give the place a new image. Inside a year, however, they had second thoughts and opened the doors to the sport again, following pressure from boxing people not only in New York but across the US as well. Now they had been confronted by a full-scale riot.

Not surprisingly there was condemnation of the disgraceful scenes from all quarters, with politicians and people in high places calling for a complete ban on boxing, not only in New York City but in the state. The *New York Times* came out strongest in attacking the riot. 'Four low blows produced an even lower blow for boxing last night,' wrote Dave Anderson, who criticised the Garden authorities' slowness in controlling 'the ugly incident'. He continued, 'The sport incurred another major injury to its dwindling image.' Gerald Eskenazi in the same paper wrote, 'The bout that dissolved into a frightening brawl evoked the darkest evenings of boxing's controversial past.' Under the heading 'What A Riot!' in *Ring* magazine, Steve Farhood wrote, 'Those who care about boxing could only shake their heads in frustration and disgust.' Farhood not only blamed Bowe's manager Rock Newman for his inability to control his cornermen from rushing across the ring to Golota's corner but also stated that 'the Garden's security was grossly ineffective'.

Jack Hirsch in *Boxing News* said, 'In all my years of attending shows, I have never felt my safety threatened to such an extent. People were attacking one another for no apparent reason, not only at ringside but in other parts of the arena as well. We waited for the Garden's security force to get things under control. When it became apparent that they were understaffed, the criminal element inside the arena took over.'

Glyn Leach, in *Boxing Monthly*, wrote, 'As a veteran of a few of these disturbances now, I can easily say that this was the worst violence I have witnessed at ringside. As for the police, where the hell were they? It was 15 minutes into the riot before I saw any police presence, and there was none of any value until nearly half an hour of fighting had passed – and they were ham-fisted when they did arrive. I saw one man, who must have been at least 65, pushed through a crash-barrier by one of New York's finest.'

As for the action inside the ring, the three judges' scorecards were not available in the sheer mayhem that unfolded, but the ringside boxing writers all had Golota well ahead, even allowing for the three points deducted for low blows. The majority of the reporters gave Bowe only one of the six completed rounds. Bowe was fined $1 million, a fifth of his purse, and the licences of Newman and Duva were suspended indefinitely.

As it happened, Bowe and his team were back five months later for the return fight but without Eddie Futch. The veteran trainer, who had been with Riddick from the start, had resigned because of 'irreconcilable differences'. Futch later recalled, 'I was shocked the way Bowe looked in the first fight. He lost focus and everything else became more important than being the best fighter around. He might have become the best heavyweight of all time. He was big,

131

strong, had a good left hand and could fight inside. He was never the same after knocking out Jesse Ferguson in 1993, shortly before he fought the return with Evander Holyfield, which he lost.

'He had lost the plot by then. The final nail in the coffin was the first fight with Golota. I could have walked away before the fight, but I said, "Maybe I can get one more fight out of him so as he can extend his career." But after that, I said to him, "I'm not going to waste my time, if you're not going to work." Bowe had a lot of ability, but he or his people didn't follow through.'

The return Bowe–Golota fight was held on 14 December 1996 at the Convention Centre in Atlantic City after Madison Square Garden officials, to the surprise of nobody, wanted nothing to do with it. Incredibly, Golota self-destructed once again and was disqualified by referee Eddie Cotton after the Pole sent Bowe writhing on his back in agony following three deliberately aimed low punches in the ninth round. The erratic Golota had earlier been deducted two points for a low blow and a head-butt.

Happily, this time there was no real trouble except for a few minor disturbances which broke out among the highly charged crowd of 12,013. They were quickly brought under control by the tight security who took full precautions to avoid a recurrence of the July riot. Bowe–Golota II had been a thriller, and the Pole had looked a certain winner before, remarkably, throwing it all away again. He had the dazed, reeling Bowe repeatedly on the verge of a knockout. Some guys never learn.

7

JAKE AND THE BOTCHED DIVE

There were few tougher men than Jake LaMotta. A rugged, uncompromising individual inside and outside the ring, he asked no favours and gave none. For years he was frozen out of a title fight because he refused to go along with the mobsters who ruled the sport in the US.

He finally got his long-overdue shot at the world middleweight championship against Marcel Cerdan in 1949 and won it but only after he deliberately lost to the moderate and weak-chinned Billy Fox two years earlier, a boxing scandal that would forever haunt him. Even at that, to get the title opportunity he had to pay Cerdan's connections $20,000, an illegal practice by any standards, before the French Algerian would sign the contract.

When Martin Scorsese filmed the classic movie *Raging Bull* in 1980, based on LaMotta's life, the general reaction when the film was released was that it was grossly exaggerated and that nobody could be that bad. Shot in black and white to capture the mood of the period, hardened critics recoiled at its violence and downbeat theme, but it won an Oscar for Robert De Niro in the leading role.

'The LaMotta character is one of the most repugnant and unlikeable screen protagonists for some time,' said *Variety*, the bible of the American entertainment industry. 'Scorsese excels at whipping up an emotional storm but seems unaware that there is any need for quieter, more introspective moments in drama. The relentless depiction of the downward slide of LaMotta from a trim contender in 1941 to a shockingly bloated slob introducing strippers in a sleazy nightclub in 1964 has all the morbid quality of a German expressionist film.'

When LaMotta saw the movie, he too was shocked, even though the screenplay was based on his autobiography *Raging Bull*, which he co-authored in 1970. He claimed the film not only misrepresented his boxing life but made him out to be a poor movie actor and nightclub comedian, which he maintained he was not. 'I want people to know that I ain't that bad,' he explained in an interview in later years. 'I'm still trying to get them to do a sequel to put things right but without success. Everything that happens to me, good or bad, is always blown out of proportion.'

Jake, who was known as the 'Bronx Bull' in his boxing days, never lost his bad-guy image. De Niro said LaMotta was 'like an animal, always going directly into a situation', and many years earlier Jimmy Cannon, the *New York Post* columnist, had called him 'probably the most detested man of his generation'.

While he battled some of the best and toughest boxers from welterweight to light-heavyweight in a thirteen-year career that included one hundred and six fights, he admitted the only people who really hurt him were his wives – and he was married six times. 'My third wife Sally divorced me,' he recalled, 'because the only thing I said to her was, "Darling, your stockings are wrinkled." Now, how the hell was I to know she wasn't wearing any?'

LaMotta was born to Italian parents in New York City's Lower East Side on 10 July 1921. When he was a child, his family moved to a poor area in Philadelphia before returning to New York, this time to the equally deprived Bronx. Out in the streets, young Jake found his way into a life of petty crime and went through reform school in upstate New York. 'I was a bum in a bum neighbourhood,' he used to say.

It was only natural that LaMotta would become a boxer. Fighting always seemed to be a way of life for him. He started as an amateur in his teens and turned professional in 1941 at the age of 19, quickly making a name for himself. By 1942, he was ranked the sixth best middleweight in the world by *Ring* magazine and began a six-fight feud with future great, Sugar Ray Robinson.

LaMotta fought his way to the number-one spot in the middleweight division, but champion Tony Zale had enlisted in the US Navy, and the title was frozen until the end of the Second World War, leaving Jake on the outside. His plight was also hampered because he would not deal with the mobsters who were beginning to move back into boxing after a brief lull towards the end of the 1930s. He refused to accept any of their nominees as his manager and looked after his own affairs, a fact which did not go down too well with 'the boys': he became *persona non grata*. However, to satisfy the two main authorities, the National Boxing Association and the New York State Athletic Commission, he named his brother as his manager, although it was no secret that Joey was merely 'a front' and that Jake arranged all his own fights.

As a result of not cooperating with the underworld, LaMotta was left out in the cold, and some promoters refused to engage him for fear of reprisals. He defeated some of the best men around – tough boxers like Tommy Bell, José Basora, Holman Williams, Bob Satterfield, Bert Lyttle and Fritzie Zivic – but he did not get a championship fight.

Even when Zale resumed his career in 1946, LaMotta was still overlooked, with Zale preferring to tie up the title with three fights against Rocky Graziano over the best part of two years. Leading boxing writers supported Jake's claims, saying he was by far the most deserving contender and that it was shameful he was being sidetracked for so long.

In 1947, Billy Fox and Blinky Palermo came into the LaMotta picture, not only changing the whole scenario but triggering one of boxing's greatest scandals. Fox, born in Oklahoma on 29 January 1926 and based in Philadelphia, was an undefeated light-heavyweight with a string of knockouts which looked impressive on paper but which in fact were mainly rigged by Palermo, his manager. Palermo tagged Blackjack onto Fox's name to give him additional publicity.

Blinky, supported by mobster Frankie Carbo, aimed to manoeuvre Fox into a world light-heavyweight title fight with Gus Lesnevich. Meanwhile, Fox was running up his knockout record, much to the suspicion of boxing commissions, who stopped the purses of some of his opponents, and ringside reporters, who wrote that many of the losers went down without being hit hard. Nate Bolden was counted out from what appeared to be a brush to the chin in the second round of their February 1946 fight as the 8,500 crowd booed, and he had his purse confiscated.

Fox would later admit that he was very dubious about the ease in which he was knocking over his rivals but did not say anything to his manager. Eventually, his suspicions got the better of him after knocking out Ossie Harris twice, in April and May of 1946. After the second fight, which Fox won in the tenth, the boxer asked Palermo if he had fixed the fight. 'Absolutely not,' said Palermo with a straight face. 'I didn't pay him to go down. Pay no attention to these kind of stories. The fight and the others were all on the level.' What he did not tell Fox was that he had slipped over to his opponent's corner during the ninth round and 'had a few words' with Harris's seconds.

In December, Fox knocked out Sheldon Bell in the fifth round as Bell took the count reclining on one elbow. The crowd of 5,887, however, did not feel that Bell had given of his best and pelted the ring with paper cups, crumpled newspapers and cigar butts. There were loud boos from all over the arena as both boxers made their way to the dressing-rooms. Newspapers the next day also raised strong suspicions about the fight.

Palermo now steered Fox into that world light-heavyweight title fight with veteran Gus Lesnevich in February 1947, but he knew he would not be able to 'persuade' Lesnevich or his manager Joe Vella to 'do business'. Gus and Joe wanted to keep the title. This was Fox v. Lesnevich on the level. In his preview, Ed Pollock of the *Philadelphia Enquirer* noted, 'Philadelphia fight fans continue to look at Fox through a haze of scepticism. They are not sure he's the fighter the book makes him appear to be.' Sure enough, Blackjack Billy was out of his class and was knocked out in the tenth round.

Undeterred by the setback, Palermo had Fox back in action less than two months later, and he notched up six consecutive wins, although he had two close calls. In April, Fox was on the boards for nine and suffered a badly cut eye before finishing George Kochan in the third. In June, he was staggered and nearly put down before knocking out Artie Levine in three.

Palermo then matched Fox with LaMotta at Madison Square Garden on 14 November 1947, and the real trouble began for both men. There were widespread rumours that something was amiss and that the contest would not be staged on its merits. There were also rumours that LaMotta would get a middleweight title fight through the mobsters if he agreed to lose to Fox. New York State Athletic Commission chairman Eddie Eagan heard the whispers and promised to investigate them, but he never did.

In the days leading up to the fight, LaMotta was a strong favourite, with the price varying, but within an hour of the afternoon weigh-in – with LaMotta scaling 11 st. 13 lb and Fox 12 st. 7 ¾ lb – the betting had shifted to even money and then took a drastic shift to leave Fox favourite at 3–1.

Shortly before the two entered the ring in front of a full crowd of 18,340, the biggest attendance of the Garden season, people were offering even money that LaMotta would not go the limit: the same LaMotta who had never been knocked off his feet, much less stopped or knocked out. A little earlier, chairman Eagan had left his ringside seat to visit the dressing-rooms of both boxers. He told them he had heard stories he did not like and warned them not to try anything or there would be trouble. Both assured him that everything would be fine.

LaMotta, several inches taller, won the opening round, battering Fox around the ribs and mid-section with strong left hooks and hard rights. Jake was able to get under the Philadelphian's left jabs and right crosses, and it appeared as though LaMotta would wear down his man and bring about either a knockout or a stoppage.

In the second round, the pattern changed. LaMotta discarded his attacks to the body and became a sitting target for Fox's left jabs and rights to the head. A hard right connected to LaMotta's head, and instead of taking it and storming back as he normally would, he reeled backwards. Fox seemed reluctant to follow through, and with Jake grimacing, his arms by his sides, the bell rang and LaMotta went to his corner on wobbly legs.

In the third, LaMotta forced the pace with a brief rally, and Fox took the blows unflinchingly to force Jake into a corner where he outfought the Bronx battler in a free exchange of body punches. LaMotta was now boxing defensively, pushing rather than punching, and sections of the crowd booed the lacklustre showing by the man regarded universally as the uncrowned middleweight champion of the world.

Referee Frank Fullam had received instructions from the commission to rule it a no contest if he felt that either man was not doing his best, but while it was obvious to everyone present that something was amiss, Fullam let the fight continue. LaMotta came out for the fourth round looking weary, and a right uppercut, not a particularly hard blow, sent him floundering into the ropes. There, he crouched and covered up without attempting to strike a blow as Fox fired lefts and rights to the head, and LaMotta's legs sagged.

Fox drove his man into a corner throwing more lefts and rights, many misjudged, with LaMotta covering up, before Fullam moved between the two and intervened. The time was two minutes and twenty-six seconds of the round. The finish was the signal for a number of angry and bitterly disappointed LaMotta supporters to make their way towards the ring. Police quickly moved in to prevent a possible riot as prolonged boos and shouts of 'Fake, fake' came from all over the famous arena.

LaMotta at first refused to allow reporters into his dressing-room. With his head buried in his hands, as he heard the angry crowd show their feelings, he said to his handlers, 'What do they want me to do, fight Joe Louis? I should have called off the fight with my injured back.' Later, he invited the reporters in and told them, 'I fought lousy, but I did the best I could. From the second round on, all the strength went out of my arms. I felt clammy and sick.'

He said that Fox hurt him with a body shot in the first round, the same spot where he had been injured in sparring a month before the fight. He did not want to ask for a postponement because he had pulled out of an earlier fight with another contender, Bert Lyttle. 'I didn't want people to think I was yellow,' he admitted. Asked about rumours of a fix and the dramatic shift in the betting, he said, 'They guessed right about the betting, but nobody can prove I lost on purpose. The truth will eventually come out.'

In the winner's dressing-room, Fox was as impassive as a buddha. Holding out his right hand which showed a swollen knuckle, he told the boxing writers, 'I got that with a good right to the head in the second round, and I'm happy I won.' Palermo intervened at regular intervals, brushing off suggestions that the fight was not on the level, and credited the finish to body shots. 'That was our secret,' he pointed out. 'The body banging was too much for Jake.'

As commission chairman Eddie Eagan made his way out of the Garden, he was asked by reporters if he felt anything was wrong. 'Not at all,' he said. 'We have no objection to paying the purses to either boxer: $22,500 each. It was a good fight. This boy Fox is a good puncher, and he's coming along. LaMotta has just gone back.' Asked directly by one reporter if he honestly thought the fight was a fix, he replied tartly, 'All I can say is that they will never fight each other again.'

In an official statement the next day, commissioner Eagan said that New York District Attorney Frank S. Hogan would investigate the fight and the circumstances surrounding it. He did feel that while there was no legal evidence that the fight was not fought on the level, he was nevertheless concerned by newspaper reports concerning the unusual actions of LaMotta as well as the sudden shift in odds favouring Fox.

Boxing writers attacked LaMotta's performance with venom. Bill Corum, formerly with the *New York Journal and American* but then with the *International News Service*, wrote, 'Your reporter regrets that he didn't like the look of last night's fight, and if this doesn't kill boxing in New York, one more like it will. Somebody got rich in the biggest betting fight in years, and our august administrators should

139

waste no time in looking into whatever link may exist between the outcome and the sinister switch in odds which made Fox favourite at ring time.'

In the *New York Mirror*, Dan Parker reported, 'Instead of fighting in close as he had done with such good results in the first round, LaMotta stood off, dropped his guard and snarled what was supposed to be defiance at Fox. From that moment on, Jake was in danger of being picketed by Equity at any moment for not having an actors' union card. Once he forgot himself and threw an authentic right cross. But when it was halfway to its target, he applied the brakes sharply and saved the night for Fox – and himself. Fullam should have called it no contest.'

James P. Dawson in the *New York Times* wrote, 'The battle was attended by many strange developments, not the least of which was a flood of reports in advance that the bout would not be waged on its merits. LaMotta's fighting style, or lack of it, was another strange incident. The husky Bronx Italian, noted for his resistance to punishment and his ability to inflict damage in a crouching style, a specialist in close-range fighting without a superior, fought up to expectations only in the first round.'

Lester Bromberg in the *New York World Telegram and Sun* reported, 'Never in his 12 previous Garden main events had LaMotta been such an unreasonable facsimile of himself. He has always been a charging bully, but he waited timidly. He is a body puncher of fire and accuracy, but he was hitting Fox on the arms. He took countless jabs without firing a return and pulled up in the third after rocking Fox with two rights to the head.'

In a column Bromberg wrote for Britain's *Weekly Sporting Review*, he commented, 'You folk may or may not know it but the fight world is seething in New York over the LaMotta–Fox affair. The tumult is in full swing. It's caused another sensation following so swiftly upon the boxing racket clean-up and the Rocky Graziano ban for not reporting a bribe.'

A month before the LaMotta–Fox fight, the 20th Century Sporting Club, America's leading promotional organisation formed by the ailing Mike Jacobs, was fined $2,500 by the New York State

Athletic Commission for dealing and negotiating with unlicensed individuals with criminal records. Jim Jennings of the *New York Mirror* reported the case and wrote, 'That the underworld has figured solidly in the boxing game as rumoured became evident yesterday.'

Solly Cantor, the Canadian lightweight who boxed in a preliminary bout on the LaMotta–Fox card and stayed on to watch the fight, was always convinced it was crooked. In an interview with the author in 1999, he recalled, 'If LaMotta intended to lose the fight, he made a very poor showing of hiding his secret. I couldn't believe what was taking place, and there was no sign of the "Raging Bull" in action. I fully expected him to storm out of his corner and take Fox apart with vicious body punches, even though Fox had a good number of knockouts, faked or real, on his record.

'The idea that LaMotta would take a dive never, never entered my mind. Not him. Not in a million years. I imagined Fox thinking that LaMotta would at least take some control, and when this failed to materialise, I think Fox might have had a fear that Jake had a trick or two up his sleeve, as the saying goes. When Fox realised there was no trick, he began to take control. Yet for me and the spectators around me, LaMotta seemed to be holding back with his punches, and the spectators voiced their feelings in no uncertain manner.'

District Attorney Hogan confirmed that the New York grand jury would be called in to investigate the affair. 'If what various boxing writers have printed is true, then a crime has been committed, and I shall investigate unsparingly,' he said. Commissioner Eagan said the purses of both boxers were being withheld, despite his earlier announcement.

LaMotta told the Grand Jury in February 1948 the same story he had given to reporters after the fight, that he had been hurt earlier in sparring and did not want to pull out, a view confirmed by his physician Dr Nicholas Salerno. Whatever opinions and suspicions the New York Commission had, they could not prove anything but they did manage to punish LaMotta. They fined him $1,000 for failing to disclose an injury and suspended him for seven months. Both boxers received their full purses.

In an interview with *Ring* magazine in 1981, Fox revealed that his manager claimed he deducted $1,000 from his purse 'to bribe the referee', a story Fox never believed. 'He just put the $1,000 into his own pocket and never went near the referee,' said Billy. 'When I put it to him that I was sure the fight was crooked, he said he would swear on his wife and children that everything was on the level, but when I got home to Philadelphia, the scandal was all over the papers.

'I felt hurt. It affected my whole life. Made me feel despondent, downhearted, disgusted. Why did he have to do it to me? Why couldn't he have done it with a guy who didn't give a damn? Then I read in the papers that most of my fights were fixed. I discovered that Palermo made up my supposed record of 49 knockouts and doubled up with some of the names. When I put it to him, he said, "Look, you do the fighting, I'll do the managing." That was his line.'

Fox was threatening to leave him when Palermo got Billy a return fight with Lesnevich for the world light-heavyweight title at Madison Square Garden in March 1948. Palermo assured Fox that everything would be on the level this time. It was, with Lesnevich doing the levelling, knocking out the challenger in one minute and fifty-eight seconds, up to then the shortest-ever title fight in the division and a record that would stand for thirty-eight years.

Not surprisingly, Fox left Palermo after the fight and joined Hymie Caplan's stable on the advice of the Philadelphia promoter Herman Taylor, only to discover that Caplan, like Palermo, was in the numbers racket and had just come out of prison on swindling charges. Fox's career, however, was more or less over by then, and with only five wins in thirteen fights after the second Lesnevich bout, including four knockout defeats, he retired.

LaMotta returned to the ring after his seven months' suspension with five wins in 1948, seemingly none the worse for the scandal experience. The mobsters kept their promise, and Jake got his world middleweight title fight in Detroit in June 1949, stopping the French Algerian Marcel Cerdan in ten rounds.

The LaMotta–Fox controversy may well have been eventually forgotten by the general public, or dragged up only occasionally in boxing magazines with space to fill, had it not been for a US Senate investigation into professional boxing 13 years after the fight. There had been growing demands for an official probe into the gangster element in the sport throughout the 1950s, but it was not until 1960 that things got moving with the setting up of the Senate Anti-Trust and Monopoly Sub-Committee under the chairmanship of Senator Estes Kefauver.

The committee began their hearings in Washington in June 1960, and the first witness called was LaMotta. Under oath, he admitted for the first time that he took a dive in the Fox fight on the promise that he would get a middleweight title chance. He said he turned down a $100,000 bribe 'because money didn't mean anything to me. I was not poor. All I wanted was the title fight.'

Even when he got the title shot, he said he still had to pay $20,000 cash in advance to Cerdan's people through Jake's brother Joey, his formal manager on record. When he took the stand, Joey refused to answer any questions as to who offered him the bribe or who received the $20,000. He also denied he acted as a go-between for the $100,000 in connection with the Fox fight. Committee members made it plain that they believed the LaMottas were withholding the all-important names because of fear of the Mob – although Jake insisted, 'I'm not afraid of any of those rats.'

Jake admitted that Joey told him about the $100,000 bribe offer to lose to Fox during a training session in Bobby Gleason's gym in the Bronx. In further questioning, he thought that his brother had mentioned the names Blinky Palermo and Bill Daly, but he could not swear to it. Both Lew Burston and Samuel Richman, Cerdan's US representatives, flatly denied receiving all or part of the alleged $20,000 from Jake's brother or anybody else.

Asked to describe the Fox fight, Jake said, 'I just stood there helpless in the ring. Fox was pounding away, and the referee stopped it. I was play-acting. I agree that at the time I told New York commissioner Eagan in sworn testimony that the fight was not fixed. I know now that this was an untruth.' In reconstructing the events, Assistant District Attorney John G. Bonomi suggested that Joey LaMotta made all the arrangements for the Cerdan title fight when he went to the numbers racketeer Thomas Milo, the man who held the key to the championship match and who had since died.

Senator Philip Hart of Michigan exploded at the whole bizarre story of bribery, coercion and fixes. After failing to get any information from Jake's brother as to his alleged role as the middle man, he proclaimed, 'If this enquiry could serve to remove from this business the kinds of persons described here, it will have been worthwhile.'

LaMotta would elaborate on the Fox fight in his 1970 autobiography *Raging Bull*:

> I suppose there's a way to fix a fight, but not by LaMotta. I'm too stupid. The way I fixed it was in Madison Square Garden in front of a packed house, and so phoney that the New York Commission caught on and the District Attorney. I'll tell you something about throwing a fight. The guy you're throwing it to has to be pretty good. It has to look like a fight. Fox can't even look good.
>
> The first round, a couple of belts to his head, and I see a glassy look coming over his eyes. Jesus Christ, a couple of jabs and he's going to fall down? I began to panic a little. I was supposed to be throwing a fight to this guy, and it looked like I was going to end up holding him on his feet. I don't know how we even got through the first round without me murdering him. Sometimes I thought the air from my punches were affecting him, but we made it to the fourth round.
>
> By then, if there was anybody in the Garden who didn't know what was happening, he must have been dead drunk. There were yells and boos from all over the place. All I wanted to do with this fight was to get it over. The only thing I could figure to do was just let him hit me, but even that didn't work out because, like I said, this kid didn't have a punch, and all around the Garden they were yelling 'Fake, fake.' Finally, the referee had to stop it. What else could I do? I was against the ropes with my hands down pretending I was taking a beating.
>
> Fox hit me about 15 times with everything he had, which wasn't enough to dent a bowl of yogurt. He couldn't beat your

sister Susie. He had two weaknesses as a fighter. He didn't have a punch, and he had a glass head. Every time you hit him, something jarred. He looked good to the average slob in the three dollar seat, plenty of action and windmill style of fighting. A headhunter, always going for the other guy's chin. The Mob just built him up with a string of knockouts.

Many prominent boxing people, including boxers like Joey Maxim, openly criticised LaMotta for his actions. 'I felt ashamed for what he did,' said the former world light-heavyweight champion, shaking his head. 'He let boxing down very badly.' When LaMotta was a surprise guest on a radio show, former world heavyweight champion Jersey Joe Walcott walked out when Jake came into the studio. An angry LaMotta said, 'Didn't Walcott ever read what people had to say about his managers and their affiliations?'

LaMotta later defended his actions in throwing the Fox fight. 'I did what I had to do,' he told the press. 'I was uncrowned champion for years. Nobody wanted to fight me, so I felt that losing to Fox was the only way I could get a chance. I had to lose the fight, which I never wanted to do, but I thought this was the way you had to do it. Everyone, all of a sudden, was acting as if I had leprosy.

'Yes, I was ashamed when it was all over, but I did get the chance at the title, and I won it. It wasn't the 100 grand that made me go through with it. I rejected that, but I was warned that I would never get a chance to fight for the title unless I agreed to their proposition. So what could I do? With my career and my life in jeopardy, how could I fight the mobsters?'

The boxing world never quite forgave LaMotta for his admissions, particularly New York. He was now 'Mr Bad Guy Number One'. Shortly after Sugar Ray Robinson had his last fight in November 1965, Madison Square Garden officials thought it would be a nice gesture to give Robinson an official farewell. After all, the former great world champion in two weight divisions had many of his most important fights in the Garden, including his debut twenty-five years earlier.

A month later before a crowd of 12,146 who had come to see

Emile Griffith defend his world welterweight title against Manuel Gonzales, Robinson climbed into the ring and got a rapturous reception. He was followed through the ropes by four of his championship opponents: Carmen Basilio, Carl 'Bobo' Olson, Gene Fullmer and Randolph Turpin. In an emotional occasion, they embraced each other and were photographed together. Missing was LaMotta, who was not invited, even though he had fought Sugar Ray six times, once for the title.

'That one hurt deep,' recalled LaMotta in his autobiography:

> I was the first guy to lick Robinson when he was on top, and, what the hell, I was the only former champion who could have walked to the Garden. I lived only ten blocks away. I still ask myself, what the hell did I do so wrong that I deserved such treatment?
>
> So I threw the Fox fight – OK. That's the cardinal sin that I have always been punished for committing. But did anybody think about the cardinal sin that was being committed against me for so many years? I couldn't get a title shot unless I threw the fight. I'd been fighting the establishment, the Mob, for four years, and where had it gotten me? Fighting guys like Tony Janiro and another tough cookie like Cecil Hudson for less than 15,000 bucks.

Meanwhile, Fox had retired after being knocked out by Joe Blackwood in four rounds in January 1950. His career had been going nowhere fast at that stage, and it seemed a wise and sensible decision. He quickly faded into the obscurity from which he had come, a forgotten contender, a yesterday man.

Gilbert Rogin, a writer for *Sports Illustrated*, discovered Fox in New York on a rainy summer's morning in 1956, living on the edge – desolate, vagrant, despairing. His only possessions, besides the soiled clothes he wore, were a pipe and a scrapbook. This was the black, ugly side of boxing. Fox told Rogin his sad story, but the magazine could not publish it at the time without corroboration. The article only made its appearance after the Kefauver hearings in 1960:

When I was boxing, I was living high, buying expensive clothes, buying cars, selling them like a fool, riding around town, having a ball. I had two houses at one time, but most of my money was lost in cars and houses. Taxes I didn't figure. After I retired, I tried to get my licence back, to get somebody interested in me, but nobody was interested. If I had some money, I would have gone out of town and fought under a different name or something.

I got a job in a factory, and I was a porter in a restaurant. I also went back to setting up pins in a bowling alley, which I had done as a kid. I started playing the horses, and I had a lot of arguments with my wife. Finally, we agreed to separate. I walked the streets at night, hung around bowling alleys that stayed open all night. I just didn't give a damn. One day, I was setting up pins and who should walk in but my old opponent Gus Lesnevich. He was very nice about it. [He] shook my hand, wished me luck.

I worked all over the city in the last four years, setting bowling pins. Now I'm not doing anything. I got fed up setting pins. I keep to myself these days. Maybe I shouldn't, but that's the way it is. Guys stare at me in the street. I don't know if it's the way I look, or maybe they remember who I was. I've got no appeal for living. Never had it in me, though, to commit suicide.

Rogin lost touch with Fox after the interview, and nobody knew his whereabouts in 1960 when the Kefauver Committee wanted him to appear before their investigators. They searched for several months before learning that he was a patient in King's Park Mental Hospital in Long Island, New York, after being found wandering the streets with barely enough to eat.

Though he was not allowed any visitors, he had told a friend before being admitted that the LaMotta fight was the cause of all his troubles. Up to then, he had believed himself to be a wicked puncher, but LaMotta's dive brought suspicions into his mind that he might not be as great as he had been led to believe. The medical staff said

Fox was in no condition to give reliable evidence before the Kefauver Committee or any other committee. 'He might not even know who Jake LaMotta is,' said Dr George Volow, assistant director at the hospital. Fox took various jobs on his release from hospital. He died in the late 1980s.

LaMotta's life went downhill after he retired from the ring in April 1954, following a loss to journeyman Billy Kilgore. He went on heavy drinking binges, which included two bottles of whiskey a night, and by his own estimate went through over $30,000. He spent six months in jail after being found guilty in a prostitution case and was divorced again, losing custody of his children.

While the old champion mellowed in later years and the intensity of feeling towards him gradually cooled down, the 1980 movie *Raging Bull* brought all the bad guy images, including the Billy Fox scandal, back again. However, the fight fraternity remembered him, and he was elected into the International Boxing Hall of Fame in 1990. Nevertheless, in interviews before and after the induction, he was not allowed to forget what had happened at Madison Square Garden on 14 November 1947. The kid born on the mean streets of New York was seemingly destined to stay on the wrong side of the tracks.

8

BITE OF THE CENTURY

With rumours flying about like seagulls around a fishing trawler, the big fight was definitely on. A month before they were due to enter the ring at the MGM Grand Garden Arena in Las Vegas, Mike Tyson called a media conference to dispel the scare stories that his world heavyweight championship rematch with Evander Holyfield was off because of reports that he was not fit.

The fight had originally been scheduled for 3 May 1997 but was postponed for eight weeks when a sparring partner opened a cut over Tyson's left eye – a different one to the cut he had received in the Holyfield contest the previous November. The injury had healed, but there were many sceptics who thought that the psychological scars of that first encounter, when 'Iron' Mike was sensationally stopped in 11 rounds and lost his title, would remain. These doubters would point out that George Foreman sustained an eye injury in training for his world heavyweight title defence against Muhammad Ali in 1974, and after a month's postponement, he was knocked out in the eighth round.

Tyson went through a 40-minute public workout in the ring at the hotel ballroom. He did three rounds with assistant trainer Stacy McKinley, who wore body padding, while Richie Giachetti, his main coach, stood by shouting instructions. The assembled media agreed Tyson looked in top shape. Promoter Don King was also present. 'We're putting the rumours to rest and saying here and now that the fight will take place,' he said. 'They say Mike Tyson is fat, out of shape and out carousing. You be the judge.'

Later, Tyson sat down with boxing writers and answered questions. 'My confidence is never shaken,' he said of his dramatic defeat by Holyfield in their first fight. 'I have a great deal of respect for Holyfield's boxing skills. With that respect alone, I would be a lot more intense for this fight.'

What he was saying was that he took Holyfield lightly in the first match, which ended after Tyson was floored in the sixth round, saved by the bell in the tenth and rescued from further punishment and humiliation by referee Mitch Halpern at the start of the eleventh. This time, he promised, there would be a different result and a new champion.

Holyfield trained at a camp in Houston, Texas, where he was said to be in the finest condition of his career. Known as the 'Real Deal', he said he was not concerned as to what kind of shape Tyson was in and that he planned to fight his own kind of fight regardless. 'I don't know if Tyson can do any better,' he told reporters. 'For his sake, he better hope he can, because he knows what he did the first time was not enough.'

In their earlier match, Holyfield was considered easy pickings for Tyson, an ogre who was mowing down opponents in the heavyweight division. It had been Tyson's second coming as champion after losing his title on a tenth-round knockout to James 'Buster' Douglas in February 1990 in another remarkable upset. The big question was: could Mike end the Holyfield of dreams?

In many ways, Evander remains one of the most remarkable men to have held the world heavyweight title. Undersized in an era of super-heavyweights, a suspected heart condition threatened to finish his boxing career in the run-up to his first fight with Tyson. It was only an unprecedented step by the Nevada State Athletic

Commission, who ordered him to have a full battery of tests at the Mayo Clinic in Minnesota, that saved the day – and the fight.

Even at that, an extraordinary provision was written into the fight contract that empowered the commission's chief physician Dr Flip Homansky to arrive unannounced at Holyfield's training camp in Houston to conduct a spot-check on the challenger's condition.

Holyfield's recent past had been tarnished by heart scares. Following his 1994 points loss to Michael Moorer, in which Evander inexplicably ran out of gas over the last half of the 12-rounder, he was diagnosed with a mysterious cardiac malady described as a 'non-compliant left ventricle'. Under medical orders not to box again, he announced his retirement.

Thirteen months later, he was back boxing again, his heart problem having been cured, he claimed, following a session with a faith healer. A deeply religious, God-fearing man who carried a Bible around with him and much given to the power of prayer, Holyfield believed his mysterious recovery to be an authentic miracle. More bewildering was that America's foremost doctors were unable to detect any recurrence of the heart ailment, even though the Nevada boxing commissioners were not fully satisfied about his condition. The situation was not helped by a phone call from former world heavyweight champion Larry Holmes to Holyfield's trainer Don Turner – later made public – imploring his old coach not to allow Evander to absorb any unnecessary punishment. 'I understand why he's doing this,' Holmes told Turner. 'Make sure he gets paid – but don't let him get hurt.'

After a series of panic attacks by the commission, Holyfield was finally given the official all-clear by John P. Scott, medical director of the Mayo Clinic, who told the commission, 'It is my conclusion that Mr Holyfield is in excellent health, and no cardiac or pulmonary abnormality is demonstrable.'

The youngest of eight children, Holyfield was born in Altmore, Alabama, on 19 October 1962 and made his home in Atlanta, Georgia, where he was such an exceptional boxing prospect that he was persuaded to give up his ambitions of a military career and concentrate on the glove sport. Evander became one of America's outstanding amateurs, winning a US Golden Gloves title at light-heavyweight, and was a hot favourite to collect a gold medal at the 1984 Olympics in Los Angeles. He had to settle for a bronze, however, after being disqualified in controversial circumstances against New Zealander Kevin Barry, following a punch that unintentionally landed after the bell had ended the second round.

With an overall amateur record of 160 wins in 174 contests, Holyfield turned professional towards the end of 1984 but as a cruiserweight. Though he was 6 ft 2 in., he knew his lack of bulk would be against him, and in his 11th fight in the lower weight division, he won the world cruiserweight title, as recognised by the World Boxing Association, by outpointing the favoured Dwight Muhammad Qawi over 15 rounds in 1986.

He later won the World Boxing Council and International Boxing Federation versions of the title, before casting his sights on the more prestigious and lucrative world heavyweight championship by going on a special fitness programme. This involved an elaborate diet and exercise regime which boosted his weight sufficiently to allow him to campaign for the heavier title, which he won from Tyson's conqueror James Buster Douglas on a knockout in three rounds in October 1990.

In his next ten fights, spread thinly over five years, he lost three, including an eighth-round stoppage against Riddick Bowe, whom he had outpointed two years earlier, and a points defeat by Michael Moorer, who took his WBA and IBF heavyweight belts. Hardly the form expected of a man going in against the awesome Tyson, who was hell-bent on another assault course in the division. But Holyfield won, and Tyson was now a man out for revenge against his conqueror.

Many people felt that Tyson had not taken Holyfield seriously the first time they met – and Mike would have agreed. It was said that he believed the writers and the commentators who had insisted that Holyfield was a shot fighter and would fold like a deckchair the first time Tyson landed a serious blow. All Iron Mike wanted was another chance to win back his prized crown.

At his best in the 1980s, Tyson was a boxer from the old school, a throwback to the rough and tough Jack Dempsey era of the 'Roaring

'20s'. Born on 30 June 1966 in Brooklyn, New York, Tyson grew up in an age when challenging authority was enjoying a new vogue. He never followed the crowd when he was growing up, and by the time he was 13, reform school was the only place that could deal with him.

This was where Cus D'Amato found him sparring one day. D'Amato, a 72-year-old manager and trainer, was always on the lookout for another champion to follow in the footsteps of Floyd Patterson and José Torres, whom he had guided to world titles – Patterson at heavyweight and Torres at light-heavy. D'Amato liked what he saw, and when Tyson came out of reform school at fourteen, he was placed in the care of Cus, who got two millionaires, Jim Jacobs and Bill Cayton, to bankroll the promising young boxer. Mike turned professional in March 1985 and ploughed through the heavyweight division like a tank.

Tyson was very much his own man, always entering the ring without socks inside his black boxing boots, choosing black trunks and never using a dressing gown. Within 20 months, he had become, at the age of 20, the youngest man in history to win the world heavyweight title.

Tyson kept winning, but his life both inside and outside the ring was beginning to unravel like a ball of string. D'Amato and Jacobs died, and the ubiquitous Don King ousted Cayton from his position of managerial control. Tyson sacked long-time trainer Kevin Rooney, and his stormy marriage to actress Robin Givens ended in a predictably messy and costly divorce. There were court cases, street fights, car smashes, assault charges and violent clashes with the media – a whole catalogue of incidents that suggested Tyson had his finger on the self-destruct button. He appeared to be cracking under the pressure, but it was still an astonishing upset when he was knocked out by Buster Douglas in 1990. He came back with four wins of varying quality before making world headlines again when he was sentenced in 1992 to six years in jail for raping model Desiree Washington in a hotel bedroom.

Tyson was released after three years for good conduct, though he was still on parole. He claimed he had found solace in Islam, but he had lost his fighting edge. Returning to the ring in August 1995 with an unimpressive disqualification win over Peter McNeeley in eighty-eight seconds, he followed it up with an equally lacklustre victory in three rounds against Buster Mathis Jr. and terrified Frank Bruno to defeat, again in three rounds.

In his next fight, he defeated Bruce Seldon after a farcical affair in which the challenger went down twice, once from a punch that missed by over 12 inches as shouts of 'Fix, fix' rent the air. The fight, if it could legitimately be called that, was stopped after 109 seconds of the first round. Seldon was known as the 'Atlantic Express', but this was one instance when the express went off the rails.

Obviously Tyson, who had earned a total of $105 million since his release, now needed a good, impressive victory over a seasoned opponent to restore his credibility both with the doubting boxing public and the critical media. It certainly looked as though Holyfield would provide that stern test, and he did, stopping Tyson in 11 rounds on 9 November 1996 for the WBA title – Mike having relinquished the WBC belt following the Bruno match – in a major upset.

Could Holyfield do it again? Despite the outcome of the first fight, Tyson was favourite with the local Las Vegas odds-makers at 5–2, with the most likely result being a Tyson win in the first round to bring his record to forty-six wins and two losses. Holyfield had a career tally of thirty-one victories and three defeats.

In the weeks leading up to the fight, Tyson was sullen and rarely met reporters. Most of the stories coming from the respective training quarters concerned Holyfield and how he was preparing to put up the fight of his life in order to hold on to his championship belt. Tyson's preparations were mainly kept a secret.

Whispers from his sparring partners, however, indicated that trainer Richie Giachetti was having little joy in re-educating his man in the fundamentals of 'illusive aggression' preached so often by Mike's boyhood custodian, the late Cus D'Amato. As Britain's John Rawling observed in *The Guardian*, 'Giachetti himself chose to adopt the confrontational language of the ghetto – or should that be the gutter? – when asked to assess the doubts provoked in Tyson's mind by the first Holyfield defeat.'

Emanuel Steward, trainer of Lennox Lewis, the reigning WBC champion at that time, and founder of the famous Kronk Gym in Detroit, thought Tyson was a man out of control and would have to be careful against a dangerous, competent champion like Holyfield. Tyson's former conqueror Buster Douglas, however, was fully confident that Mike would win and that 'he would come good all over again'. Legendary trainer Eddie Futch first went for Holyfield but changed his mind and opted for Tyson.

At the final press conference, there were signs that Tyson was having difficulty in focusing his concentration on the contest and the seriousness of it. He refused to make any kind of eye contact with Holyfield, who was super-confident of repeating his win over the man he described as one 'who used to be called the baddest man on the planet'.

The Tyson camp wanted to have the nominated referee Mitch Halpern, who had officiated in the first fight, replaced because they felt he would favour Holyfield. Mike's manager John Horne claimed that his man would be 'psychologically affected' by having the same referee and demanded somebody else. Veteran boxing scribes observed that Horne must never have heard of old Sam Langford, the 'Boston Tar Baby'. When he was once asked if he had any objection to a particular referee for a contest, he simply held up his right fist and declared, 'Mister, I carry my own referee, and here it is. Ain't no problems when I have him around.'

In any event, there were meetings between all the interested parties, including officials from the Nevada State Athletic Commission, and while the protest by Tyson's manager over a switch in referees was disallowed, the storm of protest produced by the challenger's organisation, Team Tyson, was noisy enough for Halpern to withdraw from the $10,000 post. This left the way clear for Mills Lane, a tough, no-nonsense former prosecutor from Reno, Nevada, who also acted as a circuit judge when he was not pulling boxers apart.

Exactly what pressures crowded in on Halpern to provoke his decision to stand down remain a mystery, but there was no doubt that he would have been a fair official. One of the foremost referees in the world, he had officiated in no fewer than 96 world championship fights and obviously knew his job.

At the weigh-in two days before the fight, Tyson still refused eye contact with Holyfield. Both men scaled 15 st. 8 lb. In the weeks leading up to the fight, Holyfield had predicted 'a great victory', saying that his work ethic and boxing ability would overcome Tyson, just as they had in the first encounter. He repeated his forecast at the weigh-in. 'I want to give Mike an opportunity to let him know that the first fight wasn't a fluke,' he said. 'This is how sportsmanship is supposed to be displayed in the ring. I truly believe the world should know who is the best fighter out there, and I believe we're the two best. I don't look on Tyson as a bully. I look on him as a fighter who has a style that works for him. It's one-dimensional, but it suits him. But I have the solution to the style he has. I will beat him each and every time we fight. I have faith in God, but I work hard too.'

Tyson was sparing in his predictions, limiting his forecasts to phrases like, 'Even the tiger will be eaten,' and, 'Believe the odds-makers; I will regain my title.' Pressed on one occasion to elaborate a bit more as to what he thought the outcome of the fight would be, he said no more than, 'I just want to fight; that's all. I'm in great shape.'

Holyfield's trainer and chief second Don Turner predicted, 'Tyson's character will let him down. He used to move his head, but when he is moving his head, he can't punch. Eight inches of movement, and he's got to start all over again. He doesn't have the patience for that. It's character.'

In the final minutes before leaving the dressing-room, Holyfield stood singing gospel songs and swaying from side to side. He was probably not only the most relaxed man in Las Vegas but in all Nevada. Tyson paced up and down in his dressing-room, banging his right fist into his left palm and looking down at the floor. Walking down the aisle to the ring, Holyfield was coolness personified. As Tyson walked down, he kept cursing his handlers and the crowd, some of whom booed.

Even when Lane called the two men and their chief cornermen together in the centre of the ring for the instructions, Tyson continued to avoid eye contact with Holyfield, contenting himself with staring at the canvas. Referee Lane told them they were fighting for the championship of the world and for them to protect themselves at all times. He asked the respective chief seconds if they had any questions and they said, 'No.' He then looked both champion and challenger in the eye and said, 'OK, let's get it on' – his popular catchphrase.

Among the audience of 16,331 there was the usual cast for a championship fight on the west coast: movie stars, show-business celebrities, high rollers, hot-dog-eating Midwesterners as well as pimps and prostitutes from the inner cities, all hungry for a slice of the action.

There was precious little of it in the first round, although whatever activity there was came from Holyfield. He came straight out and jabbed the challenger off balance with a stiff left, as instructed by Turner. Tyson attempted to work his own jab, then tried a left hook, which Holyfield deftly ducked, moving out of danger of an expected Tyson counter-punch.

Lane called the two together inside the first minute, warned them for roughing it up in the clinches and asked them to keep their punches up. This referee would have no nonsense. Tyson was having trouble connecting accurately as Holyfield was moving in and out. Mike missed with a big right and looked sluggish, clearly worried by his inability to nail the champion.

Holyfield was making his opponent miss and twice landed right-hand counter-punches over Tyson's jabs, which seemed to lack the power of old. This did not appear to be the fearsome Iron Mike who had struck terror into the world's best heavyweights in the past. Instead he looked tired, dispirited and uninterested.

Tyson was now finding himself being pushed back as Holyfield kept up the pressure, getting in close to hurt the New Yorker with jarring left hooks and sharp right uppercuts. Tyson connected with a long straight right to the chin, his first real effective punch of the fight, but the crowd seemed to be on the champion's side and chanted 'Holyfield, Holyfield' as the round drew to a close.

Early in the second round, there was a clash of heads provoked by a Holyfield charge. The collision opened a cut just over Tyson's right eye. Blood flowed down his face, and Mike dabbed the injury with his glove and complained to Mills that he had been butted. Lane indicated that the butt was unintentional and waved the two men on. Tyson landed with a few left hooks, but Holyfield not only took them but pushed the challenger back by gripping Tyson's shoulders with both gloves.

He followed through with a fast left jab and hook before some close-quarter work. Lane warned both boxers to keep it clean. At the bell, Tyson's thoughts were clearly going back to the terrible memories of the first fight and the loss of his title. He could not be beaten again. As he passed Holyfield on the way back to his stool, he finally fixed his opponent with a cold stare. As his handlers pushed a swab into Tyson's cut, he yelled out his pain with a few expletives.

All three ringside judges gave the first two rounds to Holyfield, in each case by scores of 10–9. Giachetti told Tyson he would have to do something to redress the balance and do it soon. 'You're losing this one, Mike,' the trainer barked. 'Go to it.'

At the start of the third round, Tyson was so keen to follow Giachetti's advice that he forgot his mouthpiece. He quickly had it fitted and went back to the centre of the ring with determination written all over his face. He hooked and jabbed, and Holyfield had to retreat hastily. A long right got through Evander's defence, followed by a strong left–right combination.

At that stage, Tyson looked like he might possibly win, and the crowd, who had earlier supported 'good guy' Holyfield, now began to chant Tyson's name. The champion was looking flustered and tried to keep Tyson in a tight clinch. However, he kept his chin down, and, gradually, Tyson's storm began to blow itself out.

Holyfield then reverted to jabbing and hooking as Tyson landed a big left hook followed by his right forearm, an infringement which Lane seemingly did not notice. They clinched again and Tyson tugged at Holyfield's arm. It was now becoming fiercely physical, a bar-room brawl. Holyfield began to open up again with a four-punch combination and effectively countered a burst of sudden activity by Tyson.

Mike fired in a right and left hook, and with 33 seconds left in the round, he hooked his right arm around his rival's neck, pulled him into an embrace on the blind-side of the referee, spat out his mouthpiece and bit hard on Holyfield's right ear. For a terrifying moment, Tyson seemed to be transformed into a combination of Count Dracula and Hannibal 'The Cannibal' Lecter. The pain caused the champion to leap straight into the air like a scalded cat, with blood streaming from the open wound, to the sheer horror of the crowd and millions watching it on television around the world.

Tyson spat out the torn flesh which landed on the table of Duane Ford, one of the judges, and as Holyfield turned his back on Tyson and headed for his corner, Mike, evidently maddened beyond reason, charged after him and pushed him in the back, taunting him to turn and fight.

Lane quickly came between them and consulted with the ringside physician Dr Flip Homansky. After Holyfield was deemed fit to continue, two points were deducted from Tyson. Lane had not seen the actual incident as Tyson had made sure that the referee was out of position at the time. Mike then made a lunge at Holyfield's left ear and left his teeth marks in it. By that point, Lane had no choice but to disqualify the enraged ex-champion.

There was chaos in the ring, which soon became crowded. Tyson went berserk, lashing out at his handlers and swinging punches at police officers. Holyfield, with his gloved hand held up to his right ear, stood quietly in his corner and looked on at the chaos. The crowd accepted Lane's decision and vented their fury on Tyson, one missile landing near the challenger as he made his way back to his dressing-room, where he claimed the two bites were a natural reaction to the butts he had received from Holyfield. 'He butted me in the first round, then butted me in the second,' he said, 'but nobody warned him. Nobody took any points off him. This is my career. I can't continue to get butted like that. This guy was trying to get me stopped on cuts. I had to retaliate.'

Holyfield blamed the incidents on Tyson's realisation that he had no chance of winning the fight. 'I truly believe that fear itself can call people to do that,' he said. 'It's the easiest thing: the quickest way to get out. We're in a fight already, so why do you have to bite somebody? If you think you can whup me, why can't you whup me with the gloves on?'

The official at the centre of the action, the referee, refused to be pressurised into supporting either boxer. 'The cut above Tyson's eye was caused by an unintentional head-butt,' said Lane, whose integrity was never in doubt. 'Both of them had their heads in. The fight was a rough one. There was wrestling and stuff going on way beyond what should have been. I did warn them about it. With the first bite, I called the doctor over, and he said Holyfield could continue. Tyson then bit him the second time. One bite is bad, but two bites is the end of the stretch.'

Lane would elaborate on the fight in his 1998 autobiography *Let's Get It On*:

> At that fractured moment, I truly believe Tyson went nuts. And by doing so, he disgraced all of us boxers, professionals and amateurs alike. He disgraced every honest and hard-working trainer, cutman, manager and promoter in the business, every boxing fan worldwide.
>
> When Tyson twice bit Holyfield's ears, then compounded the crime by attempting to assault Holyfield further, he not only fed the flames that constantly attempt to devour our discipline, but also negated everything so many young men and, yes, even young women, have fought so long and so hard to protect – men and women whose livelihood, because of its unmitigated brutality, is constantly assailed by its critics. And that, by its very nature, is a damned shame.

Scuffles broke out in several parts of the arena to add to the general chaos. The irony of the night was that the contest was publicised as 'The Sound and the Fury', and it certainly lived up to its name. Outside the MGM Grand Garden Arena, the scene was reminiscent of an action movie. Suddenly the street was full of shrieking police sirens, people being taken to hospital after skirmishes and police dodging about behind parked cars with guns at the ready. The venue lost millions of dollars in revenue as its gambling sections and other facilities had to shut down for the night when angry boxing fans stampeded through the hotel.

Surgeons at the nearby Valley Hospital and Medical Center attempted to sew the piece of Holyfield's ear back on but admitted defeat and had to stitch up the torn flesh. There was worldwide condemnation of the fight, with calls for Tyson to be banned from boxing for life. Even President Clinton, a keen boxing fan who watched the fight, expressed revulsion at what happened. 'I was horrified by it and I think the American people should be,' he said.

Writer Budd Schulberg commented, 'This is disgraceful. I have never seen anything like this before. For those of us who love boxing, this is a very sad night indeed.' Dr Ferdie Pacheco, Muhammad Ali's former physician and a respected fight analyst on US television, said, 'Tyson looked like a wolf that had gotten hold of a sheep. It was grisly and horrible to see. He lives life with no regulations. Tyson is very rich with no purpose in life, and no purpose is a destructive thing to the soul.'

The world's newspapers had a field day, with headlines such as 'Bite of the Century', 'Tyson Bites the Dust', 'Chew On That', 'Tyson's the New Hungry Fighter', 'From Ex-Champ to Chomp', 'Boxing's Hannibal Lecter' and 'Tyson Makes Meal of the Real Deal'. The *New York Post* had a one-word banner headline: 'Dracula'.

Two days after the fight, Tyson came out of seclusion and read to the media a prepared, four-minute-and-sixteen-seconds apology to Holyfield and everyone else he could think of, including the judge who controlled the conditions of his parole. He asked that he be given another chance and promised he would accept his punishment 'like a man'. He also aimed remarks directly at Holyfield: 'When you butted me in the first round and kept butting me, accidentally or not, I snapped into reaction, and the rest is history.'

Holyfield later responded, 'It takes a lot of courage to stand before the people and say, "I was wrong, and I'm willing to accept the punishment." Time will tell if he stands up to his word or goes on. I don't need to say anything. Time will show. However, regardless whether a person apologises or not, the commission has to do their job. They have to make up their mind what they think the punishment is. They have to realise that other people will probably take some measures if there is no task or punishment for what he has done. I thank the Lord I don't have permanent injury. To be honest, during the first break after the first bite, I wanted to bite him back.'

Many questions have since been asked about the infamous incident. Should referee Lane have disqualified Tyson after the first bite, although he claimed he did not see it from his 'blind-side'? Such a savage act would merit instant disqualification. Should he have warned or disqualified Holyfield for butting? Did Tyson find a second defeat to Holyfield impossible to accept and so resorted to animalistic tactics? Or was he falling prey to the kind of lunacy that had brought him down before, sliding back into that danger zone? Would Tyson have won without biting as he seemed to be making up ground in the third round? How would the original referee Mitch Halpern have reacted?

Tyson's $30 million purse was withheld by the Nevada State Athletic Commission pending an investigation. At a specially convened meeting nine days later, to which Tyson was invited but refused to attend, they unanimously agreed to fine him $3 million and imposed a 12-month ban from boxing, the maximum penalties they could hand out. When Holyfield heard the results of the enquiry, while on a gospel tour of South Africa, he said he had no further comment to make. He had already forgiven Tyson, but he could never forget boxing's horrific night of shame.

9

REQUIEM FOR A HEAVYWEIGHT

On 9 January 1999, the former world heavyweight championship contender Jerry Quarry was laid to rest in his birthplace, a small town near Bakersfield, California. The undersized boxer with the oversized heart – the man whose family motto was 'There's no quitting in a Quarry' – had finally thrown in the towel for the last time. He was 53 years old when he died.

At the funeral that day in the town of Shafter attended by several boxers, mourners spoke of a likeable, generous man whose success in the ring propelled a small-town family into the national and international spotlight. Another side of Quarry, the quiet man who liked to compose songs and poems expressing his deep love for his family, was also celebrated.

Along with feelings of sadness, there was also an underlying sense of relief: a relief that Jerry Quarry's suffering was finally over. For despite his supreme courage in the ring – or perhaps because of it – by the end of his life he had become a symbol for punch-drunk fighters. He was a sad victim of pugilistic dementia caused by chronic brain damage.

Too many beatings in a hell-for-leather career, too many brave stands and too many punishing training sessions had all taken their tragic, terrible toll, ravaging his brain. There was nobody there to tell him he had crossed a bridge too far, entered a ring too many or taken a punch too often. Nobody to yell, 'Stop.' Quarry lived his last few years in a haze.

Comeback fights in his mid-40s, long after his glory days were over, added to the damage already suffered as the faded and self-deluded one-time bright contender struggled to regain lost glories, to get back as a winner and hear the roar of the crowd again. It never happened. This was boxing's 'Hall of Shame' at its most cruel. Once one of the toughest heavyweights in the world and the 'Great White Hope' with a knockout punch in both gloves, in his closing years he needed help just to get dressed in the morning and to shave. One of the sport's most eloquent men, he could scarcely communicate towards the end.

Quarry's story reflects no credit on the sport. He died needlessly early. His final years were a tragic example of what boxing can do, and for those who write about the fight game, those who watch it, those who administer it and those who take part in it, whether as managers, trainers or whatever, Quarry's fate was a chilling reminder that it can often take much more than it gives. For all the successful ring stars, there are, unfortunately, many Quarrys.

The sport that made Quarry famous also destroyed him. A drink and drugs problem and the emotional battering of three failed marriages could not have helped his condition – but he had more than his share of bruising battles, most notably two each against Muhammad Ali and Joe Frazier. In his final fight, at the age of 47, in a state which did not even have a boxing commission, he was badly hammered by an obscure opponent and had his front teeth knocked out and his right eye cut.

Ferdie Pacheco, the medical practitioner and cornerman known as 'The Fight Doctor' who worked with hundreds of boxers from four-round preliminary kids to eight world champions, including Ali, recalled, 'Jerry Quarry was inordinately strong and proud and exemplifies what I've been saying about the need for stopping fights in time and for fighters not to stay around too long.

'He took bad beatings, especially when he fought Frazier the second time, with an incompetent and out-of-it 60-year-old Joe Louis as referee. Louis couldn't control anything – he had his own mental problems at the time – and it netted Quarry one of the worst beatings I have ever seen. But he took beatings from everybody.

'When you stay on too long, it's the same old story as it was in the 1920s, '30s, '40s and '50s; you name it. When a guy stays on too long, takes a big beating and lives a high lifestyle, he figures to end up in a nursing home. It's a never-ending story. That's the nature of the sport, and in our litigious community, it seems there is no way to stop someone fighting on to middle age. Repetitive blows to the head over a long period of time cause brain damage. When you're old, it's bigger brain damage, faster brain damage.

'[What happened to] Jerry Quarry was no surprise. He was just another in the long parade of people who won't accept that fact: the punch-drunk syndrome. That's all there is to it. There's nothing new to say about it. On Quarry's drinking, it wasn't healthy. It isn't healthy. It certainly soddens the brain. If you're getting hit and you've already got a damaged brain, it accelerates the problem.'

Quarry was undoubtedly one of the best heavyweight contenders in the world during the mid-1960s and early '70s. Up to his first retirement in 1975, he had a professional career of sixty-three fights, with fifty-one wins – thirty either on count-outs or stoppages – eight losses and four draws. As well as Ali and Frazier, he took on the best heavyweights around, and his record is dotted with the names of the foremost men of his day.

In one fight, he outpointed the former world heavyweight champion Floyd Patterson and in another boxed a draw. He smashed the unbeaten records of top contenders Mac Foster and Ron Lyle, and demolished big hitter Earnie Shavers in the first round – but 'Lady Luck' was not on his side. Quarry lost the big ones, to rugged George Chuvalo, slippery Jimmy Ellis, versatile Ken Norton and the two defeats apiece against Ali and Frazier. Perhaps it was Jerry's misfortune that he came along in the wrong era, a man in the wrong place at the wrong time.

A decade later, when the world heavyweight championship started to be fragmented and there were as many as 15 boxers claiming the title from 1980 to 1990, Quarry may well have hit the jackpot and won the crown. There were several ordinary champions around then, plus there was no Ali or Frazier. Having said that, he would have had the talented Larry Holmes to contend with at some stage, and then there was the emergence of the explosive Mike Tyson in the latter part of the 1980s.

A proud man, Quarry's problem was that he believed he was better than he really was, although there is nothing whatsoever wrong with confidence, even supreme confidence. Despite the fact that Gil Clancy, who managed and trained Jerry in the latter stages of his big-fight career, always felt Quarry was surprisingly prone to self-doubt, the Californian's bravery and his dogged hit-or-be-hit style in the toughest contact sport in the world would prove his undoing. Quarry earned $2.1 million in purses but lost it all through drug and alcohol abuse, bad investments and three failed marriages. At 38 years of age, broken in mind and body, he lived on social security.

Jerry inherited his fighting spirit from his father Jack, who did a bit of amateur boxing and tried to pass on the rudiments of the sport to his four sons, lacing up their gloves and pushing them into the ring at the local gym in Bakersfield, when each of them turned five. By the time Jerry was eight, he had won the local Golden Gloves junior championship at the 3 st. 3 lb division. By the age of 16, he had taken part in over 100 amateur bouts.

Four years later, he won the Californian heavyweight championship and finished up with one hundred and seventy wins and thirteen defeats before turning professional in May 1965. Within a year of leaving the amateurs, he had seventeen wins, no losses and one draw before being outpointed by the crafty veteran Eddie Machen in Los Angeles in July 1966. Quarry bounced back, however, and won six on the trot before the former world heavyweight champion Floyd Patterson held him to a draw in June 1967.

Four months later, they would meet again, but, by this time, the heavyweight scene had changed dramatically. The division had been thrown into confusion when Ali was stripped of his world title by

America's two ruling bodies for refusing to enlist in the US Army to fight in Vietnam. The World Boxing Association promptly set up an eight-man tournament, which included Quarry and Patterson, to find Ali's successor.

However, the number one contender, unbeaten Joe Frazier, opted out. 'Joe doesn't need any elimination tournament,' declared his manager Yancey 'Yank' Durham. 'He's the best around, anyhow, and doesn't have to prove it.' Frazier himself added, 'I'll whip the winner when it's all over.' Frazier and Durham got support from the rival New York State Athletic Commission, who saw their chance to avoid being pushed out of the heavyweight picture. They promised Joe he would get a crack at the 'New York heavyweight title', though nobody could remember when that synthetic title had been fought for, if ever. The main thing as far as New York was concerned was that they were in the frame.

Big-time wheeler-dealer promoters like Don King and Bob Arum had not yet come onto the promotional scene to tie up the boxers with contracts, so each contestant would receive $50,000 for the opening matches, $75,000 for the semi-finals and $125,000 for the championship match. Luckily, all this happened in the 1960s when there were only two main organisations, and the various state commissions would either go along with New York or the WBA. The two respective champions would then meet up, usually within a reasonable time, and there would be one undisputed champion.

Alas, if it were only as simple today. Regrettably, nowadays there are not two but a whole clatter of 'world' organisations known by their initials and referred to collectively as the 'alphabet boys'. With the New York State Athletic Commission virtually pushed out of the picture as far as being a major ruling body is concerned, we have four major organisations: the WBA, WBC, WBO and IBF. These are followed by the IBA, IBO, WAA, IBS, IBB, WBU, WBF, IBC and a few other stragglers, all rushing to the fore with plastic belts when a title becomes vacant and quickly installing their man as 'world champion' or setting up their own 'title fight'.

It is also interesting that in the 1960s there were only eight weight divisions and naturally eight world champions, with a few junior divisions sometimes cropping up. Today, there are no fewer than 17 divisions and at least 170 boxers given the title of 'world champion'. No wonder boxing is in such a terrible mess.

Quarry got through the first series of the WBA tournament by outpointing Patterson over 12 rounds in Los Angeles in October 1967. By this stage he had a beautiful wife and had also acquired a top trainer. Silver-haired Teddy Bentham, a New Yorker, had coached a string of top boxers, including world champions Davey Moore (featherweight) and Jimmy Carter and Carlos Ortiz (lightweights). Bentham was a man who knew his way around the boxing business.

Watching the Quarry–Patterson fight at ringside was the WBA's leading contender Thad Spencer from Oregon, who promised to knock out Quarry when they met. He got his chance in February 1968 at the Oakland Coliseum, California, but it was Quarry who came out the winner, stopping his man in the twelfth round following an impressive two-handed barrage.

The stage was now set for the tournament final, with Quarry going in against Ali's former sparring-partner Jimmy Ellis from Louisville, Kentucky, a twenty-eight-year-old father of six. In the early stages of the tournament, the fast, shifty Ellis, trained by Ali's man Angelo Dundee, had stopped Leotis Martin in nine rounds and outpointed Oscar Bonavena over twelve.

Quarry and Ellis met at the Oakland Coliseum in April 1968, with the WBA world heavyweight title on the line, but Quarry lost the decision, which was booed by the 12,000-strong crowd made up mainly of Jerry's supporters. When he realised he had lost, Quarry leaned over the top rope with his head down, disconsolate and dejected, and was consoled by his father. He had lost the big one, his first championship chance, but there would be another day.

Jerry returned to the ring in November 1968 with a new, aggressive style. He said his days as a counter-puncher were over, even if his father warned, 'OK, fight like Frazier and you may wind up as champion, but your brains may be scrambled.' He had four low-key wins, three in the fifth round, before gaining a lopsided points decision over Buster Mathis in New York, delighting the Madison Square Garden crowd with his attacking, hard-punching style.

Meanwhile, Frazier, known as 'Smokin' Joe', had consolidated his claims on the New York version of the title with three wins. When an offer came to defend his title, which was also recognised by several other states, against Quarry, he readily agreed. The match was set for 23 June 1969 at Madison Square Garden and was considered something of a grudge fight. Quarry had called Frazier 'yellow' because he had refused to enter the elimination tournament while Frazier said Quarry was ducking him.

Twenty-five-year-old Smokin' Joe was a tough cookie who came to personify the left-hooking, aggressive Philadelphian style of fighting. He was born in South Carolina, but his family moved north when he was a boy. He won the heavyweight gold medal at the 1964 Tokyo Olympics, turning professional in 1965. Managed by a group of wealthy businessmen, he made fast progress, and going into the Quarry fight, he had won all twenty-three of his fights, only three going the scheduled distance.

Predictably, Frazier came out smokin', but Quarry met him punch for punch in some heavy infighting. Jerry won the round, but, in effect, he was playing into Frazier's hands without realising it. Joe would prove to be the stronger and often had Quarry holding on like a drowning man clutching a lifebelt. The Californian fought stubbornly, but Frazier was too strong, and it was all over in the seventh. Quarry's face was blood-smeared and his right eye practically closed, prompting the commission's physician, Dr Harry Kleiman, to instruct the referee Arthur Mercante to stop the slaughter.

Quarry howled in rage, 'Doc, give me one more round, please. If I'm going out, I'll do so on my back, like a man.' Mercante, however, had already waved that it was all over. It was the most punishing fight of Quarry's career, and undoubtedly contributed to his condition in later years. Ruefully, Quarry would subsequently recall, 'They never thought I had a heart until that fight. Damned shame I had to show 'em that way.'

Two months later, he rebounded from the shattering loss with a one-round stoppage of John Carroll followed by a knockout of Brian London in two. Quarry, however, was now becoming disillusioned with boxing. Despite the two wins over opposition which was anything but strong, he admitted the old fire was gone and that he was retiring to pursue an acting career.

Quarry put his planned Hollywood career on hold when Madison Square Garden made him a $20,000 offer to fight the rugged Canadian heavyweight-contender George Chuvalo in December 1969. A win would make a nice Christmas box. Besides, Chuvalo was no Frazier, and Quarry thought he could take him.

It was another brutal fight, a brawl, with both men using what can only be described as street tactics: butting, hitting on the break, the use of elbows, wrestling and continual punching below the belt. Ahead on the scorecards going into the seventh, Quarry was hit by a desperation left hook. It was a long, lazy punch that landed on the side of his head and sent him to the canvas on the seat of his shorts.

Dazed and confused, he got up at the count of three, then dropped down onto one knee, apparently to take advantage of the mandatory eight count. Just as referee Zack Clayton completed the count, and with one second remaining in the round, Quarry jumped up and stormed around the ring, frantically complaining to Clayton that he should be allowed to continue – but to no avail. The fight was over, and Quarry was a seventh-round KO victim.

The consensus of opinion in the newspapers the next day was that the dazed, surprised Quarry simply misjudged the count and left it too late to get to his feet. It was a finish that would haunt him for the rest of his life. 'A lot of people accused me of taking a dive against Chuvalo,' he would recall, 'and that I quit because the going was too rough. No, I just wasn't concentrating on the count. The ending was such a weird, freaky thing.'

Quarry vowed he would never again box at the Garden or anywhere else in New York for that matter. Yet six months later, he was back in the same ring to stop big Mac Foster, an unbeaten Californian, in six rounds. He was back in contention and very much in the championship picture, although he was not to know that the scene was about to undergo a major change with the return of one Muhammad Ali . . .

When Ali had refused in April 1967 to wear an army uniform and join American soldiers in Vietnam, he lost three of his prime years. He cited his religion and allegiance to the pacifist Nation of Islam as the reason. 'Why should they ask me to put on a uniform and go ten thousand miles from home and drop bombs and bullets on brown people in Vietnam while so-called Negro people in Louisville are treated like dogs?' he told *Sports Illustrated*. Nevertheless, the World Boxing Association took the title off him. Soon afterwards, he was brought before the courts, sentenced to five years in jail and fined $100,000.

He was freed pending an appeal but prevented from practising his profession, and to ensure that he did not box again, the government took away his passport. However, America was gradually becoming uneasy and disenchanted about the war. Perception was shifting – in Ali's favour. Young Americans burned their draft cards, and older citizens were coming around to the same viewpoint. The authorities also felt guilty for the way in which Ali had been punished for his religious beliefs in a supposedly democratic country. There was also respect; the boxer had put his money where his mouth was. He had walked out on millions of dollars in purses because of what he believed in. As opinion softened, the first glimmer of a willingness to allow him to box again appeared.

Ali was still the 'bad boy', however, something that boxing promoter and publicist Harold Conrad discovered as he hawked the idea of an Ali return across the US. State after state rejected it. Eventually, almost as a last hope, Atlanta, Georgia, agreed to stage the fight, and Quarry was selected as the opponent. So, on 26 October 1970 at the Civic Auditorium, an old arena with large pillars that looked like something straight out of *Gone with the Wind*, the fight was set.

Quarry would get the biggest purse of his career: $300,000 against Ali's $600,000. The fight was scheduled for 15 rounds, an unusual distance for a non-title contest but an indication of its global importance. In an interview with *Boxing Illustrated* before the match, Quarry said, 'This fight represents the opportunity of a lifetime for me. I've everything to gain and not too much to lose.'

On boxing generally, he was fiercely critical of the sport: 'Boxing has been good to me, but if I'd known in the beginning what the real odds were and just how tough a business it was going to be, I would never have gone into the ring to make a living. It's too tough a racket to get started with. If you ask me for serious advice for young pros, even for my own brother Mike with all his ability, the only answer I can give is to tell 'em to get out of boxing and find another business.'

Once again, Quarry failed in the big test. With his face a red mask from a bad cut over his left eye, Jerry was battered to defeat in three rounds when referee Tony Perez intervened to stop the fight. 'The eye was so bad, cut to the bone, I couldn't let it go on,' he said. The wound required 11 stitches, and Quarry seriously contemplated hanging up his worn gloves for keeps. Yet like so many before and after him, the call of the ring would be too great, and he was back fighting eight months later. He won six more bouts before taking on Ali again, in Las Vegas in June 1972. 'He won't rile me this time,' said a defiant Quarry.

Alas, it was the same story all over again, with Ali at the top of his form. Outpunched, outboxed and simply outclassed, Quarry's coordination and game plan to overpower the former champion fell apart like scaffolding erected by a bunch of amateurs before referee Mike Kaplan shouted, 'That's enough,' in the seventh round. Quarry was not badly marked, but he was being reduced to a human punch-bag. He may have been the world's leading white heavyweight, but this was one night when he was very definitely and very painfully second best.

The next day, Quarry told boxing writers that he was disgusted with his showing, having failed to beat Ali for the second time. He was 'fed up with the fight game' and was going to do something else with his time, although he did not elaborate what that 'something else' was. He may well have kept his promise to quit the sport had it not been for a call from Gil Clancy, one of America's leading trainers who had taken Emile Griffith to the world welter and middleweight titles. 'You are only 27 and too young to quit,' Clancy told him. 'You can still make some good money in boxing.'

Quarry pulled on the gloves again in January 1973. He was considerably overweight but still managed to stop Randy Neumann in seven rounds in New York, leaving the way clear for a big-money clash with the unbeaten Ron Lyle, a heavy-punching former convict from Denver, Colorado, who had battered his way to nineteen straight wins, seventeen by knockouts or stoppages.

The brooding Lyle was being tipped as a likely challenger for new world heavyweight champion George Foreman and was fully expected to wipe out Quarry, who was considered washed up. The Madison Square Garden crowd, however, saw a different Quarry on a cold night on 9 February 1973. In what turned out to be one of the finest performances of his career, Quarry outboxed and outpunched Lyle over 12 rounds and received a standing ovation from the delighted crowd of 16,571.

Quarry was back in business and continued his winning form in 1973 with a two-round stoppage of James J. Woody in Las Vegas and a four-round win over Tony Doyle in Los Angeles. He credited his rejuvenated outlook and better form to the new woman in his life, his second wife Arlene Charles, a stunning blonde and former Miss Indiana. They married in Las Vegas in September 1973 after a whirlwind romance.

'When I'm mentally right, nobody out there can beat me,' he said. He also asked reporters to call his new wife Charlie, who he said was the primary reason for his new attitude. They had their picture taken together for magazines and newspapers, and seemed the ideal couple. The fighter and his lady. 'She's 100 per cent for my career, 100 per cent for me,' he said.

Meanwhile Quarry's career kept steamrolling on, and Clancy matched him with the formidable heavyweight contender Earnie Shavers at Madison Square Garden a few days before Christmas 1973. Shavers was a feared hitter, with 46 wins in 48 fights, 45 either on count-outs and stoppages, and future world champion Larry Holmes said of him: 'Earnie hit me harder than any other fighter, including Mike Tyson.'

It was all over in the opening round, with the ferocity of Quarry's attack coming as a big surprise to the crowd of just under 15,000. Going against Clancy's advice to box, box, box and move, he simply went in, battered Shavers to the boards with a barrage of blows for a

173

mandatory eight count before a crunching left hook and right cross sent Earnie staggering helplessly against the ropes. Referee Arthur Mercante intervened after two minutes and twenty-one seconds of the round.

In an interview with the author nearly 30 years later, Shavers' memory of the massacre was still vivid. He explained: 'Shortly after the bell, Quarry came rushing at me and gave me a pummelling like I'd never experienced before. He beat me like a bass drum without any retaliation on my part. On that night, Quarry was at his very best. [He was] a good puncher, but he took a lot of punishment over the years.'

Quarry laid off for five months and returned with a win in two rounds over the undistinguished Joe Alexander, but it was another Joe who would provide totally different opposition. Clancy secured a match with former champion Joe Frazier at Madison Square Garden for 17 June 1974 with the winner promised a shot against the victor in the George Foreman–Ken Norton championship fight. Frazier had given Quarry a bad hammering in the same ring five years earlier, but the experts felt that Jerry's renewed good form would overcome the former champion who had been pounded to defeat in two rounds by Foreman almost eighteen months earlier and, in his previous bout to the return match with Quarry, had been outsmarted and outpunched by Muhammad Ali.

However, Smokin' Joe had lost none of his fire, and he pounded Quarry almost at will. By the fourth round, Jerry was taking a horrible beating. His left eye was badly cut, his nose dripping blood and he was dropped to his knees by a vicious left hook when the bell rang. Frazier was still battering his man in the fifth when referee Joe Louis finally intervened at one minute thirty-seven seconds of the fifth round. There was widespread criticism after the fight that the former Brown Bomber – then 60 and long past his sell-by date as a referee – should have stopped the one-sided fight much earlier than he did.

Quarry blamed the loss on his wife's nagging. 'She was always telling me who I should have as friends and [who] I shouldn't have around,' he would recall. 'The thing she liked best about being married to me was the fame and the fortune. She loved me at her pace, but as soon as I left the limelight, I became just another guy to her.' They were divorced in October 1978.

Seven months after the Frazier hammering, Quarry was back in the Garden against Ken Norton, who had been pulverised in two rounds by Foreman in a title fight a year earlier. The scheduled 12-rounder was a back-up to the Muhammad Ali–Chuck Wepner world heavyweight title fight, Ali having taken the championship from Foreman in the famous Rumble in the Jungle the previous October.

Before a crowd of 12,000, it was another war, with Quarry again on the losing side. Norton, a slick operator with a solid punch in both gloves, simply took Quarry apart. Jerry looked in terrible shape. He was sloppy, with bushy sideburns and unruly hair; his face was red and puffy, and he had a spare tyre of flesh hanging over his trunks. Norton played matador to Quarry's bull, snapping back the former White Hope's head with hard left jabs and buckling his knees with solid rights.

In the fifth round, his face a mask of blood, Quarry looked all in, with Norton pounding him at will, when referee Johnny LoBianco intervened after two minutes and twenty-nine seconds. In the dressing-room, a dejected Quarry said, 'I tried, goodness knows, I tried.' A news-agency story later came out to the effect that when Quarry had received the call for the Norton fight, he was drunk in Hawaii. He had gone to Honolulu four weeks earlier for a fight with George 'Scrap Iron' Johnson and had edged out a decision which was booed. There were also reports back in the US that he was hitting the bottle harder than his opponents.

Not long after the Norton bout, Quarry met Ken on the street and challenged him to a fight there and then. 'If I had trained better, I would have knocked you out,' he told the surprised Norton. 'Let's see who is the better man. Let's get it out right here on the street. The street is one place I have never lost a fight.'

Not surprisingly, Norton declined, saying that they could get well paid for a return match in the only suitable place for a fight, the boxing ring. They parted, and the repeat match didn't take place, but the bad feeling Quarry had for his rival never really went away. Jerry

175

retired, yet again, but the lure of the ring was too great, and over two years later, he pulled on the gloves in Las Vegas in November 1977 against a moderate Italian, Lorenzo Zanon.

Weighing a paunchy 14 st. 13 lb, Quarry looked anything but impressive. Always behind on points, he floundered for much of the fight as the Italian peppered him with left jabs and right shots with hardly any return. Luckily for Quarry, Zanon was not a particularly hard hitter, and he was running out of steam in the ninth when Quarry finally caught up with him with some effective blows. With the tired Zanon in distress, the bout was stopped. 'This was a dismal exhibition at best,' Howard Cosell told his TV audience from ringside, an opinion shared by Frank Sinatra who was alongside him.

Quarry retired once again. Everybody, including the boxer himself, was losing count of the number of times he had quit, but he said that he meant it this time. He wed for the third time, but the marriage did not last long. Nothing was ever easy for Jerry Quarry.

Back in California from New York, things were not looking good for him. Though he had earned $2.1 million in the ring, three divorce settlements, alimony, child-support payments, non-stop partying and the loss of his principal source of income took a heavy toll. He had to cash in the investments that were meant to support his retirement years. Houses in Hawaii and Orange County, California, went. So did his small retirement nest egg.

Quarry struggled to hold down a number of jobs, including one as a television commentator for CBS. He was also a bodyguard and road manager for the pop group Three Dog Night, an actor, a public relations man and a lounge singer. He was also a salesman for mobile homes and a beer salesman of all things, considering his problems with alcohol. He either hated the work or couldn't make the grade, but nothing stuck. He said that he missed the spotlight and was even thinking of yet another comeback, much against the wishes of his family and friends.

Meanwhile, a new division, cruiserweight, had been formed by the World Boxing Council in 1979. The WBC reckoned that a substantial number of good boxers who were too heavy for the light-heavyweight limit of 12 st. 7 lb and too light against genuine heavyweights would welcome the new in-between division. They set the limit at 13 st. 8 lb, and while they raised the limit by nearly half a stone three years later, the rest of the organisations stayed with the original until it was subsequently raised to 14 st. 4 lb universally.

When Quarry heard about the new division, he decided to return to the ring and give it a go, even though he was then 38 and his great days were only a faded memory. He said his aim would be the world title. 'If the cruiserweight division existed when I was in my prime, that's where I would have been fighting all along,' he said. 'I weighed under 200 lb – 14 st. 4 lb – for most of my fights.'

So, in August 1983, after being out of the ring for six years, he made his return as a cruiserweight with a win in the first round over Lupe Guerra in Albuquerque, New Mexico. The hapless Mexican had been a one-round victim of Frank Bruno when the Brit launched his career a year earlier. Guerra was no real test for a faded Quarry, who finished him with a left hook – though Jerry's body absorbed tremendous physical punishment.

He planned to have his second fight as a cruiserweight in Scranton, Pennsylvania, against Steve Mormimo, another no-hoper, but the local state commission refused him a licence. Undeterred, he got a fight in November 1983 in Bakersfield – his old Californian home town where it had all begun – and won a disputed decision over the average James Williams, prompting an angry Williams to cry, 'Robbery, robbery. I reckoned I won every round.'

Quarry paid a high price for victory, such as it was, receiving over 60 stitches to facial cuts. His son Jerry Lyn recalled, 'It scared the hell out of me. It was so bad that the Red Cross set up camp outside his dressing-room.' On the advice of family and friends, he hung up his gloves for what he said would be the last time. 'I've had enough,' he commented. 'That's it. I just don't have it anymore.'

The California State Athletic Commission announced they had withdrawn his licence. Quarry said he would remain in boxing and took over the management of his kid brother Robert. The younger Quarry had only experienced modest success as a heavyweight and would now campaign as a cruiserweight under his brother's guidance.

Jerry was also working as a bartender in Las Vegas but had dreams of opening his own club on the west side of the gambling town. He would call it Irish Jerry's Main Event. Alas, like many other top boxers who made big money during their careers, Quarry was close to broke, living day by day, week by week. 'Charlie, my second wife, did a job on me,' he lamented. 'Anyway, I never made really big money. The most I ever made was $300,000 when I fought Ali the first time, and out of that, I only netted $95,000 after all the expenses and cuts.'

Sadly, Quarry's life was spiralling out of control. He was drinking heavily and was using cocaine. In 1983, he agreed to undergo a CAT scan and neurological examinations in Los Angeles as part of a *Sports Illustrated* investigative report into brain injuries in boxing. The scan showed enlarged ventricles in the brain and a suggestion of cortical atrophy. His neurophysical results were poor.

Nevertheless, in an interview shortly after the story appeared, Quarry was able to impress writer Doug Krikorian with a near photographic memory. Nevertheless, by 1988, he admitted that he had attended a detoxification centre to combat alcoholism. He was by then well into the final downward slide.

Nothing was heard of him for a few years, and he was one of boxing's sad, forgotten contenders. Then, in September 1992, his name came up in an agency report that he was astonishingly planning yet another return to the ring after being away for nine years. 'Jerry allowed some former business partners to talk him into another comeback,' recalled his brother Jimmy. 'They were telling him that he had to get into shape as Hollywood was planning a big movie about his life, but all they cared about was making money by getting him back into the ring. He was no longer a fighter. He was trying to please his so-called friends. He wouldn't listen to his family.'

The California State Athletic Commission ordered him to appear before them, but he refused, and they continued to withhold his licence. Nevada also turned him down. Colorado, however, was prepared to stage his latest comeback fight, against Ron Cranmer, yet another no-hoper, who had won only two of his eight fights and had been hammered in the first round of his last engagement before meeting Quarry. It was convenient, too, that Colorado did not have a boxing commission so no questions needed to be asked, or answered.

Some reports listed him as Crammer, but what's in a name? He was no more than an average club fighter, yet he gave Quarry a systematic beating in six rounds, with Jerry coming home with his front teeth knocked out, his right eye badly cut and a glaze in his eyes. All for $1,000.

His brother Jimmy remembered that Jerry's disabilities became evident later. 'He would get up from the couch and say he was going home,' said Jimmy. 'When I would say, "What do you mean, you're going home? You are already home," he would say, "Oh, I was just checking you guys out." That's the way it was.'

Jerry's sister Dianna took him to see Dr Peter Russell, one of California's leading neuropsychologists, and his examination revealed that the boxer had 'suffered significant cerebral atrophy and neurological impairment'. Further testing showed a severely impaired short-term memory. The cause, according to Dr Russell, was repeated trauma to the head. 'He [Quarry] is at third stage dementia and has the brain of an 80 year old,' the doctor said.

The connection between Quarry's condition and boxing echoed findings that had begun to appear in the 1980s in the *Journal of the American Medical Association*. Advances in technology and testing allowed researchers to confirm medically what had for years been anecdotal speculation about so-called punch-drunk boxers. According to one study done in the New York area at the time, more than 60 per cent of professional boxers who had fought a large number of fights would end up with chronic brain damage, although not many made their disabilities public. The report found that chronic brain damage often results from an accumulation of blows over a long period rather than from a quick knockout which registers the boxer unconscious immediately. Chronic brain damage is gradual, more subtle and hard to measure. It was also reported that other factors that contributed to the severity of the condition included the number of fights undertaken and the age that the boxer began and ended his career. The study found that the more fights a boxer had fought, the more likely he was to end up with brain damage, with ageing only exacerbating the condition.

Quarry was now damaged goods: a poster boy for punch-drunk

boxers. He had memory loss and difficulty with his equilibrium. He could not follow directions and was unable to perform even simple chores, such as taking a shower, lacing his shoes or shaving. Because he had problems with depth perception, he struggled to remember where he was and as a result would get easily lost. Nor could he live alone.

With no source of income, other than a monthly $614 social-security cheque, and little chance of finding a job, he lived with his elder brother Jimmy, who looked after him and paid for his medical treatments. Despite his 13-year career and the money he made, Quarry had no pension. Nor did he receive any health-care benefits.

Jimmy became bitter that his younger brother had literally boxed his brains out, made a lot of people a lot of money and had nothing to show for it. Jerry was now exposing the essential contradiction of the sport – its heroes are, of necessity, also its victims. The poundings he had taken in the ring had turned him into a confused, child-like man.

The two brothers shared a small townhouse in San Jacinto, some 95 miles from downtown Los Angeles, at the foot of the San Jacinto mountains. It was peaceful there, and the turf was familiar to Jerry. He had often trained along those roads. Jimmy also set up the Jerry Quarry Foundation, a non-profit organisation aimed at paying pensions and providing health-care coverage for disabled boxers. Whenever there was a fundraiser, Jerry would go along, sing a few songs and recite some of the poetry that he used to write. Otherwise he would spend afternoons alone but for a live-in nurse, watching television or tapes of his old fights.

'He would have to be watched 24 hours a day,' said Jimmy. 'On his own he could not find the bathroom or his bedroom. He couldn't shave himself. He would walk out of the house, and the police would have to be called to find him. He would leave at five o'clock in the morning. If he got milk out of the fridge, he couldn't remember where it went back. He wasn't violent. He would hallucinate and hear voices. He lived in a small world [of his own]. He was missing the accolades, and he would walk around saying, "I'm going to be a hero again."'

180

David Davis, a freelance writer, visited Quarry in 1995 to interview him about his career for an article to appear in the magazine *Fight Game*, spending several hours watching videos of his fights and poring over a scrapbook filled with yellowed newspaper and magazine clippings. At one stage, Quarry, genuinely puzzled, asked Davis, 'What did you say you were here for?' Jerry told Davis, 'Boxing is a very cruel sport, and getting in the ring is not an easy thing to do. But the situation after you retire is hellacious.'

Davis would write in the piece, 'Jerry's face and words and deteriorating mind reveal him as a man whose dedication to boxing cost him everything: the sport that made Jerry Quarry also destroyed him.'

Quarry had to be introduced to friends at boxing functions because he could not remember their names. He was so disabled he could not sign autographs. His old foe George Chuvalo met him twice in Los Angeles, but Quarry did not recognise him either time. 'It was very tragic,' the Canadian recalled. 'I was forewarned that his condition was kind of unsettling after knowing him the way he once was. Jerry was always a cocky fighter, and he was a smart guy when he was young. To see him at the end was a mind-blower.'

Many people were pointing out that boxing could not be blamed entirely for Quarry's sad plight; alcohol and cocaine had dulled his reflexes and left him virtually defenceless in the closing stages of his career. Three bitter divorces also extracted an emotional toll. However, it could not be denied that he took some brutal hammerings, even in his prime, and was shamefully allowed to have at least three fights at the end of his career when his memory loss and motor skills had deteriorated so noticeably.

On 28 December 1998, Quarry developed pneumonia and was admitted to Twin Cities Community Hospital in Templeton, California. He had a heart attack and never recovered consciousness. When doctors said that he might survive but would be bedridden and would have to be fed by tube, the family agreed to switch off the life support machine. He died on 3 January 1999, aged 53. 'Jerry won the last fight of his life by going home to God,' said his tearful mother Arwanda to her husband Jack.

The funeral was in his native Bakersfield, and he was buried at nearby Shafter Memorial Park. 'Jerry's legacy is that he gave 100 per cent of himself in all his fights,' said Ray 'Boom Boom' Mancini, the former world lightweight champion, who was among the mourners. 'As a boxer you leave pieces of yourself in every fight, and after so many fights, how much of you is left? It's unfortunate that the sport wasn't as gracious to him as he was to it.'

Johnny Ortiz, a former co-owner of Main Street Gym in downtown Los Angeles where Quarry used to work out, said, 'He was one helluva fighter, a big puncher with a terrific left hook. But he took a lot of punishment. He should have retired, but he didn't because he was broke and just kept coming back. If he were fighting today, he would have been a champion, with all the fragmented titles around.'

Jerry Quarry loved to sing, often with the Stars and Stripes draped around his shoulders in the ring, and recite poetry. Some of his poems were read by his three children Jerry Lyn, Jonathan and Keri at his funeral. It was probably the most fitting way for this very brave man to make his sad, final exit.

10

THE FIGHT NOBODY WANTED

Lewiston, Maine, with a population of 41,000, was as obscure a boxing town for a big fight as you could possibly get – especially one for the heavyweight championship of the world – and St Dominic's Youth Center an even more unlikely venue. Mainly used for hockey matches, it was a place very, very far removed from venues in New York, Chicago, Philadelphia, Los Angeles, Las Vegas, Atlantic City or any other big-fight town across the US. The building had 2,803 permanent seats which could be extended to a maximum of 5,000.

Yet it was here in the spring of 1965 where Muhammad Ali defended his heavyweight title, boxing's richest prize, against former champion Sonny Liston. It was the first heavyweight title fight in Maine – and, as it happened, the last. It started and ended controversially, and the reverberations are still being felt in boxing circles today.

The fight was originally scheduled for the 16,000-seater Boston Garden for 16 November 1964, but it came under attack from the World Boxing Association, who said that the fight would be a violation of their strict ruling on return-fight clauses in contracts.

They promptly stripped Ali of the title, dropped him and Liston from their ratings – ignoring the fact that they were the two leading heavyweights in the world – and set up an elimination tournament to find a new champion. This was eventually won by lanky Ernie Terrell, a former Liston sparring partner.

Despite this, plans still went ahead for the return fight in Boston, with or without WBA recognition. Then, three days before fight time, Ali was rushed to hospital for a hernia operation, and the fight was postponed for six months. When Liston got the news, he spat out in disgust, packed his bags and flew home to Denver, Colorado. 'I'll wait,' growled the man christened the 'Big Ugly Bear' by Ali. 'It could have been worse. It could have been me.'

There were further problems in the run-up to the new date of 25 May 1965. With just three weeks to go, there was the threat of a grand jury investigation into alleged malpractices and irregularities by Inter-Continental Promotions, Inc., who were putting on the fight, and the bout was placed in jeopardy again. It seemed that before the first fight the previous year, the same promoters had paid Ali $50,000 as an advance on his first title defence should he win the championship and that the chief stockholder in the group was a certain Mr Sonny Liston. Nudge! Nudge!

Inter-Continental Promotions, Inc., then decided to move the contest away from Boston to avoid any awkward and possibly embarrassing questions and look for another venue. Pittsburgh was considered, but they opted to move the fight into the safety of the state of Maine. It may have been a boxing backwater, but the whole thing would be given official approval by Governor John H. Reed.

In their first contest, in Miami on 25 February 1964, Liston had sensationally retired on his stool when the bell rang for the seventh round, claiming an injured shoulder. There were widespread reports that he threw the fight, although those claims were never substantiated. Many states, particularly those affiliated to the WBA, refused to stage the return match because they had banned Liston due to his underworld connections.

Liston's unsavoury past was well known to the FBI, and he had a string of convictions, including two prison terms and nineteen arrests. Sonny was simply one of boxing's baddies, although he always maintained that society was against him and nobody ever gave him a fair chance.

Born Charles Liston in a shanty town in St Francis County, Arkansas, on 8 May 1932, he was one of twenty-five children, part of the second family of an impoverished cotton picker. He ran away from home at the age of 13 and made his way to St Louis, where he quickly got into bad company. He was later apprehended and committed to a reform school, where he picked up the rudiments of boxing. He never fully recovered from his bad start, however, and much of his professional career was lost because of trouble with the law.

The brooding Liston did not get a shot at the world heavyweight title until 1962, nine years after he turned professional, because of his association with hoodlums. This period was in the immediate aftermath of the US Senate's investigations into boxing's underworld, and anybody with a shady past such as Liston's was on the outside track as far as getting a chance at a world title was concerned, whether they deserved an opportunity or not.

That's how it was with Sonny Liston. Even when he had convinced the authorities that he was on the right road and that his past was where it should be – in the past – he still had to hang around and wait for a title shot. Despite having convincingly beaten all the leading heavyweight contenders, he was forced to lie low while Floyd Patterson and Ingemar Johansson played ping-pong with the title in three fights.

Eventually, Patterson's canny manager Cus D'Amato was forced by the ruling authorities to accept Liston as the number-one contender. Sonny made no mistake, knocking out Patterson in 126 seconds in September 1962 and flattening him again in a return fight the following July, this time in 130 seconds.

Liston now looked indestructible and unbeatable, with 35 wins in 36 fights, 26 either by knockouts or stoppages. Marty Marshall, the only man to defeat Liston at that point – he had broken Sonny's jaw in the process – was subsequently knocked out in six rounds in a return match and convincingly outpointed in a third bout. There seemed nobody around to even test 'Old Stone Face' let alone take his title, and boxing writers predicted a long reign for him.

There was little doubt that he would have remained champion much longer had a brash, young former Olympic light-heavyweight gold medallist named Cassius Marcellus Clay not come along. Only seven months after blowing Patterson away for the second time, Liston lost the title to Clay in a stunning upset in Miami in February 1964.

The day after the fight, Clay changed his name to Cassius X in honour of Malcolm X, a well-known African-American activist who was born Malcolm Little and later changed his name to Al Hajj Malik Al-Shabazz. Two months later, the extrovert boxer changed it again, this time to Muhammad Ali as a mark of respect to Elijah Muhammad, leader of the Nation of Islam, the most militant of the civil-rights groups then at work in the US.

Ali would tell sportswriters that his original name denoted slavery, it had been forced on his father, grandfather and great-grandfather and he took pride in denouncing it. He was now a true follower of the Islamic faith as taught by Elijah Muhammad.

In the ring, Ali was the most exciting young heavyweight to burst onto the big fight scene since Joe Louis in the 1930s. He became boxing's greatest showman of the twentieth century, and arguably the finest heavyweight of all time. A fast, skilful boxer with a tough chin, he transcended sport and became one of the most famous people in the world.

The youngest of two children born to a Louisville, Kentucky, sign-writer and his wife on 17 January 1942, the future ring great was one of America's top amateurs when he went to the Rome Olympics in 1960. After returning with the gold medal hanging around his neck, he promptly turned professional and under the guidance of a syndicate of millionaire sponsors, made fast progress. He also made headlines by predicting the rounds in which his opponents would fall and by reciting his own poems.

Inside four years, and a month after his twenty-second birthday, the future Muhammad Ali took the world heavyweight title from Liston. It was an astonishing night as 43 of 46 boxing writers around the ringside had picked 7–1 favourite Liston to keep his title by demolishing the young upstart.

Before the fight, the former Olympic champion had mounted a campaign to unsettle the slower Liston, insulting him at every opportunity and causing a disturbance outside his house in the early hours one morning. It was claimed that the challenger was demented, that the fight was a degrading mismatch and that he would suffer serious injuries if it went ahead.

His eccentric behaviour reached its peak at the weigh-in. With bulging eyes, he pranced around, screaming at Liston. His pulse rate shot up to 120 beats a minute, and it was said he was scared to death. After being medically examined, however, it was found that it was all self-induced hysteria, and his pulse soon returned to normal. On fight night, he predicted that Liston would go in seven, and he did.

By the time the return fight came around, the boxing public were still not convinced that Ali was the better man. Neither were most of the boxing writers, who tipped Liston to recapture his title inside the distance. Sonny set up his training quarters at Poland Spring, Maine, and after former world heavyweight champion James J. Braddock watched him sparring for six rounds and doing another nine on a punch-bag, he said, 'I expect Liston to win in about nine rounds.'

Liston's three sparring partners, Amos 'Big Train' Lincoln, Willie Richardson and Wendell Newton, agreed that Ali was in for some trouble. Lincoln, at 6 ft 4 in. and 15 st., said after a brisk workout with Sonny, 'I hit him with a powerful left hook with all my weight behind it today, and he just shook it off. He's in great shape. He's not taking Ali lightly. He's got larceny in him: not the police kind, but the kind that makes him hungry for the title. There's nobody around who can punch with him.'

Liston claimed he had trained harder for the return fight than for the first one. 'I have a surprise for Ali,' he told reporters. 'After all, he is only a fair fighter, not nearly as brave or as good as Floyd Patterson. I fought a stupid fight in Miami. I shouldn't have run after him. I had something he wanted, and I should have waited for him to come to me.'

'I'm not making any conditions,' he said, then quickly corrected himself, 'or predictions I mean. I'm keeping that secret for Ali. But I think I'll come ahead. Am I bitter? Yes, I'm bitter at losing my title but not bitter enough to lose my head. When I catch him, he'll know all about it. All I know is that I'm going to regain my title. I can go no further than that. I'm not a man for making predictions, anyhow.'

If there was a sombre atmosphere about Liston's training camp, Ali's quarters at Chicopee, Massachusetts, had a carnival feel about them. The champion was in his usual talkative, lively mood and entertained the visiting media with his entire poetic repertoire as well as by throwing in a few songs at the piano.

He also found time to telephone Jersey Joe Walcott, the former world heavyweight champion, in New Jersey and chided him for picking Liston to win the first fight. Walcott assured Ali that he was not going to make any prediction this time. Nobody was to know, least of all Jersey Joe, that Walcott would be named as the referee shortly before the fight.

The tenor of the Ali camp changed with the murder of Malcolm X. The erstwhile voice of the Nation of Islam had not seen eye to eye with the pacificist approach of Martin Luther King. Indeed, Malcolm X had alienated many blacks, including the prophet Elijah Muhammad, and he left the Nation of Islam in 1964. His demise nonetheless coincided with the outbreak of renewed black unrest.

A month after Malcolm X's murder, King led 25,000 marchers to the steps of Capitol Hill in Montgomery, Alabama, where he presented Governor George Wallace with a list of grievances, mainly directed at the sluggish pace of electoral reforms intended to give blacks the vote in a state where whites were outnumbered by six to four.

In Selma, Alabama, where an attack on three liberal clergymen by a white gang had provoked six nuns to front a demonstration, bombs were discovered in a black church, in a funeral parlour and at the home of a prominent black lawyer. King and some 300 of his supporters had earlier been arrested in Selma for staging a protest parade without a permit.

It was no surprise, therefore, that Ali, whose own leanings were towards Elijah Muhammad, should begin to fear for his own safety.

Word got around that a group of Malcolm X's associates were bent on avenging the assassination by rubbing out the most popular Muslim in the Nation of Islam. Two carloads of assassins were reportedly heading for Maine from New York, with Ali the target.

The day that Ali arrived at his camp, five FBI agents turned up and installed a twenty-four-hour guard. Every morning, two police cars would accompany him to the track where he did his roadwork. They would scamper across the field and check for ambushers before he could begin running. Police snipers were concealed behind the bushes, while plain-clothes policemen circulated among the crowds at the gym where Ali worked out.

This was no cheap publicity stunt dreamed up by promoter Fred Brooks, front man for Inter-Continental Promotions, Inc.; this was for real. The life of the undefeated heavyweight champion of the world was in danger. Brooks took the threats seriously enough to take out a $1 million life-insurance policy on the boxer. Several policemen were also assigned to Liston's camp. The former felon understood the power of gunfire and realised, too, that assassins cared little if they shot him as long as they got Ali as well. There had never been a more remarkable scenario for a world title fight.

Ali took the reports of threats to his life seriously at first but later dismissed them. On his days off, he took the opportunity of listening to his large collection of records. His favourites were those made by Sam Cooke. The two had been close friends before the rhythm and blues singer was shot dead in a Los Angeles hotel in mysterious circumstances five months earlier.

Two days before the fight, Angelo Dundee, Ali's trainer, slipped unnoticed into Liston's camp to do some spying on the challenger. As he recalled later, 'Nobody stopped me. They must not have known who I was. I stayed at the back of the gym and watched Liston sparring with Amos Lincoln, and he looked terrible. Then he tried to skip rope and got his feet all tangled up.

'Maybe just to do something, anything, to impress the spectators, Liston let his trainer Willie Reddish throw a big medicine ball into his stomach. Boom, boom, boom. Some of the people were oohing and aahing like he was really terrific, like what shape he must be in.

I turned to the guy next to me, who didn't seem to know me, and I said, "Why doesn't he throw the medicine ball at his head? That's where Ali is going to hit him." There was no response. Maybe the guy felt like telling me to mind my own business. I don't know.'

Both men wound up their training three days before the fight, and while Liston relaxed in the mansion at his camp, Ali decided to drive the 200 miles to his final campsite at Auburn 'just to sharpen up in a different atmosphere for a day or so', as he put it. He had planned to travel in 'Big Red', an old tomato-coloured bus in which he and his entourage of 15 had come from Miami Beach and which had been given a fresh coat of paint. Ali had wanted to drive the bus himself, but the police objected to the world champion becoming a sitting target for snipers while seated at the wheel of such a slow-moving and conspicuous vehicle. So, 'Little Red', Ali's scarlet Cadillac, was tuned up and used as a safer form of transport for him, while his entourage travelled in the bus. It was clear that Ali, while not nervous, was now irritated and embarrassed by the need for protection, though he admitted he had been worried when he first heard that Malcolm X supporters were heading to Maine from New York.

'Why didn't the police pick up these men if they were really coming for me?' he said at a press conference. 'I believe it's all lies just to keep people away from the arena. All people, black, white, brown and yellow love me. Nobody wants to kill me.' He then turned the conversation towards a lighter mood: 'If they shoot me, the gun will explode in their hands, the bullets will turn, and Allah will protect me. Stop these lies or you['ll] scare poor Liston, and he won't show up for the fight. I don't want that to happen. I want this fight to go on.'

At his final press conference in Auburn, he claimed that Liston was a dirty fighter who purposely tried to blind him in the first fight, Ali having had difficulty seeing during the fifth round. 'He blinded me with carbolated Vaseline,' he said. 'It was on his face and body, and I came into contact with it. It got in my eyes, and I could've gotten killed. I couldn't see a thing.

'This return fight is going to be dirty too. He's planning certain punches to the body. Foul punches. If I lose that way, it's unfair, but I won't be ashamed. If he whips me, let him whip me clean. No dirt. I'm a clean fighter. I scared the hell out of him last time so he won't come out charging and thinking he's going to knock me out. I took all he could hand out, burned him out and whipped him. I'll fight to the death.'

Liston talked to the media the day before the fight but only briefly. 'I'll regain the title,' he said. 'I'm sure of it. As I told you guys earlier, I have a surprise for him. All I can say is that it will be over quickly, and I'll be the new champion. I want that title back real bad, believe me.'

Though most boxing writers, unconvinced that loudmouth Ali could win again, tipped Liston to regain the title, former champions were divided as to the outcome. Jersey Joe Walcott thought that Liston would win 'anytime after the seventh round'. Sugar Ray Robinson, who had helped Ali train for the first fight, was going for him again, though he declined to name a round.

As was the custom at the time, the weigh-in took place on the day of the fight, and this time there were no hysterical scenes at the ceremony as there had been for the first bout. This time Ali was very subdued. Wearing a white bathrobe with the words Muhammad Ali inscribed on the back, he shadowboxed as he waited for officials to prepare the scales. Liston, in a plain white robe, stood quietly with his handlers, ignoring the champion. Ali made one attempt at clowning as Liston stepped onto the scales, which registered 15 st. 5¼ lb. He made an inaudible remark but got no response from the unsmiling challenger. Ali then stepped up and weighed 14 st. 10 lb. They were both lighter than they had been for the first fight.

After the ceremony, Ali said to Liston, 'I'm going to be faster this time. I'm going to whip you.' Liston shook his finger at the champion, smiled contemptuously as he prepared to leave and said, 'Shut your big mouth. I'll take care of you tonight.' Sonny, at the age of thirty-one, was eight years older than the champion but was nevertheless installed as the 8–5 favourite by the odds-makers, proof that few people believed that Liston was ready for boxing's slag heap just yet. On the way out of the weigh-in area, Ali overheard that the odds were favouring Liston. He turned back and shouted for all to hear, 'This is ridiculous. I should be a 7–1 favourite. Now I'm more determined than ever to whip him.'

Shortly before the fight was due to begin, it seemed that there were more people outside the arena than inside it. There was heavy security at the gates, with close on 300 police on duty because of the reported threats on Ali's life. Women's handbags were searched, with a patrolman explaining to boxing writers, reporters, and television and radio commentators that they had been given strict instructions to check anything that looked suspicious. They apologised for the delays.

Fight officials would later release figures to say that the official attendance was 2,434, the smallest crowd for a world heavyweight championship fight in history. However, Inter-Continental Promotions, Inc., were not too concerned if the 5,000 seats at St Dominic's Youth Center were not filled. They had already sold the closed-circuit television rights worldwide, with an estimated audience of 80 million in the US alone. Closed-circuit television and radio rights pushed the receipts up to a tidy $1,602,190. Boxing was moving into the satellite age in which the size of a ringside audience did not matter any more. The sport was moving away from big, open-air fights in ball parks before crowds of anything up to, and sometimes over, 100,000. Smaller venues with lucrative television revenue would soon be the norm.

Each boxer's share was $480,657. Why the champion, who usually earned more than the challenger, was content to earn the same figure as his opponent has never been fully explained. It is another mystery of the strange events surrounding the fight.

The rules were changing, too. Instead of the referee being given the sole responsibility of naming the winner, the points scoring would be left in the hands of three judges, in this case Joe Bolvin, Coley Welch and Russell Leonard, all from Maine. Referee Jersey Joe Walcott would have no say in the scoring. It was the first time in history that the final authority was taken from the third man. As it happened, the sole arbitrator of the contest would be the knockdown timekeeper Francis McDonough.

The introductions from the ring sounded like a roll-call of legends.

Included were former world heavyweight champions Jack Sharkey, James J. Braddock, Joe Louis, Rocky Marciano and Floyd Patterson as well as two past world featherweight kings, Willie Pep and Sandy Saddler. Also introduced was reigning world light-heavyweight champion José Torres, a Puerto Rican, who was reporting the fight for a Spanish radio station in New York. Canadian heavyweight champion George Chuvalo, who would meet Ali nearly a year later, was also introduced.

The Canadian singer Robert Goulet, being touted in clubs and on television as the 'new Frank Sinatra', set the tone for the evening by forgetting the words of the American national anthem. It was 'a smeared, syncopated version', said the British broadcaster and writer Alastair Cooke, 'unmatched for musical gall since Bing Crosby put out his first recording of the Christmas carol "Adeste Fideles"'.

Liston climbed into the ring and was given a good round of applause. A few minutes later, Ali entered, and he received a mixed greeting of boos and cheers. When Walcott called the two men together for the final instructions, the champion and challenger exchanged cold stares – now becoming almost a ritual in world heavyweight title fights – before they went back to their corners to await the bell.

The pattern of the fight was set in the opening seconds, with Ali dancing around the ring in reverse, with the lumbering Liston shuffling forward, jabbing out a long left and endeavouring to get close enough to swing to the body. Liston planned to use his weight advantage of over half a stone to the full, particularly in the clinches. First, however, he had to draw Ali in before he could put his plan into action. Was this the big secret Liston had talked about before the fight?

As George Whiting wrote in the London *Evening Standard*, 'Ali dropped his red gloves to somewhere near the seat of his white pants, twitched his shoulders like an ambitious snake dancer and sped smoothly away in a clockwise direction – with seldom less than a yard between his torso and the groping, ungainly lunges of the discomforted Liston. Thus might a cheeky schoolboy run from an irritated prefect in the playground.'

Ali stopped dancing for a few seconds to step in and send a left and a right to Liston's head before sliding back out of range and continuing with his flicking left jabs to the head and face. A straight right stunned Liston, who continued to plod forward in a flat-footed manner. He was short with two left jabs and grazed the jaw of the fast-moving champion with a left hook.

Old Stone Face seemed to be putting more power into his blows, although he was not connecting solidly. Ali was dancing and moving, with his hands at his sides, flicking out left jabs and throwing the occasional rights, but with little power. Muhammad's plan was seemingly to frustrate Liston and tire the older man out.

Liston was still trying to pin Ali in a corner or against the ropes to set him up for some of his ponderous lefts and rights. The trouble was that the champion was a constantly moving target. Ali did recoil to the ropes for a few seconds but bounced back with a short left hook and a hard right to the jaw, ringsiders noting that it made the challenger blink.

Sonny retaliated with a strong left jab to the face and a heavy right to the ribs which Ali clearly did not like. The crowd, small as it was, was now calling for more action. Liston's corner was shouting for their man to move in and out on Muhammad and cut short his movements. Ali was still dancing, but now he was taunting Liston to come in and fight. Liston replied with a glancing left hook to the jaw and a right to the body.

Ali suddenly stopped dancing and taunting. He flashed a right to the jaw followed by a left hook that merely swished through the night air, and Liston sank down like a felled bull. 'Liston's middle-aged paunch folded, the reflexes spread in all directions,' wrote George Whiting, 'and the once-menacing ex-champion collapsed into a heaving heap of misery. He thudded into the canvas with a bump, rolled over, sought to recover some sense of balance by pushing upwards on one huge arm as the count reached six, then deflated once again. One was reminded of a jug of spilt chocolate.'

Lying on his broad back, his arms beyond his head, Liston did not move, and Ali, who had been walking around the ring with his gloves held high in a display of victory, stood over his prostrate rival with a snarl on his lips as he yelled, 'Get up. Get up, you bum.' Cries of 'Fake, fake', 'Robbery' and 'Shame' reverberated around the hall.

Liston still made no effort to move, and he explained later that had he got to his feet, he would have been undoubtedly subjected to a merciless attack from the berserk champion. Walcott seemed temporarily at a loss to know what action to take, and the noise from the crowd was almost deafening. The whole picture was one of sheer bedlam.

Walcott showed his inexperience as a referee. The correct procedure would have been to order Ali to a neutral corner the moment that Liston had hit the canvas, then to take up the count from timekeeper Francis McDonough, who was monitoring the knockdown by banging his gavel on the canvas. He wasted valuable time, however, in arguing with the wild Ali, even trying to use force to get him from standing over the fallen challenger. Ali was behaving like a demented person, shouting for Liston to get to his feet. Eventually he allowed himself to be pushed back by Walcott, by which time Liston had risen to his feet.

Walcott wiped Liston's gloves in the customary manner but suddenly realised that *Ring* magazine's Nat Fleischer was shouting up at him from the ringside press row to say that McDonough had already counted out the challenger. The timekeeper had been striving frantically to attract Walcott's attention but could not be heard above the din and chaos.

Jersey Joe walked over to the ropes and eventually located McDonough, a retired printer, who shouted up at him, 'I've counted Liston out twice. The fight's over.' The boxers were now swapping punches in a free-for-all, much to the delight of the fans. Walcott quickly turned around, moved between them, told Liston to go to his corner and raised Ali's right hand as winner and still champion.

At that stage, all hell broke loose among the angry crowd who felt they had been cheated of a decent fight between the world's two best heavyweights and that it was all over before it had really begun. There was prolonged booing as the solemn-faced Liston was jostled through the crowd and back to the solace, not to mention the safety, of his dressing-room. Meanwhile, Ali, still in the ring, was yelling

195

and gesticulating about how great he was, how he had proved superior to the Big Ugly Bear for the second time and who he wanted next. He continued in this manner for the best part of 20 minutes to a mixed reception of booing and cheering.

'Where's Floyd Patterson?' he screeched in reference to his next likely opponent. 'I want Floyd Patterson.' The fans could not have cared less about who Ali wanted next – whether it was Patterson or Popeye – at that stage of the proceedings. All they wanted was their hard-earned money back and to throw anything that was not nailed or bolted down into the ring as a squad of police tried to restore some kind of law and order to the situation.

The time of the knockout was given as 60 seconds, but that was sheer guesswork on a bizarre night when nothing seemed to go right. It was later announced as one minute and forty-two seconds, which is now considered to be the official time. Walcott was heavily criticised for his handling of what can only be described as a fiasco – it was obvious that he was too confused to know what was going on – and yet another nail was hammered into boxing's coffin.

Timekeeper McDonough laid all the blame on Ali for the manic confusion. 'If that bum had gone to a neutral corner instead of running around like a maniac, all the trouble would have been avoided,' he told reporters later. 'I started my stopwatch when I saw Liston hit the canvas and banged off the count until the watch showed that 12 seconds had elapsed when I shut it off.

'When Jersey Joe came over to me, I made it clear that Liston had been counted out. Also, that in my view Liston had stayed down 20 seconds in all. I made it clear that Liston had been counted out. Walcott then turned back to the centre of the ring when the fighters had resumed battling, separated them and declared Ali the winner.'

When Ali met the press in his dressing-room, he had his wife Sonji by his side. He solemnly assured all and sundry that the punch which put Liston down and out had come from the grave of the great Jack Johnson, the former heavyweight champion of the world and someone whom Ali admired. 'The comedian Stepin Fetchit taught me the short right-hander that Johnson took to the tomb with him,' he said. 'You cannot throw a punch until a guy comes near you, but I practised it for several months and gave it a special twist of my own. My corkscrew punch.

'But don't blame Liston. He's a good loser. Any man has to be a loser when Muhammad Ali hits him. Once he went down, I got excited and forgot the rules. I know I should have gone to a neutral corner. I was having fun. I wanted to give the people their money's worth because everybody said the first fight was fixed. I wanted him to get up so as I could show everybody how great I was.'

Over in Liston's dressing-room, the former champion insisted he did not quit. 'I got hit and hurt good,' he said. 'Ali's right caught me high on the cheekbone, and I felt all screwed up. To be honest, I figured I could have beaten the count, but I looked up and saw Ali standing over me, waiting to hit me again when I got up. Ali is a nut. You can tell what a normal guy is going to do, but you can't tell what a nut is going to do. I figured I was safer on the floor.'

Walcott, the man in the middle of the controversy, explained to the press, 'The punch was a short right to the chin. It was no phantom punch. This guy puts his punches together better than anyone I've ever seen. The reason I stayed with Ali was that I was afraid he was going to kick Liston in the head. He was acting like a wild man, running around and shouting for Liston to get up. He might have even hit Sonny while he was getting up, but it was definitely a solid punch that put him down.' In an interview with the author in later years, Walcott said, 'Liston was definitely knocked out. The more I think about it, the more I'm convinced.'

Nat Fleischer was not convinced it was a genuine knockout. 'I was as much surprised as were the spectators to think that the giant challenger could be toppled from apparently far from a devastating punch,' he said. 'The punch was one seemingly not sufficiently powerful to put a 215¼ lb hulk on the canvas. He had stood upright from many tougher exchanges with spar mates.' Almost a year to the day later, when Fleischer was in London for the Ali–Henry Cooper title fight, the author asked him his views on the one-rounder. 'Ali definitely hit Liston with a right,' he said. 'How hard a blow, only Liston knows.'

Radio commentator José Torres, the reigning world light-heavyweight champion, did not agree with Fleischer's assessment. He told his listeners that 'a perfect shot to the jaw' had floored Liston, although his producer Nahro Diaz had been screaming with the crowd and yelling, 'It's a fix.' Seven years later, Torres wrote in his biography of Ali, *Sting Like a Bee*, that while he thought the punch was not a powerful one, it had separated Liston's senses 'because of its quickness, its sharpness and its accuracy. Liston's mind could not function to prepare him for the impact.'

Dr Ferdie Pacheco, the doctor in Ali's corner, said in an interview for *The Times* in February 2004 that his man should have been disqualified. 'There should have been a disqualification against Ali,' he said. 'The rules say you have to go to a neutral corner in the event of a knockdown. But you have Ali standing over Liston and shouting for him to get up, a dumb, old fighter Jersey Joe Walcott as a referee who doesn't how to referee and Liston saying he wasn't getting up unless Ali got away from him.

'Liston was right. He should not get up with this kid standing over him. He was quite correct to stay down and he did for 17 seconds. Can you believe it? Seventeen seconds? Ali had no right to stand over him, and that's why I say he should have been disqualified and the title given back to Liston.'

The fight, or should that be fiasco, pushed world news off the front pages. It became an international incident. Even a major story and normal page-one lead such as six men being arrested in an assassination plot to kill the French president Charles de Gaulle as he laid a wreath on a monument commemorating war dead while on a provincial tour was relegated to the inside pages in many newspapers.

Arthur Daley of the *New York Times* wrote, under a heading 'Comedy of Errors', 'There was no way in which Ali could have won with one punch. Tongues will wag in the Big Apple about this wretchedly mishandled, bush-league production for many years to come.' The *New York Post*'s Jimmy Cannon noted, 'I saw the punch that had Liston floundering on the canvas. I can tell you that it wouldn't have crushed a grape.' Down in Mexico, *La Afición* railed about 'a coarse and indignant farce'.

Former world heavyweight champion Gene Tunney was quoted in

the *New York Journal and American* as saying, 'This is the worst, most offensive debasement of boxing I have ever seen.' James J. Braddock, one of Tunney's successors, said, 'I think Liston was genuinely knocked out,' and Rocky Marciano, another ex-heavyweight champion, commented, 'I just can't understand it.' The *Corry Journal* of Pennsylvania had an apology on its front page: 'Due to the nature of last night's fight, the *Journal* feels it does not warrant coverage. Don't look for it on the sports pages.'

When Ali was in Dublin in 1972 to fight Alvin 'Blue' Lewis, and two years before he sensationally reclaimed his title against George Foreman, he told the author, 'I hit him with my corkscrew punch. It jarred him. It was a good punch, but I didn't think I hit him so hard that he couldn't have gotten up.' He said much the same to his biographer Thomas Hauser in 1991.

British boxing writer Peter Wilson, who condemned the farce in the *Daily Mirror*, would recall in his 1977 autobiography, *The Man They Couldn't Gag*, 'In all honesty, I do not believe that particular punch would have knocked me out, although it might well have knocked me down. It seemed to be quite incredible that Liston, a supposedly fit man who had trained for months and who weighed over 16 st., could be taken out with one punch in the very first round.'

So what really happened on that infamous night described by former world heavyweight title challenger Tommy Farr as 'the blackest night for boxing'? Who was telling the truth? Did Liston take a dive, or was it a legitimate blow that floored him? If the latter, could Sonny have regained his feet in time? Was he truthful in saying that he was afraid to get up and face an enraged Ali? Was Liston threatened by the Nation of Islam to lose or else? Why, too, was an inexperienced referee like Walcott allowed to handle such an important fight? Why did timekeeper McDonough not have a microphone so that he could be heard in the event of any noise? Did large sums of money change hands in the betting? Liston's managers Joseph 'Pep' Barone and Blinky Palermo were well-known fight fixers, and with odds of 8–5 on Sonny, they would have made a killing. However, Liston's wife Geraldine always insisted that besides getting his purse, her husband was no wealthier after the fight. 'He would have told me if he was,' she recalled. And what can be made of the FBI investigation which revealed that, in fact, the fight was a fake? Fraud or fair?

The only person who could finally solve the mystery of what really happened and explain the strange events that surrounded the fight in the backwoods town of Lewiston, Maine, in the spring of 1965, was Liston himself, and he was found dead in his luxury home in Las Vegas on 5 January 1971. Even then, there was a mystery. The coroner's verdict was suicide but many people dispute it, maintaining that Liston was murdered by persons unknown. They also claim to have evidence to prove it. We may never know the full truth.

11

DIRTY WORK AMONG THE FEATHERS

Legend has it that the great world featherweight champion Willie Pep once won a round in a fight without throwing a punch. It is said to have happened in a non-title fight with Jackie Graves in Minneapolis, Minnesota, in July 1946. Pep swears it is true and claims it was in the third round. He says he did it for a bet.

Known as 'Will o' the Wisp', master boxer Pep says he feinted with his head, threatened to throw punches, allowed Graves to rush him into corners, turned him around, bobbed and weaved, ducked and danced, taunted and twirled, and never once permitted the frustrated Graves to hit him.

Pep stopped Graves in the eighth, and when he leaned over the ropes to check the judges' scorecards, there it was. He had won the third round without landing a blow. Fact or fiction? There is no filmed evidence available for proof. Nevertheless, it is a testament to Willie's fluid athletic ability and superb defensive skills that such a notion would even be entertained as truth for so many years. His style of skilful boxing was likened to tap dancing with gloves on.

Willie's great rival was Sandy Saddler, a powerful puncher who at 5 ft 8½ in. was taller than many boxers in heavier divisions. As a result of his long arms – 70 in. outstretched from fingertip to fingertip – Saddler's probing left jab, backed up by his hook and right cross, was an awesome weapon of ring destruction. Of his total of 162 fights – more than any other featherweight in history – 103 opponents failed to last the distance.

Saddler had only sixteen losses and two draws, a magnificent record by any standards. He could hand out the rough stuff, too. In his book, *The Sweet Science*, A.J. Liebling said, 'Saddler is relentlessly aggressive. He seldom takes a step backward, and if an opponent occasionally gets a foot under one of his descending ring shoes, he hospitably allows it to remain there.'

Pep and Saddler had four fights together, Sandy winning three, but Pep's lone victory, in February 1949, was a masterful exhibition of boxing at its best. He outboxed and outsmarted the harder-hitting Saddler over 15 scintillating rounds. Unfortunately, their third and fourth meetings, in 1950 and 1951, were marred by fouls and roughhouse free-for-alls, particularly the last one, described by Nat Fleischer as 'a disgraceful brawl, and the poorest apology for a world championship fight I have seen in close to half a century of attendances at boxing matches'.

Each blamed the other for starting the fouls, but whatever the cause, the fourth fight between the two has gone down in boxing annals as the dirtiest in the gloved history of the featherweight division formed in the closing years of the nineteenth century. It was a fight that disgraced the sport. It was certainly as rough as, if not rougher than, any of the bare-knuckle brawls of the 1800s when an antagonist could win a fight by lifting up an opponent and slamming him into the hard turf. 'Pep and Saddler should have been ashamed of themselves,' wrote Pep's biographer Brian Hughes in 1997.

Saddler was considered by all to be a rough customer, but it was uncharacteristic of Pep to resort to foul tactics as he was generally considered to be a clean boxer, even allowing for the somewhat slack rules of the American boxing scene. Saddler was a tremendous puncher, particularly to the body. He could rough it with the toughest if the need arose, and he was not averse to foul methods himself. Pep, as fine a boxer as Saddler was a puncher, was a skilled technician with one of the most accurate left jabs in boxing. It seemed that Sandy and Willie just brought out the worst in each other and boxing suffered.

Pep was born Gugliemo Papaleo on 19 September 1922, the first child born to an Italian couple who emigrated from Sicily to the US as teenagers. They settled in Middletown, Connecticut, and later moved the 16 miles to Hartford with the promise of better jobs. He became William, the English for Gugliemo, and was called 'Peppy' by his schoolmates, though he had little formal education as he had to go out to work and bring in money for the family. He worked at all kinds of jobs: running errands, delivering newspapers, sweeping the pavements for local shopkeepers and shining shoes.

Willie got into boxing after bigger kids started bullying him and stealing his money. He went down to the local gym on the advice of his father who told him about the great Hartford featherweight Battling Battalino, who was a hero to the Italian community all over Connecticut. Willie became a boxer, and in an amateur career, he went on to win 63 of his 66 fights.

On 3 July 1940, Pep turned professional, two months before his eighteenth birthday, and outpointed James McGovern over four rounds in Hartford. It was the beginning of one of the finest and busiest careers in boxing history. Willie signed up Lou Viscusi as his manager. Viscusi was a hustler who promoted wrestling tournaments, ice shows, circuses and football matches, and he had the right connections on the US fight scene. Viscusi also happened to be involved with the underworld and was a close confidant of the mobster boss Frankie Carbo. Dan Parker, the fearless boxing writer and columnist in the *New York Mirror*, would openly describe Viscusi as a 'henchman of Frankie Carbo'. The manager's name would be mentioned frequently in the Senator Kefauver hearings in 1960, although he did not have a police record and was not connected with any criminal activities.

Recalling his manager in later years, Pep remembered, 'I had to share my purses with Viscusi 50–50, though it wasn't like that at the beginning. The contract stated I would get two-thirds, Lou would get one-third and expenses would then come off the top. There was something in the small print, though, which said that should I become world champion the split would become 50–50. Now being a world champion seemed somewhat far away at the time.

'Lou was a good manager, though, and he always treated me fairly. He never interfered with my training in any way. He just booked the fights, did all the negotiations and left all the training, coaching and corner work to Bill Gore. There was never any friction between us. It was a good relationship, and we worked together well as a team.'

Gore was something of a legend in boxing and was one of the finest trainers around. He trained two world light-heavyweight champions, Mike McTigue and Melio Bettina, and would go on in later years to coach two more world champions, lightweight Joe 'Old Bones' Brown and light-heavyweight Bob Foster. He would also train top contenders including Cleveland 'Big Cat' Williams, Roy Harris and Manuel Gonzales.

With Gore doing the training and Viscusi the managing, Pep made fast progress and at the age of 20 he won the world featherweight title at Madison Square Garden in November 1942 by outpointing the favoured Albert 'Chalky' Wright. Pep's beaten opponent was a hard-punching Mexican, who had been boxing for 14 years and was a former chauffeur for movie queen Mae West. Wright and Pep would have three more fights together, all wins for Willie, two in 1944 and one in 1946. Wright tragically died in 1957 when he was found drowned in a bathtub at his mother's apartment in Los Angeles. He was 45.

Pep ran up 63 consecutive wins before losing a decision in a non-title fight in March 1943 to the cagey Sammy Angott, who had retired as the undefeated world lightweight champion four months earlier because an injury to his right hand had not responded to treatment. But the offer of a fight with Pep came along, and after testing out the hand, he decided to make a comeback and would, in fact, continue boxing until 1950. He was too strong for Pep and won a ten-rounds decision. Pep would not lose again for another five years. When he did it was to a certain Sandy Saddler.

After knocking out his old rival Chalky Wright in three rounds in Milwaukee in November 1946, Pep took a Christmas and New Year break in Miami with a few friends before planning to get back home to see his family. When he got to Miami airport to book a seat home on one of the scheduled airlines, he was told there were no seats available that evening. Instead, he could have a seat with one of the unscheduled companies that ran flights to New York, with two stops along the way: one in Newark, New Jersey, which would suit him.

Pep booked a ticket on a two-engine plane. There was a four-hour delay because of bad weather, but when conditions improved, the plane with its twenty-one passengers and small crew took off. The weather deteriorated, however, as the plane neared Philadelphia, with a downpour of heavy snow, sleet and rain. The pilot also discovered that he was running low on fuel and would have to make an emergency landing at a small airport about 45 miles south of Philadelphia, which had been used as a training base for fighter pilots during the Second World War.

As it happened, he failed to locate the airfield and decided to fly on to another one in southern New Jersey. Continued bad weather, however, was hampering his directions, and the plane crashed into tree tops in a densely wooded area in Midvale, New Jersey, smashing in two and scattering most of its human cargo among the branches and snowdrifts. Miraculously, only the pilot and four passengers were killed; the rest were badly injured, including Pep.

'I was asleep when the plane came down,' he recalled. 'The first I knew of the crash was when I woke up and found I was lying on a stretcher inside the broken plane with the state police standing by and telling other survivors to remain calm until more help arrived. My back and legs were killing me, and all around, people were moaning and hollering.

'Pretty soon, some workers who had cut their way through the woods put us in the back of a truck and took us to the local hospital. It was a miracle there were any survivors. Being asleep saved my life. I still had my safety belt on when we came down, and that cushioned the crash for me. I came out of it with multiple injuries. My left leg

205

was broken and so were the fifth and sixth vertebrae in my back. There were cuts and bruises all over my face.'

Dr Howard Brannon, one of the attending physicians at Millville Hospital, told Pep, 'You know, you are very lucky to be alive.' Willie had to agree. A week later, still in his hospital bed, he asked Dr Brannon when he could start training again. 'Willie, forget about training; forget about boxing,' the physician said. 'We just don't know. You will be here for a few months, but there's no guarantee you'll ever box again. My advice is to just look to your recovery.'

Five months later, with the casts on his leg and chest taken off, and much to the amazement of Dr Brannon and the medical staff at Millville, Pep was back in the gym. In June 1947, seven months after the crash, he returned to the ring with a points win over the tough Puerto Rican Victor Flores at the Hartford Auditorium before a capacity crowd of 4,184 fans who gave him a tremendous welcome.

Pep continued on his way with two successful defences of his title and a string of non-title bouts, but looming on the fistic horizon was the menacing figure of Sandy Saddler, who would become his nemesis. An exceptional boxer–fighter with gunpowder in his gloves, the rangy Saddler was born in Boston on 23 June 1926, one of five children, his father being a West Indian immigrant and his mother an American. When Sandy was three years old, the family moved to Harlem in New York City, where Saddler would get his start in boxing in his teen years. 'I reckon I had about fifty amateur bouts and lost around three or four,' he recalled.

Saddler turned professional as a bantamweight in March 1944 and ran up an impressive and busy record, moving up to featherweight and qualifying for a shot at Pep's world title at Madison Square Garden in October 1948. Pep's manager Lou Viscusi insisted that his boxer got 50 per cent of the boxers' 60 per cent overall purse, leaving Saddler very much on the short end. Viscusi also had a return-fight clause in the contract.

As the fight drew near, there were persistent rumours of a fix, fuelled by the fact that two days before the pair were due to enter the ring, large bets were being placed on the challenger who had been the underdog all along. The fact that the Pep party had the return fight guaranteed, and could afford to lose and collect another big purse the second time round, led to further allegations and concerns. Viscusi totally rejected the stories as 'completely false'.

At the weigh-in, New York Commission chairman Eddie Eagan, who had heard of the fix rumours, told both Pep and Saddler, 'Boys, I am holding you responsible to uphold the good name of boxing. There are rumours of a fix before every fight, but we don't pay any attention to them. You are two honest athletes, fighting in a great class, for a great championship. You will represent boxing tonight.'

Pep's lacklustre display did little to dispel the fix rumours. He did not seem able to avoid Saddler's long jabs and hooks, had no spring in his legs and was ultra cautious, as if he secretly knew that the younger man was wired with an explosive device and one punch would set it off. Pep took a heavy beating in the first two rounds, was floored twice in the third and knocked out in the fourth. It was his first loss inside the distance in 137 fights.

'I was just caught cold,' Pep recalled in later years. 'I started out by feinting as I usually do to get the feeling of the other guy, but Saddler surprised me by just ignoring my feints and walking in right on top of me.' Saddler gave credit for his upset win to future world light-heavyweight champion Archie Moore, who was in his camp as both were managed by Charley Johnston. 'I followed Archie's advice to stay on top of Pep all the time,' he remembered, 'and knocked him stone cold.'

In the return fight in February 1949, again at Madison Square Garden before a packed crowd of 19,079 who had paid a combined $87,563 to see the fight – a record at the time for the featherweight division – Pep put on one of the greatest displays of skilful boxing in the history of the 9-st. division. Jabbing, hooking, ducking, twisting and turning, Pep outsmarted Saddler over 15 rounds to win back the title. Grantland Rice of the *New York Herald Tribune* called it 'the greatest exhibition of boxing I have seen in more than a half-century of covering the sport'.

There was naturally widespread public demand for a third meeting, but Pep's stalling gave rise to stories that he was giving Saddler the run around, preferring to take on easier challengers.

Eddie Compo was knocked out in seven rounds, Charlie Riley in five and Ray Famechon, one of three French fighting brothers, was outboxed in a dazzling exhibition of ring wizardry over fifteen rounds.

The New York State Athletic Commission finally demanded that Saddler be given another deserved chance, and the outdoor match was scheduled for 8 September 1950 at New York's Yankee Stadium. Sandy had kept busy in the meantime, packing in twenty-three fights, all wins, and only five going the full route.

This time, 38,781 fans passed through the turnstiles, paying a new featherweight record of $262,150 in gate receipts. Pep was ahead in all three scorecards but retired as the bell rang for the eighth round when he claimed an injured left shoulder. Saddler was furious at the claims, shouting across the ring, 'Dislocated shoulder? Nuts. It was my kidney punches that did it.'

There were allegations that Pep simply quit, knowing that he had received the biggest purse of his career – $93,000 – and that he would get another fight with Saddler as he was still the leading contender. Pep and Viscusi would deny any wrongdoing, insisting that the shoulder injury was caused by Saddler's illegal wrestling tactics and rough work inside, and was causing too much pain for the boxer to carry on.

Not surprisingly, a fourth Saddler–Pep fight was arranged, this time scheduled for the Polo Grounds, another New York outdoor venue, on 26 September 1951. It would enter boxing's infamous Hall of Shame, showing the fight game at its worst. The Marquess of Queensberry, who gave his name to the rules drawn up in 1867 by John Graham Chambers of the London Athletic Club, must surely have squirmed in his grave at what was being done to his beloved sport. The fight turned out to be the brawl of brawls.

Saddler, ahead 2–1 in the series, climbed into the ring as 9–5 favourite. The feeling among New York boxing writers was that Saddler would either win on a knockout, a stoppage or a retirement in about the ninth or tenth round, with the clever Pep winning most of the earlier rounds.

The promoters, the International Boxing Club, were hoping for a larger crowd than the 13,836 who paid $75,311 through the turnstiles, but the general view was that the public were probably getting tired of the Saddler–Pep serial, which seemed to be going on forever and was getting rougher and dirtier with each instalment.

Referee Ray Miller, a former lightweight with close on 200 fights, raised more than a few smiles when he called both boxers to the centre of the ring for their instructions, greeting them with a courteous, 'Good evening, gentlemen, and I want a good clean fight from both of you.' Wishful thinking, surely.

At the bell, Saddler started the action with a long left hook to the jaw, but Pep went into his familiar style, peppering the champion with left jabs and right shots, and drilling in hard left hooks to the body. Saddler got his first warning when Miller cautioned him for hitting and holding. A sign of things to come?

A vicious left hook cut Pep's right eye in the second round. In a clinch in Saddler's corner, the champion whipped home another smashing left hook to the body, his most potent blow, and Pep went down like a stone tossed into a river. Saddler watched intently as Pep took a count of eight on one knee. Getting to his feet, Willie resumed his jabbing and moving, staying outside the range of that blitzing left hook from Saddler.

'From the spectators' view, the second was the outstanding round of the fight,' wrote Eddie Borden of *Boxing and Wrestling* magazine. 'They battered and slashed away at each other with neither giving ground, and the round was marked by an enthusiastic response from the fans.'

From the second round on, however, the fight deteriorated into what James P. Dawson of the *New York Times* would describe as 'a sorry spectacle. Both fighters were guilty of the collar-and-elbow, rough-and-tumble fighting made famous on the waterfront. By some oversight, they failed to bite each other or to introduce that quaint kicking game *la savate*, at one time popular in France.'

The pattern never varied. In the third, Pep, who now had a cut right eye to contend with, back-pedalled when he could, boxed when he could and stalled when he could as Saddler stormed forward. The champion missed many blows, but whenever he landed, Pep knew he had been hit. Both were guilty of blatant infringements with Pep pushing the heel of his glove in Sandy's face and Saddler pulling Willie into punches by putting his glove around Pep's neck. Miller's warnings went unheeded, and by that stage, the referee must have felt like an unwelcome guest at a wedding.

By the fourth round, the affair had deteriorated into a full brawl, with heeling, butting, wrestling and any other illegal trick being employed. Saddler was also making a play for Pep's damaged right eye. Miller did not appear to be doing his job properly, only occasionally giving them a reprimand. Why both were not disqualified and the fight, if it could be called that, declared a no contest – views shared by all the ringside boxing writers – will forever remain a mystery.

Pep, at twenty-nine and the older by four years, seemed to get his second wind in the fifth round, gliding in and out of the range of Saddler's heavy bombs, making the champion often miss and countering with his own left jabs, right crosses and uppercuts. Pep won the round on the cards of Miller and judge Arthur Aidala, though the second judge Frank Forbes strangely gave it to Saddler, presumably by virtue of his aggression, however ineffectual.

It was all Pep again in the sixth, one particularly good right turning Saddler completely around and nearly dropping him. He was dazed for a few seconds and fumbled around trying to get at his rival, like someone in a dark room looking for the light switch. Once he reached Pep, however, he banged in some hefty wallops with both gloves. On one occasion, the two became tangled up in each other and tumbled to the canvas like circus clowns.

Pep won the round on all three scorecards. It was also a round that transpired to be the turning point of the fight. From the seventh on, it was all downhill for Pep. Despite those two excellent rounds, Saddler's body punching and intense pressure were slowly wearing the challenger out. The speed was draining from his legs, the strength from his body.

With less pep in Willie now, he seemed to be losing all interest and appeared to want Miller to take him out, even disqualify him. Warned for heeling, he twisted his leg around Saddler's in an attempt to trip him. When Miller stepped in and attempted to pull the two apart, Pep grabbed the referee and Saddler, and all three stumbled to the floor. Miller was the last to get to his feet, and shoving Saddler aside, he pointed his finger at Pep and shouted, 'Do that again and you're out. I have the power to disqualify you and deprive you of your purse. Do you want to start a riot here? You can fight. Do so.' Why Miller waited until the seventh round to show some authority was a mystery, as the fouls started as early as the second. Also, why warn only Pep when both were at fault? His admission later that Pep started the fouls did not justify his reluctance to reprimand Saddler earlier than he did.

By that stage, the crowd was in uproar, and several fans rushed towards ringside, demanding that Miller leave them alone and let them get on with it. Saddler's manager added to the chaos by getting up onto the ring apron, pointing at the commission physician Dr Vincent Nardiello, who was sitting next to judge Aidala, and shouting, 'You're trying to influence the official. You're trying to dictate the judging of the rounds.'

Both boxers were guilty of further fouls in the eighth and ninth. 'Willie did not show any inclination to continue at the beginning of the ninth,' wrote Eddie Borden for *Boxing and Wrestling* magazine, 'and was literally forced out by his seconds. The injured eye was of great concern to him, but, apparently, he was alone in that thought. The round was another roughhouse session in which the principals forgot the cardinal rule of boxing, resorting to the crude, elementary method of doing everything the wrong way.' Borden felt the cause of the foul fighting was the considerable personal ill feeling between the two men as the result of their previous three title fights.

Pep returned to his corner at the bell ending the ninth round and slumped onto his stool, arguing with trainer Gore, who wanted Willie to fight on. With about 15 seconds remaining in the rest period, the referee went over to Pep's corner and warned him, 'If you don't cut out the wrestling and hauling, I will call the fight off and declare it no contest.' Miller was turning to go to Saddler's corner and issue a similar warning when Pep said, 'I can't go on. My eye is paining me.'

Miller then walked across the ring, bent down over the ropes and asked Dr Nardiello to go to Pep's corner. The doctor got the same answer: Pep was retiring. Nardiello told Miller that Pep's eye injury did not seem to be bothering the challenger. 'The eye is all right,' he said. 'He can see, but he is refusing to continue.' Miller then waved the finish, awarding the fight to Saddler on a ninth-round knockout under New York rules.

The officials differed in their scorecards at the finish. Miller had Pep in front by five rounds to four, while judge Forbes put Saddler ahead by the same margin. Judge Aidala had them level with one round even but put Pep ahead on points, eight to six. In the dressing-room, Pep complained that he had to fight the officials and his opponent. He said the referee had favoured Saddler, but he made no excuses for his foul tactics. 'I only did what Saddler was doing, fighting rough,' he explained. 'Besides, my eye was cut. An eye is more important than a fight.'

Saddler admitted complicity in the fracas, maintaining that he had to resort to the same tactics that Pep used or take the consequences. 'He started it,' said Sandy. 'I wanted a clean fight, because I can lick him every day of the week, but he wouldn't fight cleanly. When he stuck his thumb in my eye, what was I to do? Let him continue? I wouldn't let him get away with it.'

The referee said Pep was responsible for the dirty fight. 'He started it,' said Miller. 'He's clever. He knows all the tricks and all the holds there are. Saddler knows only one and held Pep behind the neck with his right and pummelled him with his left. Pep deliberately kept on fouling, even after warnings. I think he wanted to save face by having me disqualify him. That's why I went to his corner after the ninth round to warn him. It's too bad there was so much wrestling, holding, pulling and tugging. I also saw some of the finest boxing skills displayed in a ring.'

Miller would recall in later years, 'I won't go into all the details as to whether it was Pep who threw the first illegal punches or Saddler who retaliated, but there were few holds barred. This was a championship fight, remember, and it is a referee's duty to see that the crowd gets their money's worth. I'm not sure if they did. At one time it was hard to tell if they were wrestling or boxing.

'I was in a peculiar position as I did not want to stop the fight because of the other's illegal roughness. Nor did I want to disqualify them both. It was only when I went over to Pep's corner that I sensed the fire had gone out of him and he quit. After that bout, I was considered a leading authority on the art of tug-o'-war.'

Not surprisingly, the fight came in for scathing criticism, with *Ring* magazine headlining its report 'Pep–Saddler Brawl Disgrace to Boxing'. Nat Fleischer wrote:

> Wrestling, heeling, eye gouging, tripping, thumbing, in fact every dirty trick known to the old-timers in the days of the bare-knuckle bruisers was on display. Both boxers should have been tossed out of the ring long before the ninth round. What need for a referee in the ring when the contestants pay no attention to his commands?
>
> Though Pep was more to blame for the fouls, Saddler was far from blameless. If ever a fight drove a sword into boxing and aided those who want the sport killed, this was it. Every code of sportsmanship and decency was ignored, yet the perpetrators walked out of the Polo Grounds, Sandy richer by $61,243 and Willie by $36,401.

Fleischer also warned off any notions of a fifth Saddler–Pep fight: 'Boxing and boxing regulations could not stand another dock brawl between Sandy and Willie.'

In the *New York Herald Tribune*, Jesse Abramson wrote:

> This bout was the roughest of all the Saddler–Pep fights, involving so much wrestling, pulling, twisting and heeling that referee Miller could not pry them apart round after round, though he used all his strength. He was wrestled to the floor himself once. Pep was to blame for most of the fouls, though his hit-and-getaway style was admirable.
>
> Far less admirable were Pep's crafty, underhand tactics when he realised the game was up and couldn't stand the pace against his younger, stronger rival. He heeled, kneed, twisted,

spun and grabbed Saddler in hammocks, wristlocks, cobra
holds, leg locks, anything ever known to the wrestling art.

Rocky Graziano, the former world middleweight champion, told
reporters, 'No street fight was ever like this. They wrestled, they
tripped each other, they butted, they elbowed – and if the referee had
let them, they would have added their corner stools to their brawling
tools.'

A week after the fight, Pep and Saddler appeared before a meeting
of the New York State Athletic Commission and had their licences
suspended: Pep for life and Saddler indefinitely. The commission
clearly pointed the finger at Pep as being the main perpetrator. The
state ban was lifted on Pep after 20 months and Saddler's ended after
30 days. In any event, Sandy would soon be called up for service in
the US Army.

Not present at the meeting was Eddie Eagan, who had retired as
commissioner after a six-year stint in the job. Eagan, in effect, had
been forced out of office following pressure from politicians and
government top brass that he was not doing enough to rid boxing of
its hoodlum element and monopoly practices. There was also
criticism that he was lax on safety measures, as three boxers had died
in recent contests. It was, therefore, left to the new commissioner,
Robert K. Christenberry, to tell the two boxers, 'You have brought
disgrace on the good name of boxing, not only in this state but all
over America.'

Pep told the hearing, 'It seemed there was no referee in this fight.
He was getting in too late to break us up. The only way I could get
away from Saddler was to wrestle him. He was holding me by the
head and banging away at my eyes.'

Saddler admitted complicity in the fouls but added, 'I had planned
a clean fight, but what can you do if Pep didn't? I wouldn't let him get
away with it. I had no choice when he plays it rough, trips, stabs his
finger into your eye, heels you.'

In an interview with author Pete Heller in 1970, Pep said, 'I never
boxed rough or tough with anyone except Saddler because he made
me lose my head, and then you're fighting the other guy's fight.

Whenever I lost my head, I was playing right into his hands. This was my mistake. I should never have boxed that way. I couldn't overcome the guy. He was very strong. I had to outsmart him, which I was able to do when I tried it, but when I fought his game, he just took me right over. People say I quit in that fight: I didn't. I just couldn't continue because Saddler was a very dangerous fellow, and he might have killed me.'

In 1971, Saddler told Heller, 'Pep was just in there slipping and ducking until I caught up with him. Also, I never got the recognition I deserved. They introduce Pep at fights [now] as "one of the greatest featherweights" and me as "another retired champ". I whipped him in three out of four fights. Why not "Sandy Saddler, the undefeated featherweight champion of the world"? That's why I don't care to get introduced in the ring. It's just plain ol' prejudice.'

Referee Miller would make headlines again. Four months later at Madison Square Garden, he was the third man in a fight between world middleweight championship contenders Rocky Castellani and Ernie Durando. In the seventh round, Castellani was floored by a powerful right uppercut. He barely arose at the count of nine, his eyes were glassy and he looked in real trouble as he wobbled against the ropes, his arms dangling by his sides.

As Durando moved in for the kill like a bullfighter going for the *coup de grâce*, Miller, fearing Castellani might be seriously injured or even fatally hurt, stopped the fight. This did not go down well with Castellani's manager Tommy Ryan, one of the they-can't-hurt-us school. Climbing into the ring, he physically attacked the lighter Miller before being restrained by some quick-thinking cornermen.

Then, in June 1952, almost a year after the fourth Saddler–Pep battle, Miller was in the news again when he officiated at the world light-heavyweight title fight between champion Joey Maxim and Sugar Ray Robinson at Yankee Stadium. After ten rounds, on what was the hottest New York night on record, referee Ruby Goldstein stepped down from exhaustion and was replaced by Miller. It was the first and only time two referees handled the same fight. A completely drained Robinson failed to answer the bell for the 14th round, leaving Joey still champion.

As for Saddler and Pep, they did swap punches together again – but only for fun in their retirement years. At Madison Square Garden in March 1973, nearly 22 years after their infamous brawl, Saddler, 46, and Pep, 50, boxed a one-round exhibition. This time there were no elbows, butts, leg or arm locks, or wrestling tactics. Not a single infringement. One report the next day said, 'Saddler and Pep performed like true gentlemen of the ring, a credit to the noble art.' It's just that nobody believed it.

12

DURAN'S SHOCK SURRENDER

Every era produces its boxing superstars, ringmen who had talent and box-office clout to push the sport to new heights and create a bit of history along the way. Legendary boxers like Sugar Ray Robinson, Muhammad Ali, Stanley Ketchel, Benny Leonard, Henry Armstrong, Joe Louis and many more would still have become great irrespective of what age they boxed in.

During the 1980s, five men dominated the world scene: Marvelous Marvin Hagler, Thomas Hearns, Roberto Duran, Mike Tyson and Sugar Ray Leonard. Each had talent in abundance, and, equally importantly, they had that indefinable asset that separates the great ones from the good – charisma. Of the five, Leonard was arguably the best. Handsome and clean-cut with a dazzling smile, supreme boxing skills and a knockout punch, he was hailed as boxing's saviour to replace the fading Ali.

Leonard succeeded with a series of brilliant fights, even if he also managed to upset the establishment by the ease in which he selected his own contests and called the shots as far as his massive purses were concerned. He was the man who became known as the champion who made up his own rules as he went along. It was often said that Sugar Ray was very much his own man.

A gold medal winner at the Montreal Olympics of 1976, Leonard returned to the Canadian city in June 1980 only to lose his prized world welterweight title to the rugged Panamanian Roberto Duran in one of boxing's biggest shocks. Before a crowd of over 40,000, who paid from $500 for ringside seats down to $20 to sit under the rafters in the Olympic Stadium, Duran outpunched and outlasted Leonard over 15 thrilling rounds for the World Boxing Council belt.

For his own reasons, Sugar unwisely elected to fight rather than box Duran, who had been beaten only once in 72 fights over 13 years; Leonard could never hope to match the tough challenger in street fighting. Duran took an early lead, and although Leonard fought back well and won the last two rounds, the verdict to Duran was not unexpected to those present. Despite the fact that it was a unanimous decision, it had been a close contest all the way.

A second match was inevitable. Return-fight clauses were officially illegal by that time and no agreement had been reached or signed between the two men before the fight, but the public demanded a rematch. So did Leonard and Duran, to really decide who was the better. They met again five months later, this time at the New Orleans Superdome, the venue which came back into the world's news in tragic circumstances in 2005 as a result of the floods brought about by Hurricane Katrina.

When they climbed into the ring on 15 November 1980 with Duran's title on the line, Leonard was again the favourite. Duran, however, felt that what he did once he could do again, and he was determined to prove it. In the Panamanian's eyes, Leonard was no superman and would be vulnerable to Duran's style of non-stop aggression.

Boxing analysts, however, warned in print that Sugar Ray could never be underestimated. A crowd of 35,000 in the Superdome watched as the two boxers climbed into the ring; the atmosphere was electric. A classic was promised. Here were two of the sport's greats in action. Nobody was to know that the sensational ending would bring further shame on boxing with allegations that the fight was crooked.

Sugar Ray's schoolboy idol was Muhammad Ali, and he patterned his slick style on the man who called himself The Greatest. The fifth of seven children born to a couple in the racially segregated city of Wilmington, North Carolina, on 17 May 1956, Leonard was christened Ray Charles because of his parents' admiration for the blind singer and musician. The family later moved to Palmer Park, Maryland, when Ray was ten, but it was the boxing beat rather than the music beat that appealed to young Ray, and he followed one of his brothers into the sport at the age of fourteen. He discovered that he had a natural talent and would soon develop into one of America's outstanding amateurs.

Leonard's winning of the Olympic gold medal as a light-welterweight in Montreal in 1976 was the pinnacle of a brilliant amateur career in which he lost only five times in one hundred and fifty-five contests. Every top manager in the US wanted him to sign professional forms, but he opted to set up a syndicate called Sugar Ray Leonard Incorporated to guide him through the murky waters of professional boxing. He hired lawyer Mike Trainer to handle his business deals and tax affairs and engaged Angelo Dundee to be his trainer and to oversee the managerial duties. Dundee was one of the world's leading coaches and had worked with a string of world champions, most notably Muhammad Ali before and after he won the heavyweight title. Ray's early amateur trainer Dave Jacobs and adviser Janks Morton were also on the payroll. The rollercoaster was ready to roll.

Leonard turned professional in spectacular fashion on 5 February 1977. Playing on the publicity and goodwill generated by his Olympic success, he collected a $40,000 pay cheque – a record at that time for a professional debut – when he outpointed Luis 'The Bull' Vega, who took home just $650, over six rounds at the Baltimore Civic Centre before a crowd of 10,170 – another record.

He soon became known as 'America's Sweetheart'; he was a hugely popular boxer–fighter and was gaining a large following. His flashing fast hands and fluid movement meant that he won as he pleased. His wide smile, however, belied the hard-edged competitiveness and arrogance that would not surface until he started fighting for world championships.

219

Leonard got the 'Sugar' tag from the original owner, the great Sugar Ray Robinson, when he went to the former world welterweight and five-times middleweight champion and politely asked if he could use it. 'Sure, go right ahead,' said a smiling Robinson. 'But make sure you look after it.'

After twenty-four consecutive victories, Leonard won the first of his five world titles in November 1979 by stopping Wilfred Benitez with only six seconds of the fifteenth and final round remaining. The fight, for the World Boxing Council welterweight championship, earned Leonard $1.2 million, with Benitez getting $1 million. Four months later, Sugar Ray successfully defended his belt against Dave 'Boy' Green with a one-punch knockout in the fourth round, before agreeing to put the title on the line against Roberto Duran in June 1980.

Leonard was handed a cheque for $9 million, but it did not compensate for the loss of his title to the gritty Panamanian, who had handed Sugar Ray his first defeat in 28 professional fights. The points loss would have to be reversed, vowed Leonard. Duran had other ideas.

There have been few men tougher than Duran in ring history. Boxing writer and historian Harry Mullan once described him 'as close to being a pure fighting animal as a man can get'. Duran was, to quote Mullan, 'a rugged brawler who could box with the best when he had to but loved nothing more than getting down in the trenches and breaking his opponent's spirit'.

Certainly Duran's ruthless style of fighting – you could hardly call it boxing – was in complete contrast to the Sweet Science. He would enter the ring unshaven and went about battering his opponents with a style resembling a street fighter. He personified the hungry boxer more than anybody else had since Jack Dempsey, the 'Manassa Mauler', half a century earlier. A poor youngster of mixed Native American and Spanish heritage, Roberto clawed his way up from grinding poverty to financial security.

Duran was born in the slums of Guarare, Panama, on 16 June 1951 and grew up in the equally deprived El Chorillo. His father walked out when Roberto was a young boy, leaving his mother to raise nine children alone. By the time he was 13 years old, his limited schooling had ended, and he was hustling money in any way possible to help his family. On one occasion, while he was stealing fruit from an orchard, he was caught by the owner Carlos Eleta, who would, ironically, become his manager. At the age of 14, Duran drifted into amateur boxing, but after winning 13 of his 14 contests, he decided that if he was going to fight, he would get paid for it.

Duran's sheer ferocity in the professional ring was enough to intimidate his early opponents, and he had 21 wins, 16 inside the distance, before meeting up again with Eleta. The wealthy landowner bought his contract for a mere $300 and hired Ray Arcel and Freddie Brown, two of boxing's most famous trainers, to hone and polish the Panamanian's raw talent.

Roberto won what would be the first of four world titles in a spectacular career when he challenged Scotland's Ken Buchanan for the lightweight championship at Madison Square Garden in June 1972. As the bell rang to end the 13th round of a vicious battle, Buchanan sank to the canvas, clutching his groin and claiming a foul blow. He was unable to continue, and the fight and title were awarded to Duran, despite protests from the Scot's corner that the challenger should have been disqualified. Duran had won the belt in his typical manner with a savage and merciless attack, taking no account of the rules or even basic sportsmanship.

The fight was recognised by the World Boxing Association as being for the title and Duran, known as 'Hands of Stone', went on to clean up the lightweight division with eleven successful defences over the next seven years, equalling a record for the 9 st. 9 lb class, before unifying the title by knocking out Esteban De Jesus in the twelfth round of their Las Vegas bout in January 1978. Duran relinquished the title just over a year later because of increasing weight and campaigned as a welterweight. He had five impressive wins, including a points defeat of the former world welterweight champion Carlos Palomino, before successfully challenging Sugar Ray Leonard. The big question now was: could he do it again?

Both men looked impressive in training. Leonard worked out at his own camp in New Carrolton, Maryland, and Duran trained at a camp in Miami, Florida. Promoter Don King had suggested to Duran that he train at Grossingers, a luxurious resort in the Catskill Mountains in upstate New York, but he declined, saying that the weather would be too cold up there and that he preferred Miami.

Leonard planned to box Duran at long range the second time around rather than engage in close-quarter work and admitted that taking on the Panamanian at his own game was wrong. 'That is not to say I won't slug it out with him,' he told reporters, 'but only in the later stages when he's probably tired. I have just found out I have a left jab. I guess I'll just pace myself more carefully this time.'

His trainer Angelo Dundee said, 'Sure, we're going to fight him but this time when Ray takes the steam out of his legs. There will be no mistakes this time. Ray will also repay in kind any rough tactics employed by Duran. The only foul Duran did not commit was to hit Ray when he was down, because Ray wasn't down.'

After a heavy session on the bag in Miami, Duran, who spoke no English, told reporters through an interpreter, 'I don't think he can give any more than he did in the first fight. If he does anything more, you can bet I'll be ready for him. There'll be no new champion in this fight. I'm fully confident of repeating my win, and my handlers feel the same way.'

Leonard and his entourage arrived in New Orleans a week before the fight to do light workouts and to visit the Superdome. New Orleans was a historic fight city. It was there that the famous Carnival of Champions was staged in 1892 with three world title fights on successive nights, culminating in James J. Corbett's successful challenge against John L. Sullivan in the first heavyweight championship fight with regulation gloves.

Dundee made a point of visiting the offices of the Louisiana State Athletic Commission, where he expressed concern about two things. The first was the length of Duran's beard, which Dundee claimed Duran had used as a weapon in the first fight. 'I want it trimmed,' said the trainer, but the commission did not think that this was a reasonable request and turned it down. The second point Dundee wanted clarified was the commission's definition of fouls such as butting, grabbing and holding, explaining that he wanted their definitions to accord with his. He reminded officials that Duran had repeatedly fouled in the first match and had used his head so much that he should have been required to put a glove on it. Dundee was assured that the appointed referee would be very vigilant with regards to fouls.

Duran later arrived in New Orleans, but after working out at the Superdome, he decided two days before the fight that the arena was too cold to train in and moved his final sparring sessions to an old wooden schoolhouse in a poor neighbourhood of the city. It was used by the local jail as a prisoners' workhouse, and uniformed New Orleans policemen unlocked the door to let locals in to watch the world champion.

The gym was tiny, and onlookers had to line the walls to see the action. In a way, Duran was returning to his poverty-stricken beginnings back in Panama. Leonard's people regarded it all as a publicity stunt. 'The whole Duran mystique is a bunch of crap,' remarked Leonard's lawyer Mike Trainer. Meanwhile, Sugar Ray shadowboxed silently and purposefully in a makeshift gym set up in a spare back room of the Superdome.

There were reports that Duran was having difficulty in making the stipulated weight of 10 st. 7 lb, and it was no secret that he was a heavy eater. He had gone up to 11 st. 6 lb three weeks before the fight, but he had dieted so well that when he stepped onto the scales on the morning of the contest, he registered 10 st. 4 lb. Leonard had no problems with his weight and balanced the scales at 10 st. 4 lb as well.

In the first fight, Leonard had been favourite at 9–5. For the return contest, the odds were also in his favour but a lot closer at 3–2. He came down the aisle preceded by cheerleaders wearing pom-poms and chanting 'Sugar Ray, Sugar Ray', as his enthusiastic supporters joined in the chant. He smiled and waved to the crowd.

As if to underline his determination to be tough this time, he had departed from his usual custom of wearing white and had dressed entirely in black: trunks, socks and boxing boots. Before the fight, Leonard had asked Mike Trainer how he looked and had been pleased when the lawyer had responded, 'Like the Grim Reaper.'

Duran then made his appearance to the blare of salsa music and the waving of hundreds of small Panamanian flags. The cheering was not as loud as it had been for the challenger. Sugar Ray's namesake Ray Charles sang a rousing rendition of 'America the Beautiful', and Leonard smiled as he listened to it, looking relaxed and confident. Duran scowled, but he too looked confident.

Both had reason to be happy, at least in a financial sense. Duran would be getting an $8 million purse and Leonard $6 million, as compared with the first fight when Sugar picked up $9 million and Roberto $1.5 million. Leonard's smaller purse this time was not an inconsiderable sum for a man who was wealthy beyond his wildest boyhood dreams. Duran was not exactly a poor man either, his wealth a far cry from his humble beginnings in the abject slums of Panama.

Duran, at twenty-nine, was five years older than the challenger. He had an impressive record of only one loss in seventy-three professional bouts, including fifty-five inside the scheduled distance. His championship fight record was 13–0, and he was on a 41-fight winning streak. Leonard had a shorter career, but his record was still impressive, with twenty-seven wins and one defeat, eighteen of his victories by the short route. His championship fight record was 2–1.

After referee Octavio Meyran gave the two men their final instructions, they returned to their corners to await the bell. The crowd's expectations were high. This was a natural rivalry, promoter Don King billing it as 'Spectacular Two – the Rematch'.

Leonard was depicted as the good guy: the clean-cut kid who brought an Olympic gold medal back to the US. Duran was the mean and moody ex-slum kid and owner of a mystique that included stories of him knocking over a horse, an opponent's wife and a sparring partner's father. One of his nicknames was 'El Diablo', meaning 'The Devil'.

The fight started cautiously, and for the first minute, they just sparred around, looking for an opening. Leonard used the ring, circling Duran and moving in and out. He was employing a different method this time. Unlike in Montreal, he was boxing the rugged Panamanian in an attempt to prevent Duran from using his heavy punches and greater strength in close. Duran was moving forward,

224

but he found Leonard an elusive target. After two minutes of the round, referee Meyran urged them to put a little more effort into their work. Duran responded with a solid right to the body which made the challenger back away, but, a few seconds later, Leonard moved in smartly with a neat left–right, which brought a smile to Duran's face, as if to say, 'Is that the best you can do, Ray?'

In the second round, Duran bulled Leonard into the ropes, but Meyran quickly separated them. Leonard reverted to moving around the ring, jabbing the dour Duran at long range. Whenever they got close, Sugar Ray effectively tied up the champion. Roberto's plan of action was to keep on the inside as much as possible and wear down Leonard with body punches and shots to the head. Leonard, however, was not going to get involved in any close-quarter exchanges. Angelo Dundee had told him in the interval between the first and second rounds, 'Move, move, let him come after you. Frustrate him. Tire him out.' Towards the end of the round, Duran again bulled his man to the ropes and landed a good left hook to the head. Leonard was now circling the ring again and caught the champion with two fast lefts: a jab to the face and a hook that landed solidly on Duran's bearded chin.

The Panamanian came out fast in the third round, rushed Leonard to the ropes with a two-handed attack and looked like a man about to finish the job. The satisfied, menacing smile seemed to emphasise that he was doing what he loved best – fighting. He had some success with a solid right smash to the body near Leonard's corner. Sugar Ray wrapped his left arm around Duran's neck to prevent him from doing much damage but got a stern warning from Meyran.

Near the end of the round, the crowd enjoyed a real slugfest as both boxers punched it out for nearly 30 seconds to great cheers. Leonard knew he could not engage in too much close-quarter work, but he also wanted to show that he could fight when it was called for. Duran scored mostly to the body and Leonard mainly to the head. They went at it again along the ropes before the bell rang.

In the fourth, Leonard was again forced onto the ropes but moved off them to catch Duran with a left hook on the belt-line. He followed through with a burst of fast punches – jabs, hooks and uppercuts – and the champion backed away. Leonard went after him. Duran got through with a long straight right to the head, but many of his blows were beginning to fall short of the target.

Leonard was mixing his punches well at that stage, although it was difficult to know if his well-placed blows were really hurting or having any effect on the rugged champion. Duran was clearly the harder hitter, and he landed a good left hook to the body after Leonard was short with his own long left hook. Roberto charged like a bull against a matador but missed and ended up halfway through the ropes near Sugar Ray's corner at the bell.

In the fifth, Leonard's work rate dropped, but he was able to get up on his toes and jab the oncoming Duran with precise lefts while moving smartly around the ring. The Panamanian caught Leonard with a solid right, but the challenger took it well. He continued to circle the ring, staying far away from Duran's counter-punches but still close enough to land telling lefts to the head and body.

Duran was now pushing Leonard with both hands when the action got to close quarters. On one occasion, he drove the challenger into a neutral corner, and Leonard slipped trying to extract himself. Both men touched gloves, and it was good to see that sportsmanship still prevailed between the two deadly rivals intent on destroying each other.

By the sixth, it still looked like anybody's fight, with neither man having a clear advantage. All the boxing was coming from Leonard, all the fighting from Duran. Sugar Ray was still circling, Roberto still stalking. Leonard landed two good left hooks, but Duran merely knocked them aside as though they were rolled-up newspapers. Duran was using his weight to wear down Leonard in the clinches. The challenger, however, was still boxing well behind his left jabs and hooks to the body with both hands. Near the end of the round, Duran landed some heavy hooks to the body, followed by a stiff right lead to the head. Leonard was trapped momentarily on the ropes but was soon back in the centre of the ring, moving and circling.

In a dramatic seventh round, Leonard simply stood off and taunted his man. Before the fight, Duran had said that Sugar Ray was a clown, and that he did not like clowns in the boxing ring, only the

226

circus ring. He also gave the opinion that Leonard was trying too hard to be another Muhammad Ali and that 'all imitators are losers'. Leonard dropped his hands by his sides, and it was clear that he was intent on inviting Duran into a mistake: it was a trap. He swayed from side to side, shrugged his shoulders and wobbled his legs, finally sticking out his chin and daring Duran to throw a punch. This was the showboating Leonard, and he had it down to a fine art. Duran merely responded with a smile, but it was clear that he was bemused. Leonard then produced his most outrageous act of disrespect by winding up his right hand, swinging it in windmill fashion and then back-pedalling swiftly around the ring before stopping to toss in a few left jabs. The sportsmanship he had displayed earlier was disappearing like a puff of smoke. Duran closed in, and they finished the round by swapping punches freely. The Panamanian returned to his corner, shaking his head in disbelief at the sudden turn of events.

The real drama came in the eighth. Leonard started the round in his usual fashion, moving around the ring and jabbing on the retreat. Duran landed a solid right to the body but took a fast left jab to the head in return. Sugar Ray's jabs were working very well at that stage. Duran was still powerhousing his way forward but was caught by a solid right hook. Both men exchanged furious blows in the centre of the ring, and as Duran started to bob and weave, he suddenly straightened up. Still scowling, he shook his right hand in a dismissive manner and said, 'No más' – or 'No more.' He half turned away and Leonard, with an open target in front of him, drove in a right to the body and a left hook to the side of the head.

The referee jumped between them but then hesitated, as if he could not believe that Duran wanted to quit, and waved the two men to resume activities. Leonard obliged, delivering a hard left and right to Duran's body, but Roberto turned his back again, shaking his right glove and repeating, 'No más, no más.' This time Meyran did not hesitate and stopped the fight. The time was two minutes and forty-five seconds of the eighth round.

Leonard raced across the ring and leapt onto the ropes in a neutral corner, shouting, 'I'm the champion of the world, I'm the champion of the world,' as Duran trudged back to his own corner. All three

227

judges had Leonard ahead at the controversial finish, marking the completed rounds 68–66, 68–66 and 68–67. The Associated Press news agency gave it to Leonard by four rounds to three at the end of the seventh, and United Press International marked it five to Leonard, one to Duran and one even.

At first, a stunned silence fell over the crowd bemused by the bizarre ending. There was an uneasy murmur as people turned to each other and asked, 'What happened?' Some cheered Leonard, but the boos for Duran drowned those mild acclamations as 'Fix, fix' rent the air. Was this durable fighter, known as Hands of Stone, hurt badly enough to quit? It did not look like it. Nobody could have imagined this bearded, brawling ring warrior, who learned his trade in street fighting in the ghettos of Guarare and El Chorillo, just walking out. One of the great champions, Duran was a fighter who, in the words of author and historian Gerald Suster in his book *Lightning Strikes*, 'could take as much physical pain as any fighter who ever lived. One could take a machete to cut off his left arm, and he would still be fighting with his right.' So, was the fight fixed?

Many people in the angry crowd grouped outside the Panamanian's dressing-room were yelling that Duran had quit and had let his faithful fans down. Roberto, however, was safely inside. The door was locked and only some of the press were admitted. The ex-champion was composed and subdued as he answered questions through an interpreter: 'At the end of the fifth round, I started getting cramps in my stomach. I felt my body and my arms getting weaker – but this was my last fight. I don't want to fight anymore. I have been fighting for a long time. I've gotten tired of the sport.'

Was he ashamed that he had seemingly tarnished, if not entirely ruined, one of boxing's deservedly great reputations by going out in this fashion after 74 professional fights? 'No,' he said emphatically. 'Why should I be ashamed? I still consider myself a better man than Leonard, but he just beat me on this night. However, I'm not fighting anymore.'

When Ray Arcel, Duran's 83-year-old trainer and a legendary figure in boxing, was asked if his man had been complaining of cramps, he shook his head. 'No,' he said. 'He's a young, strong fellow, always full of joy, always happy. I almost fainted when he quit. I thought he had broken his arm. I think it was a question of Duran not being able to take command of the situation. He couldn't get off. The other fellow played with him, made him look silly. It's not like Duran to be handled that way. Sure, I was surprised he quit. This is the last guy in the world I would have ever thought this would happen to.'

In Leonard's dressing-room, the new king of the world welterweights held court. 'I've no idea why he quit,' he said. 'Something must have happened to him. But I'm the champion. That's the important thing. My friends back home in Maryland bet against me, but I surprised everybody. I boxed scientifically. I beat one of the greatest fighters of all time: beat him mentally and physically. I don't wreck men's bodies. I wreck their minds. Look, I beat Roberto Duran. Can people not accept that?' When a boxing writer suggested that Duran had quit for no apparent reason and that he was not visibly hurt or cut, Sugar Ray snapped, 'Hey, man, don't knock him. He quit of his own free will. He's still a champion in my eyes. He's still the great Roberto Duran, remember?'

The next day, the Louisiana State Athletic Commission met and decided unanimously to withhold Duran's $8 million purse pending an investigation. 'I thought it was a very unusual performance for a fighter to give his title away,' said chairman Emile Bruno, in one of boxing's classic understatements. They also ordered him to be medically examined by the commission's physician, Dr A.J. Italiano.

Dr Italiano concluded that Duran had suffered an upset stomach, apparently because he had two or three steaks and a lot of orange juice before the fight. Questioned by reporters, Dr Italiano said he could not say if the stomach upset was reason enough to just hand in his world championship belt.

Following the investigation, Commissioner Otis Guichet fined Duran a mere $7,500, a sum considered to be paltry by boxing people. 'The fine was for not performing up to par,' explained Guichet. 'He was saying he had cramps, but if he had cramps, none of his corner asked for a doctor. The fans rightly felt that they had been jilted. We feel the fine is an adequate penalty for a non-performance.' Once Duran paid the fine, Guichet announced that his purse was being released.

So, what really happened in that ring? Did the Panamanian throw the fight as part of a big betting coup? Boxing insiders found it exceedingly hard to believe that one of the gutsiest champions of all time could just quit like he had. An upset stomach? Weren't there conflicting views on this by the commissioner and the doctor? In any event, was an upset stomach enough reason to quit? What about the men who carried on with broken jaws, smashed hands, bleeding faces, severely lacerated eyes? Where was all the heart that the great Duran had been associated with? Did he simply quit because of his frustration in failing to contain the shifty Leonard? Did he decide to just take the money and run?

Duran did not help the delicate situation by announcing two days after the fight that he was changing his mind about his earlier retirement statement – 'I don't want to fight anymore' – saying that he now wanted a third match, much to the embarrassment of the humiliated Louisiana Commission and the World Boxing Council. Not surprisingly, they rejected his plea.

There was universal condemnation of Duran's walk-out. Author and novelist Budd Schulberg, writing in the *New York Post* the next day, said, 'With the exception of Sonny Liston quitting against Muhammad Ali in 1964, I cannot recall a single fight in which a champion has done an *el foldo* like Duran's dump to Leonard.' Calling the fight a scandal, he added, 'Champions have obligations to paying customers and loyal betters, and cramp or no cramp, ex-macho Roberto should give them back their pesos. In the mean time, if there is a shred of honour left in the boxing commissions, they should hold up his purse and give to the poor the $8 million this man flunked away.'

Boxing writer Ted Green of the *Los Angeles Times* revealed that the commission could not realistically have withheld Duran's purse because a letter of credit for the $8 million was already safely in his bank account in Panama before the bout, a claim supported by promoter Don King. How then could the commission have held onto his purse if he had already received it?

Duran's long-time friend and former translator Luis Henriquez added to the controversy and mystery by admitting later that Roberto had asked him to invent an excuse immediately after the fight. Henriquez then came up with the story of the stomach cramps. 'He didn't have cramps at all,' he said. 'He just quit and that was it.'

Ray Arcel never believed the story about the alleged cramps either. 'Leonard's taunting angered him,' Arcel would recall. 'Duran wasn't used to being treated that way. Who knew what was going on in his head? He needed a mental examination, not a physical one.'

Some big Las Vegas gamblers claimed the fight was most definitely crooked and that Duran and his handlers had cleaned up afterwards, an allegation strenuously denied by the boxer and his camp. This denial was supported by local matchmaker Mel 'Red' Greb of Caesars Palace, who felt that Duran was simply frustrated and quit. Many top boxing writers disagreed, however, and still insist that the fight was not on the level.

For Duran, the consequences were disastrous. Not only had he left his title in New Orleans, he lost respect universally. In Panama, he had been a national hero, and after his first win over Leonard, the president had telephoned him to offer congratulations. Now a mob came out of the slums and stoned the house Duran had bought for his mother. Those who had cheered him were now jeering him. How the once mighty had fallen.

Duran would recover from the shame in New Orleans, however. He was back in the ring within a year as a light-middleweight and proved he was anything but finished. In 1983, on his thirty-second birthday, he won the WBA world title by knocking out Davey Moore in eight rounds. In 1989, he captured his fourth world championship by outpointing Iran Barkley for the WBC middleweight belt.

Leonard was also starting to pick up world titles the way philatelists collect stamps. After unifying the welter championship by stopping Thomas Hit Man Hearns in 14 rounds in 1981, he won titles at light-middle, middle, super-middle and light-heavyweight. He even found time to take on Duran for a third time. In 1989, he outpointed the Panamanian in a fight for Sugar Ray's WBC super-middleweight title.

Neither boxer has since talked at any great length about what really happened in that highly controversial second fight in 1980. Today, they both feel that everything that had to be said was expressed at the time and that no more need be added. So, it seems as if the mystery surrounding the shame in New Orleans may never really be solved.

13

ROCKY'S FURY IN FRISCO

There may have been better all-rounders among the world heavyweight champions down the years, but for sheer power, explosive hitting and true grit, few if any could match Rocky Marciano. He was limited in skill and finesse, and he was short and light, but he had a devastating punch. No opponent could halt his non-stop advance.

Rocky was the only world heavyweight title-holder who remained undefeated throughout his entire career, winning all 49 of his professional fights, although wars might be a more accurate description. Even when he was battered and badly cut, he was able to summon up the will and the sheer power to overcome his rival – and only six of his fights went the scheduled distance.

Jersey Joe Walcott, one of Rocky's championship opponents and someone who shared rings with most of the leading heavyweights of his day, said, 'Rocky was extraordinary because he didn't understand pain.' Peter Wilson of Britain's *Daily Mirror* described him as 'the twentieth-century caveman of the ring'. He certainly was a primitive champion – his one aim being to get in there and batter down the opposition in the shortest possible time.

Marciano's wade-in, swarming style of roughhouse fighting was modified by little Charlie Goldman, his faithful Polish-born trainer who grew up in New York's Brooklyn. Goldman could not stop Rocky getting hit or cut, but he taught him how to get in close and hurt his man. Marciano had a true warrior's heart and a pitiless instinct for not only surviving but winning at all costs.

The remarkable thing about the 'Brockton Blockbuster', as he was known, was that he was the gentlest of individuals outside the roped square – kind, considerate and soft-spoken. During an interview with the author in London in 1966, the retired former champion turned out to be extremely modest about his achievements. He was more concerned about his family back home in the US, hoping that they were not lonely without him.

Once the bell sounded, however, 'Nice Guy' Rocky turned into 'Killer' Rocky, and all hell broke loose. Most of his fights were brawls, and he could never in anyone's wildest imagination be called a clean fighter. He was at his roughest against Britain's Don Cockell in their 1955 title fight in San Francisco. In that infamous encounter on a night of shame, Marciano broke every rule in the book and many that had not even been written yet. Even the American boxing writers, used to seeing illegal tactics in their rings, were appalled.

Marciano hit low, punched on the break, butted, used his elbows and even struck the Brit when he was down. Why he was not disqualified is a mystery to this day. Just as peculiar was the fact that Rocky didn't remember resorting to foul tactics. It seemed his natural way of fighting, and afterwards he was all apologies for a fight that remains one of the dirtiest in heavyweight history since men first fought with padded gloves at the end of the nineteenth century.

The Marciano–Cockell fight is a shameful chapter in American boxing history and one that made a complete mockery of the concept of fair play for foreigners in US rings. In his book, *England's Boxing Heroes*, Frank McGhee wrote, 'Marciano thought the rulebook was for cissies. If some of the criminal acts committed against the brave Englishman that night had taken place in the street, Rocky would have been arrested.'

Gilbert Odd, the historian and author, put it like this:

Marciano's brand of belligerent destructiveness had to be seen to be believed. There was no art or finesse about his work. He just bulldozed in and took his opponents apart with his hooks, swings and uppercuts, not taking any aim or placing his shots, merely saturating the other man with leather until he had been battered into submission.

In his eagerness to plaster an opponent with as many punches as could be got into every round, Marciano had no time for discretion. He hit them anywhere. It was a good man who could survive the scheduled distance with such a human tank. Some did, and six of Rocky's pro contests went all the way. The rest either called for the timekeeper's services or the referee's charity.

The first of five children in a working-class family, Marciano was born Rocco Francis Marchegiano in the Massachusetts town of Brockton, about 20 miles from Boston, on 1 September 1923. His father Perino was a poor Italian immigrant who found work as a cobbler in one of the shoe factories in town, but life was tough in the 1920s and pay was low, with most families struggling to survive.

Rocco grew up to be a strong boy who was mad on sport, especially baseball and football, popular activities in Brockton. He left school at the age of 16 and worked at various jobs. He was employed on a coal truck and in a sweet shop, and did a short spell with his father before developing his muscles in a construction gang. The lad had no idea at that stage of becoming a boxer. He just wanted to keep fit.

In March 1943, he was called up for army service and posted to Wales for a while. It was in Cardiff that he discovered his knockout punch when he flattened a burly Australian in a bar. The big Aussie had called Marchegiano a cissy because he didn't drink or smoke. As the future world heavyweight champion would explain later, 'He insulted other American soldiers, too, so a row broke out. Suddenly there was only me and him left. I lashed into him with both fists, put him down, and I was told later he was out for over half an hour.'

On being demobbed in 1946, Rocco began digging trenches for

the local gas company. Meanwhile, his uncle Mike entered his nephew's name in an amateur tournament in Portland, Oregon, and the young boxer won his way through to the semi-finals. Despite an injured hand, he won the semi but lost the final. He also met up with Allie Columbo, a baseball fan like Rocco, who persuaded him to have one professional fight – just one – and pick up some easy money.

To protect his amateur status, Marchegiano was entered as 'Rocky Mac'. He knocked out one Lee Epperson in the third round with a hard right to the body and picked up $50. However, Rocco still wanted to become a baseball player but failed a trial for the Chicago Cubs because of trouble with his right arm and a slowness in running. He tried a few other clubs only to be turned down, so it was back to boxing – but this time to the amateurs.

Rocco entered the New York Golden Gloves but was eliminated. He then competed in the trials for the 1948 Olympics in London but injured his left thumb and had to withdraw from the tournament. The injury also prevented him working for the gas company, so there was nothing else for him to do but wait until his hand healed and return to boxing – this time as a full-time professional.

Marchegiano joined up with his friend Allie Columbo, who became his trainer/manager. They both knew, however, that they would need an influential manager and a prominent trainer, and headed for New York where they met up with Al Weill, a top matchmaker at Madison Square Garden. Weill invited them along to the CYO Gym on 17th Street and brought along Charlie Goldman, an ex-bantamweight boxer who had fought over 300 times and was one of the best coaches in the business. When Marchegiano climbed into the ring for a sparring session, Goldman couldn't believe what he saw. The guy had two left feet, and his defence was as open as a swinging gate in a high wind. 'What are y' trying to do, kid? Get yourself killed?' he barked.

In an interview a few years before his death in 1968 aged 80, Goldman said, 'I never believed in changing a guy's natural style, so I just polished his up a bit. I saw he had real natural ability right from the start. He just needed to curb his anxiety. But he had raw power, and he could punch.' Goldman taught his boxer to fight at close range and in a crouch, which would not only make him difficult to hit but would also make up for his lack of weight, height and reach. At 5 ft 11 in., he was one of the shortest world heavyweight champions of all time.

Under Weill's guidance and with Goldman always in his corner and training him at the gym, the man whose name had now been changed to Rocky Marciano made fast progress. He beat all before him, including a demolition in eight rounds of the once-great Joe Louis, an 8–5 favourite and on a successful comeback, in eight rounds in October 1951, and the following year, he finished contenders Lee Savold in six and Harry Matthews in two.

On 23 September 1952, he got his world heavyweight title chance against veteran champion Jersey Joe Walcott in Philadelphia. It was a fight that started sensationally when, in the first round, Walcott manoeuvred the challenger into the path of a smashing left hook the way a magnet draws steel filings and knocked Rocky down. It was the first time he had been on the boards in 42 winning fights. He got to his feet at the count of three, and Walcott was unable to get another clean shot at him.

For 12 rounds it was all Walcott as he outboxed and outpunched the crude Marciano, until Rocky caught the champion with a tremendous hard right in the 13th that twisted Walcott's face into a grotesque rubber mask. Jersey Joe slumped to the canvas, his left arm hooked over the rope, for all the world like an imitation of a religious man in prayer, and he was counted out by referee Charlie Daggert.

Marciano kept to his promise of being a fighting champion. He won a return match by knocking out Walcott in the first round, stopped Roland La Starza in eleven and had two wins over former champion Ezzard Charles, beating him to the decision over fifteen rounds and knocking him cold in a return in eight.

A nose injury sustained in the Charles fight kept Rocky out of the ring for eight months, but it had healed sufficiently by the early spring of 1955 when manager Weill announced that the champion would defend his title for the fifth time against Don Cockell, the holder of the British, and what was then the Empire, championship.

The fight would be held at the Kezar Stadium on the fringes of San Francisco on 16 May 1955.

Few outside the Cockell camp, however, gave the Brit the remotest chance of taking the title from the rough and tough American who looked unbeatable. US boxing writers were scathing in their forecasts in the early run-up to the fight. Even before the boxers went into serious training, the fitness-fanatic Marciano had kept in good shape all year round, and the sharp knives were out for the Brit.

Prescott Sullivan of the *San Francisco Examiner* wrote:

> One redeeming feature about the fight, which is scheduled to louse up the Kezar Stadium, is that attendance is not compulsory. It looks like the mismatch to end all mismatches. The villagers know Cockell isn't a logical challenger. Soft and fat, he has been knocked out by middleweights and beaten by bums.

Curley Grieve, also on the *Examiner*, wrote:

> Even the most casual fight fan knows the bout is a mismatch designed as a test run for Marciano's 'beezer' after being cut down the middle from a punch thrown by Ezzard Charles. There is no public demand for the fight here. Even the fight mob is fearful of the stench. It could ruin a top fight centre.

Pat Robinson of *International News Service* reported that a manager who handled two world champions had said, 'The bum won't last three rounds with Rocky.' Robinson then quoted an old-timer who told him, 'This is one of the biggest frauds ever perpetrated on a sucker public. If it goes six rounds, it will only be because they are working for the pictures.'

All this before Cockell had even left Sussex. When the caustic comments were relayed to him, he retorted angrily, 'So I'm a bum, am I? But I seem to remember that Roland La Starza was once rated as the boy to beat Rocky, and I beat him a year ago. All this only makes me more determined to show these ignorant guys how wrong they are.

'I'd rather have them against me than for me. That way I know how I stand. After our fight, Rocky's suspect nose will know that it has had more than a workout. These Yanks are finding nothing new in calling me a fat boy, but they ought to remember, I'm unbeaten as a heavyweight, and I intend to stay that way. I'm going out there to win, and you reporters can send that to these American wise guys, without my love.'

Fighting talk, but he was going to need more than words against Marciano. Born on 22 September 1928 in London's Battersea district, Cockell was originally a blacksmith, and the strength he developed working with iron on the anvil encouraged him to be a boxer. He had 26 amateur bouts and got the urge to turn professional after defeating a 14½ st. policeman. He went to Jack Solomons' gym in the city's West End and asked the promoter for advice. Solomons turned him over to a manager named John Simpson, and Cockell made a successful debut as a middleweight in June 1946, progressing well enough to win the vacant British light-heavyweight title four years later.

The European championship followed, and a bright future was predicted for him. He seemed to have natural talent, a hard left jab and a solid if not explosive right. Suddenly and inexplicably, however, something went horribly wrong with his metabolism. Everything he ate or drank turned to fat on his 5 ft 10 in. frame. Trying to boil that weight off by starving and sweating, he was leaving himself vulnerable, and when he defended his British and Empire titles in June 1952 against Randolph Turpin, who was essentially a middleweight, he was hammered to a painful defeat in eleven rounds after being knocked down three times.

Cockell went into hospital for tests, resulting in specialists telling him that he would have to settle for carrying the burden of excess weight for the rest of his life. At the age of 24, he seemed to be washed up, but the fight game is full of twists and turns, often for the better. Despite his short stature, he decided to give the heavyweight division a go, and, remarkably, he won ten straight fights, including impressive wins over the highly rated American contenders Roland La Starza and Harry 'Kid' Matthews. He also won the British and Empire titles from the skilful Johnny Williams.

Although Cockell knew that Marciano would be in a totally different league, the Brit's confidence was not lacking. He recalled going into a local cinema to watch the film of Rocky's second fight with Ezzard Charles, which Marciano won in eight rounds. 'They ought to give that an X-certificate,' he remarked to a boxing writer in an interview a week later. 'Marciano butted, hit Charles after the bell and the last punch that put him down landed smack on the back of his neck. But I'll jab him hard and often and beat him.'

Cockell was the first Brit to challenge for the world heavyweight title since the brave Welshman Tommy Farr went the full 15 rounds with Joe Louis in 1937. The challenger's training quarters were set up at the plush and expensive Bermuda Palms Hotel in San Raphael, a little town just outside San Francisco. If the hotel residents were not shaking the hand of the challenger who had the guts to take on the mighty Marciano or drinking his health in the bars and restaurants, they were lazing around outside and watching shapely blondes and brunettes diving into the blue-tiled pool.

Marciano prepared in a more spartan atmosphere, pursuing his own ruthless and remorseless way in the isolation of his camp set up in a disused fairground on the outskirts of Calistoga, a town in California's vineyard territory with strong literary connections. About 100 miles from San Francisco, it was where Robert Louis Stevenson of *Treasure Island* fame had convalesced during a respite from his life-long battle with tuberculosis and where novelist Jack London wrote *The Valley of the Moon*.

A few weeks before the fight, there was a story circulating that a Mafia underling called Ed Napoli, who was friendly with the Marciano family, had claimed that a top mobster had approached Rocky in his camp. 'You lose this fight to the 10–1 underdog, and we'll take care of you,' the mobster had purportedly said in the presence of Napoli. 'There's a lot of money to be made. You're the champ, Rocky. You place a high bet, and you'll win the title back in a lucrative rematch.'

According to Napoli, Marciano got very angry and said, 'You get away from me. How could you even suggest such a thing? You disgust me of the Italian race. I'm ashamed you're an Italian.' The story did not reach Marciano's daughter Mary Anne until several years after her father retired, and while she never mentioned it to anybody, nor ever brought it up with him, she, nevertheless, believed it to be true.

The US magazine *Sports Illustrated* took up the story in later years but did not comment on it, merely presenting the details as told by Napoli. Everett M. Skehan, Marciano's biographer, said that the whole affair seemed unlikely and could not be substantiated, although he conceded that other champions told of mobsters trying to influence them to throw fights and that the gangsters often succeeded.

Then, ten days before the Marciano–Cockell fight, a dope scare hit American boxing when Harold Johnson, the leading contender for Archie Moore's world light-heavyweight title, slumped to the canvas in the second round of his fight with Julio Mederos in Philadelphia – without being hit. The Cuban was declared the winner on a knockout. In an investigation after the fight, Johnson, a 6–1 favourite, claimed an autograph hunter had given him an orange which he had eaten and said it must have been doped. Medical tests showed traces of barbiturate in his system. Lie-detector tests were taken and police investigations would uncover that there had been a $100,000 nationwide betting coup brought off by a big gambling syndicate as a result of Mederos' surprise victory. It was also disclosed that Johnson had an undercover manager named Pete Moran.

Johnson was fined $4,113 and would not box again for 19 months. It was over two years before he fought in Philadelphia. As a result of the scandal, boxing in the state was outlawed for six months after the Pennsylvania State Athletic Commission reported to Governor Leader that, 'There was no doubt that Johnson had been drugged, that his handlers knew all about it and that the information was deliberately withheld from the commission.'

Meanwhile, the Johnson–Mederos fiasco resulted in the tightest security measures being put in place for the Marciano–Cockell fight. Rocky was personally unworried, but Cockell's camp was scared. Packets of tea sent by fans in Britain were destroyed, and only tea bought and prepared by his wife Irene was served. 'We can't take any chances here,' said the challenger's manager, John Simpson. 'We have a world title opportunity coming up.'

There were also rows about the interpretation of the rules and the size of the ring, with Cockell's camp wanting to ensure that their man got a fair deal. The arguments became so tense that the Brit's manager telephoned President Eisenhower 'to sort all this out' only for a White House spokesperson to tell him, 'The President, unfortunately, has other matters on his mind and, regrettably, cannot help.' Surprise, surprise!

Harold Mayes, boxing writer for Britain's Kemsley Newspapers which included the *Sunday Empire News*, went on record as saying that Simpson was complaining too late and that both he and Cockell should have had all these things sorted out before leaving Britain. In the end, the Americans had their way once again.

At the weigh-in – in those days held on the day of the fight, unlike at present when they are staged twenty-four hours earlier – Marciano scaled 13 st. 7 lb, the heaviest he had been since his amateur days, and Cockell was 14 st. 9 lb, his lightest for two years. Rocky, at the age of thirty, was four years older than Cockell and had the perfect record of forty-seven wins in as many fights, forty-one inside the scheduled distance. Cockell had sixty-one wins, ten losses and one draw, with thirty-seven victories by the short route.

Few challengers for sport's richest prize ever climbed into the ring labelled as much of a 'no-hoper' as did Cockell. So little did the American boxing writers, who had attacked him in print from the outset, think of his chances that odds quoted variously from 10–1 to 20–1 were being laid against him. It was 5–4 against Cockell lasting five rounds, 2–1 against him being there at the end of ten and 5–1 against him lasting the full fifteen rounds, even as the loser.

On the day of the fight, Bill Leiser, sports editor of the *San Francisco Chronicle*, wrote, 'If you see Cockell's hand raised, you will have watched the most phenomenal upset in all the history of pugilism. Cockell is a freak of the ring. He didn't become a heavyweight because, as many do, he was a good light-heavy and graduated. He was a bum at the lesser weight, famous for being knocked out, and caused laughter among his best friends when he announced he was a heavyweight and would quit if he didn't get a go at the world champion.'

Not only did the Americans dismiss Cockell's chances, the British writers felt likewise. Under a heading in the *Daily Mirror* which read 'Cockell is Fighting the Rock, the Ring, the Rules and the Racket', Peter Wilson wrote:

> I do not think that Cockell has the remotest chance of winning. There is no common denominator between the above-average boxing of Cockell and the all-in tactics of Marciano. It's like a bowman of Olde England against a Sherman tank.
>
> In sparring sessions, Marciano hit low, used the heel of his hand, his forearm and his elbow, and his head became a third glove. These things are fouls according to our rules, but there is not the slightest chance of Marciano being disqualified, whatever he does against Cockell. The men behind the scenes here are never going to allow the heavyweight title out of their possession. So, the group which controls the heavyweight champion controls world boxing.

Five former world champions were introduced from the ring – Jimmy McLarnin, Henry Armstrong, Max Baer, Young Corbett III and Willie Ritchie. Carl Bobo Olson, the reigning world middleweight champion, who was being spoken of as a possible future challenger for Marciano, was also introduced.

After referee Freddie Brown called the two men together for their pre-fight instructions, they went back to their corners to await the bell. It was the Bay Area's first universally recognised world heavyweight title fight since October 1909 when Jack Johnson knocked out middleweight Stanley Ketchel in 12 rounds in Colma. Marciano went straight into the attack and drove the bulky Brit back to the ropes where he bombarded him with blows. Cockell, on advice from his corner, moved well and scored with left jabs, but Rocky was like a bulldozer as he pounded his way forward. He missed with quite a few shots, but those that landed hurt the challenger. Before the bell,

Marciano landed a kidney punch, but there was no warning from referee Brown. Rocky was hitting on the break, which was his normal style. This was going to be a bumpy ride for the man from Battersea.

Cockell was able to land his jabs and hooks quite freely in the second round as Marciano crouched, hooked and swung, often out of range, and while Rocky landed the harder blows, Don was picking up the points by jabbing and hooking well at long range. His obvious aim was to score but, at the same time, keep away from the champion's heavy bombs.

A bump appeared on the side of Cockell's head near the end of the round as a result of a Marciano butt. Again, there was no warning from the referee for Rocky using his head as a third glove. The small ring was also a big advantage to Marciano as he was able to cut off Cockell's advances from the corners.

Marciano's suspect nose was standing the test, especially in the third round when the Brit landed three hard jabs on it. Don seemed to be encouraged by the ease with which he could connect with long-range blows, but the Rock was as dangerous as a live wire, and he made Cockell visibly wince with a powerful right to the chin. Just after the bell, Marciano landed a solid right to the body – again, no warning came.

They exchanged fast, hard blows in the fourth, but then ducking well below the belt, Marciano straightened up so that the top of his head caught Cockell's forehead and caused a nasty cut which would worry the Brit for the rest of the fight. Again, Rocky received no warning. Cockell was still boxing correctly, but Marciano was beginning to wear down his man like the bullfighter weakening the beast in front of him.

In the fifth, the world champion landed so low with body smashes that Cockell reeled back into the ropes, as usual with no warning. The Brit was taking heavy punishment now, and it seemed to be a case of seeing how long he could survive the bombardment. A strong right to the head shook Cockell, and his forehead began to bleed again. A Marciano right landed as the bell clanged, and Cockell went back to his corner on decidedly wobbly legs.

Rocky was now bowling his right like a fast bowler with a new ball, and there was no let-up in his relentless pounding in the sixth. Many of his blows missed by feet, but the ones that landed really hurt. Brown finally issued a warning, but, remarkably, it was against Cockell for a low blow! Don was supremely game and continued to take everything that the unbeaten American could hand out. Nobody could question his bravery, but courage was never enough in the rough and raw world of a Marciano title fight.

In the seventh, people were asking, 'What's keeping Cockell up?' Marciano again butted his man, and the Brit decided the only way to survive at that stage was to give Marciano a taste of his own medicine. He butted Rocky back, but, again, no warning was given to either competitor. It seemed that it was a fight in which anything would go, and it did. Rocky moved in with another butt, and this time Cockell looked appealingly at the referee, but Brown just waved them on as though nothing had happened.

By that point in the fight, Cockell was landing frequently on Marciano's once-vulnerable nose, but Rocky simply ignored the blows in his relentless drive forward. There was a maul in the centre of the ring, and Marciano was still using his head and his elbows in close. Two more smashing rights were delivered by the world champion, and it seemed only a matter of time before Cockell would cave in under the ceaseless bombardment.

Don jabbed his man at the start of the eighth, but he may as well have been hitting a tiger with a stick. Marciano punched back twice as hard, a solid straight right followed by a wicked left hook sending the challenger staggering back several paces. When Cockell recovered, a heavy overhand right shook him up again. Seconds before the bell, Marciano bulldozed his way in, and a crushing right to the head sent Cockell headlong through the ropes near his own corner.

Cockell, now looking decidedly tired and frustrated in his inability to make any impression on this iron man, came out slowly for the ninth and fired feeble left jabs before Marciano connected with a blasting right which dropped the Londoner on the seat of his black shorts for a count of nine, and the jaunty Rocky back-pedalled to a neutral corner.

When Cockell got to his feet, he was wobbling like a seasick sailor on his initial voyage. Another Marciano piledriver then dropped his opponent for a count of four. A second blow crashed against the side of Cockell's head while he was still on one knee, and, as usual, not a word of warning came from the referee. It was obvious that neither Marciano nor Brown had ever read the rule book, the Californian one or any other.

When the supremely gallant Briton arose on shaky legs, his eyes glassy, Rocky rushed across the ring with a non-stop attack, both arms flailing. The challenger took the full brunt on his head and jaw, and it was painfully clear that he was unable to defend himself. The referee then performed his first constructive action of the whole fight. He jumped in between them and raised Marciano's right glove. The time was fifty-four seconds of round nine.

Immediately after the announcement, Cockell made his way across the ring and told BBC radio commentator Eamonn Andrews, 'I'm very sorry I've disappointed you in England. I promised I wouldn't let you down, but I had hoped to do better than that.' In a crowded dressing-room, the defeated challenger repeated his remarks. Sitting on a bench and swathed in his blue bathrobe, he said, 'Yes, I suppose the referee did the right thing in stopping the fight, but I really wanted to fight some more. I gave my manager strict instructions not to stop the fight whatever happened.'

To Cockell's eternal credit, he never once complained, then or later, about Marciano's illegal tactics. 'I had been hit harder, but he hit me more often than anybody else,' he said in later years. 'But no complaints. Rocky was a great champion.'

Cockell's manager was furious. 'Marciano butted, he twice hit Don low, he hit him when he was down and twice after the bell,' Simpson complained. 'The referee ignored these fouls yet warned Don for what he said was a low blow in the sixth. I wanted to stop the fight after the sixth, but I went along with Don's wishes to let him carry on.'

Over in Marciano's dressing-room, there was jubilation. It was another win and another successful title defence for the unmarked champion. Eating an orange, he said, 'Cockell hit me on the nose several times, but it held up. I must say I never fought a gamer guy. Charles, Walcott, Louis all took plenty, but nobody took more than Cockell. I hit him something awful.'

If Rocky avoided danger in the ring, he took a hammering from the boxing writers the next day. Joe Williams of the *New York World-Telegram* said, 'Marciano violated practically every rule in the book. If, as a result of his experience here last night, Cockell should get the idea that anything goes in the American ring, short of wielding a knife or pulling a gun, you could hardly blame him altogether.' In the *New York Post*, Jimmy Cannon wrote, 'It was a dirty fight, and Marciano continually fouled Cockell. The fight developed an atmosphere of wickedness which obscured it as a sporting event.' Bill McGowran of the London *Evening News* said, 'In an English ring, Marciano would have merited disqualification half a dozen times.' A similar view was held by Peter Wilson of the *Daily Mirror*.

Eamonn Andrews, as well as doing the BBC radio commentary, reported for the London *Evening Star*: 'Make no mistake about it, Marciano is one of the toughest champs who ever rubbed a foot in resin. But he never read the rule books. He should have been taught long ago that this sort of street fighting would mean disqualification.'

The attendance of 18,000 fell considerably short of the 30,000 expected by promoter Jimmy Murray, who staged the fight in association with the International Boxing Club. Murray blamed the low gate on negative publicity plus the fact that nobody gave Cockell a chance. 'They called Cockell a bum before the fight,' he said. 'Now we know he was anything but that.'

Marciano had just one more fight. Four months later, he knocked out Archie Moore in nine rounds in New York. He would tell the author in London in 1966, when he attended the Muhammad Ali–Henry Cooper championship fight, that Cockell was the bravest man he had ever fought, paying full tribute to the Londoner's supreme courage against all the odds. 'Cockell was a really game guy: nobody gamer,' he said. 'The fouls? Honestly, I never realised I was breaking the rules. I was totally focused on winning.'

Sadly, Rocky lost his life on the eve of his 46th birthday when his light aircraft crashed into a tree in the middle of a cornfield in bad weather near Newton, Iowa, in August 1969. Among the many mourners who attended a memorial service at St Peter's Church in London was Don Cockell, the memories of that severe drubbing in San Francisco lost in the mist of time.

14

RISE AND FALL OF THE GORGEOUS GAEL

When Jack Doyle, the 'Gorgeous Gael', went to the US in 1935 to campaign for a world heavyweight title fight and pursue a dual career as boxer and international singer, his first call was to attend an official welcoming reception in New York. Among the guests was the former world heavyweight champion Jack Dempsey.

As somebody called for the genial and handsome Irishman to make a speech, he cleared his throat, straightened up and announced, 'Gentlemen, and to the ladies present, thank you for the reception, and it's great to be in your wonderful country. All I will say for the present, however, is that while I'm here, I hope to sing better than our own John McCormack and fight better than your Mr Jack Dempsey.'

On hearing this, a slightly bemused Dempsey said to a boxing writer next to him, 'Frankly, I think Mr Doyle might be better advised to take me on at singing and McCormack at boxing. It strikes me that it might be more of an even match that way.'

Doyle was certainly one of the most colourful and exciting boxers in the long history of the heavyweight division. Though he was never a professional champion or attained the heights he aspired to, he received more space in newspapers and magazines than many a world champion because of his colourful and often crazy antics outside the roped square. An idol of the fight crowds and the 'darlin' boyo' of women who thronged to his fights, his innate charm and striking good looks won over a generation of followers.

Doyle also happened to be one of the most controversial boxers who ever pushed his hands into gloves. He threw away fights he could well have won had he trained harder and not been so impetuous and woolly headed. One exasperated promoter in the 1930s said that the word impulsive could well have been created with Jack Doyle in mind.

Few would disagree that had the big, strapping Irishman with the hefty wallop in his right hand put his mind to hard, disciplined training and complete dedication to the sport, he could have been a champion and one of boxing's real stars. This was the tragedy of Doyle. With his classic features, shock of well-groomed dark hair, sparkling eyes, wide smile and brogue as expansive as O'Connell Street, Dublin's main thoroughfare, he sadly preferred to act the role of playboy instead of puncher. His was a genuinely wasted talent.

Unfortunately for Jack, the sheer grind of training in what were often spartan gyms and pounding the lonely miles of roadwork early in the morning was simply hard graft, not to mention utterly boring. He quite rightly reckoned that he had a terrific punch in his right hand, but he never realised, or perhaps did not want to face up to the fact, that there is more to boxing than a big wallop. Having said that, were he around today in this age of fragmented titles, he could have arguably won one of them.

Michael Taub, Doyle's biographer, wrote, 'Jack was a giant in stature and with a giant appetite for life. He lived his life like a hell-raiser, and by the time he was 30, he had earned and squandered a £¾ million fortune.' Boxing historian and author Gilbert Odd observed that, 'Doyle, for all his potential ability, could never quite dedicate himself to boxing and all that goes with it.'

Outside the ring, Jack was a real charmer. It was often said that he got his eloquence as a child when he kissed the Blarney Stone. The inscribed stone at the fifteenth-century Blarney Castle in Doyle's native Co. Cork is said to impart the gift of words – especially of flattery, persuasion or even deception – to anyone who kisses it. It is one of Ireland's main tourist attractions.

Certainly, it was never too difficult to realise why people liked Doyle, especially the ladies. He was a real flatterer. The author got to know him quite well in London in the early 1970s, long into Doyle's retirement years. He was living in a dimly lit, cramped basement flat in Paddington, one of the poorer areas of the city, and was battling a serious drink problem at that time. Acquaintances were renewed later when he was in Dublin for a singing tour of Ireland, and he was still the charmer, still the gentleman. It was always 'Mr Myler', never 'Thomas'. Jack had a fine tenor voice and could have made it as a singer had he not decided to split his career between boxing and show business.

Doyle was born on 31 August 1913 in the Co. Cork seaport of Cobh, from where just the previous year the *Titanic* had sailed on its ill-fated maiden voyage. He was one of six children born to local sailor Michael Doyle and his wife Anastasia. A strong youngster, Jack grew fast and at the age of sixteen he was a husky six-footer who got work as a bricklayer on a building site to add to the family's modest income.

He got into lots of street fights, mainly against bullies, and it was in these battles that he discovered his right-hand punch. However, it was not until he joined the Irish Guards, a battalion of the British Army, at the age of 17 that Doyle realised his full potential as a boxer. The avid admirer of Jack Dempsey knew that he would get nowhere fast by staying in Ireland and decided that Britain would be his base. He reckoned that being an Irish Guardsman would provide that opportunity as he had heard a lot about their boxing championships.

Based in Windsor outside London, Jack began to learn the rudiments of boxing in the forces, and he developed his fine physique even more. He tried out his limited boxing skill on opponents in army tournaments, and while he enjoyed the fancy stuff of jabbing and moving around, he always finished up by tossing his big right, which he would let loose with lusty abandon. Usually, his rivals would end up flat on the canvas and stay there. On one occasion, he knocked an opponent into the ringside lap of his commanding officer who promptly told Jack, 'Young man, you should think seriously of taking up professional boxing when you leave the army.'

While off duty, Doyle hung around the gym above The Star and Garter pub in Windsor and watched the British middleweight champion Len Harvey train. Jack pestered Harvey to give him a spar, and when they got together for a few rounds, the skilful Englishman was so impressed that the next day he advised his manager Dan Sullivan to have a look at the kid. 'Doyle's got great potential,' said Harvey.

Sullivan watched Doyle in the gym and was so impressed that he offered to buy Jack out of the Irish Guards and have him turn professional. Doyle was so keen to be freed from the regimental life he was living in the barracks that he readily agreed, but not before stipulating that he be allowed to take part in the Brigade of Guards Championships. He reasoned that he needed some experience before turning to the tougher professional side of the sport. As it happened, he did not get a lot, flattening all five of his opponents in a single round apiece to wrap up his amateur career with a record of twenty-eight fights, twenty-eight wins, all but one by knockout or stoppage.

So it was that as the highly touted Brigade of Guards heavyweight champion, Doyle made his professional debut at London's glass-domed Crystal Palace on 4 April 1932 and flattened Chris Goulding in 30 seconds, including the count. Big Jack was on his way. Over the next seven months, he won nine consecutive fights, all without the referee having to tot up his scorecard. Four were in the first round, the remainder in the second.

Of his successful run, Doyle's most significant win was over big Jack Pettifer, a Londoner known as the 'King's Cross Giant', who was all of 6 ft 7 in. and weighed 17 st. 4 lb. Pettifer, like Doyle, was also unbeaten and a hard puncher as well. On the night of 17 October 1932, a crowd of 12,000 fans packed Crystal Palace to see the action, with another 8,000 outside unable to gain admittance.

It came quickly and all from Pettifer. With his superior skill and longer reach, he made an utter fool of Doyle in the opening round, punching the Irishman all around the ring the way an angry child might knock a doll around the floor. When the glassy-eyed Irishman struggled back to his corner, desperate action was called for. Fortunately for Doyle, Dan Sullivan was not adverse to bending the rules a little here and there if one of his meal tickets was in trouble, or in Doyle's case, in serious danger of being knocked out colder than a fishmonger's slab. With all the expertness of a magician pulling a rabbit from a top hat, the canny Dan produced a small flask of brandy from the pocket of his cornerman's coat and under cover of the water bottle, tipped a generous quantity down Jack's throat.

The effect was immediate. When the bell rang for the second round, Doyle bit on his mouthpiece, went out and swung a mighty right that sent Pettifer reeling into the ropes. He followed through with a fusillade of hammer blows that shattered the Londoner's defence and sent him down for the full count. 'There Pettifer lay,' wrote Ben Bennison of the London *Evening Standard*, 'his eyes staring at the roof, the last ounce of his fighting power beaten out of him.'

The Irishman's sensational victory pushed him to the forefront of challengers for the British heavyweight title held by the popular Welshman, Jack Petersen. When a boxing writer asked Doyle if he would like to fight Petersen, the Irishman's blue eyes lit up like a Christmas tree. 'Sure I'll fight him,' he replied. 'Let them name the date.'

Secret negotiations had already started for a Doyle–Petersen fight in London between promoter Jeff Dickson and Brigadier General A.C. Critchley, chairman of the White City Stadium where the bout would most likely be staged. Critchley had acquired Doyle's contract from Dan Sullivan and would in future guide the Irishman's career, although Sullivan was kept on as Jack's official manager and retained a veto over Doyle's opponents.

Meanwhile, the Gorgeous Gael adopted the role of boxing's playboy. Still only 19 years old, the public adulation showered on him was proving difficult to handle. He began to believe in his own publicity and that with his heavy punch, he need not train. After all, he was enjoying life to the full, being invited to all the best London restaurants and most fashionable dining places, and there was hardly a big, lavish party that did not have Jack Doyle's name high on the guest list – and the 'A' list at that.

At the same time, he also wanted to keep his name in the boxing limelight. He finished off 1932 by knocking out the hard-hitting Frenchman Moise Bouquillon at London's Royal Albert Hall, although he had to climb off the canvas twice in the first round before flattening his man in the second.

There was now a snag in negotiations for a Doyle–Petersen fight. The Welshman was holding out for more money. He knew a title defence against the popular Irishman would be a financial windfall for everybody, and he wanted a large slice of the action. So, with no sign of a title shot in the immediate future, Doyle took a six-month break from boxing and devoted time to his fledgling singing career. He toured theatres and concert halls in the UK, including a prestigious spot at the London Palladium, to great acclaim. Jack even managed to cut his first record with 'Mother Machree' on one side and 'My Irish Song of Songs' on the reverse.

Meanwhile, promoter Jeff Dickson announced that negotiations for the Doyle–Petersen fight were progressing well and that the contest would be staged at the White City Stadium, an arena normally used for greyhound racing. The original date was planned for June 1933, but Doyle reportedly injured his back in training, and a new date was set for 13 July. All that was required was the two contestants' signatures.

After much haggling, Petersen agreed on a straight £5,000 fee and Doyle on £3,000, although the Irishman insisted on the money 'win, lose or draw'. Doyle considered the possibility of defeat and was making sure he was adequately covered for such an eventuality. Dickson agreed, knowing full well that the gate receipts of a fight everybody wanted to see would well cover his outlay.

Both men had warm-up fights, Petersen outpointing the Australian George Cook over fifteen rounds and Doyle knocking out the experienced but faded Belgian Jack Humbeeck in the second. Although both were undefeated, Petersen was installed a 5–4 favourite because of his greater experience, with four championship fights to his credit. He had won the British heavyweight title by knocking out Reggie Meen in the second round. The Welshman had twenty-three fights with eleven wins by the short route, while Doyle had ten victories, all inside the scheduled distance. The Irishman's supporters were quick to point out that while it had taken Petersen twelve rounds to knock out Jack Pettifer, Doyle had completed the job in two.

Petersen was a popular champion. A tall, rangy boxer with a knockout punch in his right glove, he had his father and a syndicate of sportsmen behind him in his career. He had harboured designs of being a doctor in his native Cardiff, but the lure of the ring had helped to change his mind. The Welshman had enjoyed an impressive amateur career, which included the winning of the British ABA light-heavyweight title, and it was no surprise when he turned professional in 1931. He won the Welsh heavyweight title in his 13th fight and later dropped down a division to take the British light-heavyweight championship before becoming national heavyweight champion. His main failing, however, was that he was considered too light to compete among the big men. He generally scaled around 13 st. and invariably had to concede weight to his opponents, including Doyle, who outweighed him by over two stone – 15 st. 3 lb to 13 st. to be exact.

There was considerable excitement on the day of the fight. Everybody seemed to be talking about it, and the newspapers carried full coverage of the boxers' arrival in London: Petersen from Cardiff and Doyle from Taplow, just outside Windsor. The stadium was ready for the expected capacity attendance of 60,000. Barbed-wire barriers were erected around the centre area where more than 9,000 chairs were placed for ringside seats. Some 4,000 planks were put down to form a vast wooden floor over the turf. Twelve bridges leading from the entrance gates down to ringside were built, and over three hundred signs were put up in various parts of the large stadium to direct people to their seats.

The stadium was full by the time both men made their appearance, with several thousand people outside the gates vainly looking for tickets, not realising that there was simply no room for them. By tradition, challenger Doyle was first into the ring, looking resplendent in a dressing gown of emerald green, which he removed to reveal his beautiful body, resulting in gasps of admiration from the many ladies present. His bright-green satin shorts had a white waistband, and his initials and a shamrock were embroidered on each leg.

Petersen was playing the oldest trick in the business by keeping the challenger waiting. Eventually, he came down the aisle wearing a simple grey dressing gown over plain blue shorts, in stark contrast to Doyle's colourful attire. However, the fight was not about dress sense. It was about ring ability, the better boxer, the hardest puncher, and may the best man win.

As both stood in the centre of the ring to listen to the instructions from referee Cecil 'Pickles' Douglas, a London timber merchant by profession, the contrast between the champion and challenger was very obvious. Doyle, at 6 ft 5 in., towered over the 6 ft ½ in. Petersen, and besides his weight advantage, the Corkman, aged twenty, was two years younger than the Welshman. Would these advantages help Doyle?

The vast crowd did not have long to find out, if the dramatic first round was any kind of guide. Doyle was first into the attack, hoping to unsettle Petersen before the champion could get into motion his plan of action. Petersen, nevertheless, countered Doyle's rushes with a cracking right to the jaw. Doyle simply shook his head and barged forward again, forcing the champion to the ropes under a two-handed body attack.

As Doyle surged in again, Petersen moved off the ropes and caught the Irishman with a solid right to the jaw. Doyle immediately fell into a clinch and was warned by Douglas. 'Stop holding, Doyle,' the referee commanded. The challenger nodded in acknowledgement but continued to rush in and landed a palpably low blow, although Petersen sportingly showed no obvious signs of being hurt. Douglas again warned the Irishman, saying, 'Keep your punches up, Doyle.' Petersen continued to box coolly and attempted to hold off the rushing challenger. The Welshman connected with a hard right to Doyle's jaw, but it did not seem to affect the Irishman's driving attacks. As both men were engaged in close-quarter work, Douglas barked, 'Break away, both of you.'

Towards the end of the round, Doyle lashed out with a sweeping right that landed on Petersen's temple and sent him staggering backwards to the ropes with his hands dangling by his sides. For some unexplained reason, instead of following up with more of his heavy rights to the head, Doyle switched to the body, and just before the bell, he got another warning from a stern-faced Douglas: 'Keep your punches up, Doyle.'

Douglas took the trouble to go over to the Corkman's corner during the interval and told him, 'Doyle, you will have to be more careful with your punches, or I will have to disqualify you. I can't keep on warning you, remember that.'

Petersen came out fast for the second round after being told by his corner to get the dangerous Irishman out of there as soon as possible, although it was not going to be that easy. Doyle was simply swarming in from all angles, tossing punches with reckless abandon and obviously hoping one of them would flatten the Cardiff man. Petersen simply hit back, much to the delight of the big crowd, who were now on their feet cheering.

'Petersen and Doyle lashed out at one another with lefts and rights like primitive savages,' wrote Joe Sherwood at ringside for the *Irish Press* newspaper. Petersen dodged a vicious right but walked into another tremendous right that sent him staggering back to the ropes like a drunk. However, Doyle's follow-through punches missed the target by several feet, and Petersen managed to work the Irishman back to the centre of the ring with a barrage of hard, well-timed punches.

Both men landed hammer blows on each other but neither wilted. Two heavy rights staggered Petersen, but the Welshman stormed back and got through with a stinging right to the jaw that sent Doyle stumbling against the ropes as though his legs were made of papier mâché. He recovered quickly and rushed Petersen across the ring before landing two decidedly low punches, as Douglas attempted to move in between them. So eager and deeply concentrated were the two to win the crucial championship contest that neither realised that Douglas was intervening, particularly as Petersen had shown no signs of distress from the low blows. The referee pulled the boxers apart, touched the Irishman on the shoulder and said, 'Doyle, go to your corner. You're disqualified.' The much-hyped and eagerly awaited battle had lasted no longer than thirty-three seconds into the second round.

The sensational finish of what had been a thriller took the large crowd completely by surprise, even if there had always been the constant threat of a sudden ending, judging by the torrid pace of the fight. Angry at being deprived of more of the same action, they burst into prolonged boos and whistles which echoed around White City Stadium. The din continued as the two boxers made their way to their dressing-rooms, and it went on into the following contest, drowning out the MC's announcements. It was pandemonium rarely witnessed in a British ring.

Back in the dressing-room, the happy-go-lucky Doyle was all smiles, seemingly looking or feeling none the worse for his ignominious defeat. He broke into song for the assembled reporters as he sat down and took off his boxing kit. 'I'm quite happy, despite the loss,' he said, 'though I wish we had gone another round because I would have won. I had him going. No, I don't think he was any stronger than the men I have met before.' Asked by one writer if he felt he had thrown away his big chance, he said, 'All I know is that I sailed right in, knowing that so many of the folks in Ireland were listening in to the radio broadcast, and I said to myself that I would finish it quickly. I suppose I did hit him low because everybody said I did, including the referee, but it will never happen again.' Then, as if to convince himself that the defeat was just a temporary setback in his quest for further boxing honours, he declared, 'I was disqualified because I was young and inexperienced, but I can beat any of the heavyweights around, and one day, you watch, I'll be heavyweight champion of the world.'

Doyle stayed on in his dressing-room, shaking hands with everybody, without a care in the world. Petersen got ready quickly and told reporters, 'It was a bad ending. What a pity, as I thought we were going to have a great fight – but I was always confident of winning, right from the start.'

Seven years later, in Britain's *Sunday Pictorial*, Doyle said, 'I fouled

Petersen in the first round. I admit that now, freely. I was warned that I would be disqualified if I persisted. I fouled him again in the second round, more than once. I was ordered back to my corner, disqualified and disgraced.'

Looking back on the fight when he arrived in Dublin for the start of a singing tour in the 1970s, Doyle would elaborate on that night in an interview with the author: 'I always felt I was harshly treated in that fight. You could say I was robbed, because every time I aimed a punch at Petersen he jumped up a few inches, and my punches would automatically go below the belt. The next thing I knew I was being disqualified in the second round, and, remember, Petersen did not show any sign of being hurt by the low blows as he was wearing a protector.

'There is no doubt in my mind that I would have won the title had the fight been allowed to continue. I had him rocking several times, and I'm convinced I would have knocked him out. There's no doubt in my mind about that.'

Petersen, naturally, had a different version of what happened. In an interview in 1989, during his term as president of the British Boxing Board of Control, he recalled that the frequency of powerful fists pounding his lower regions made it extremely unlikely that they were merely stray blows.

'Doyle must have hit me low 14 times in all, and the punches put a huge dent in my protector,' he remembered. 'Had I not been wearing it, I would never have been able to fight again. Doyle could have crippled me for life. The fight itself I can only describe as an absolute farce. It was a disaster as far as British boxing was concerned.

'I am certain that I would have knocked him out had the fight gone another round, but it was a travesty of a boxing match from every point of view, and I would like to forget all about it. There was no doubt that he was anxious to win, and win quickly, but poor Doyle lost his head. Let us put it down to the occasion being altogether too big for him.'

Meanwhile, despite Doyle's insistence before the fight that he be paid his £3,000 purse win, lose or draw, the money was withheld pending an investigation. This was convened a week later with Jack in attendance, and after hearing referee Douglas's damning account of Doyle's repeated low blows and holding tactics, the board felt that they were left with no choice but to suspend the Irish boxer for six months. They also ordered that he would have to forfeit £2,740 of his purse, with the balance of £260 divided between Doyle and his dependent parents at the rate of £10 a week. Doyle stood up and in an almost tearful plea, said the penalty would place 'an intolerable burden on them'. The board's decision, however, was final, and the financial arrangement would last for the duration of the six-month ban.

Doyle's biographer Michael Taub called the penalty 'appalling' and 'vicious in the extreme'. It was a feeling shared by the boxing writers at the time of the hearing, including the respected James Butler, who felt that Doyle had been treated very unfairly, not only by the heavy fine but also by having to humiliate himself before officials of the British Boxing Board of Control. Butler also made the point that other top boxers who had been disqualified for hitting low were fined very small sums. These included the prominent German heavyweight Walter Neusel. The writer said that some even escaped fines and got away with cautions. Certainly none had to appear before the British Board to explain their actions.

Doyle stood dejected outside the board's offices in London's West End and told waiting reporters that he was going to sue. With a fresh yellow rose in the lapel of his brown-check suit, he spoke sadly of being 'beaten for the first time in my life', and added, 'I am not accepting any part of their ruling, nor am I looking for charity. I only ask for justice and my legal rights, and I intend to press for them. I am going to test the legality of the board's decision.'

He took his case to London's High Court in 1934 before Justice MacKinnon and won, being awarded damages of £3,000, as well as undisclosed costs. Concerned that Doyle would have to wait some considerable time before receiving the money the court had deemed was rightfully his, and sympathetic to Jack's circumstances, Justice MacKinnon took the unusual step of allowing the sum of £500 to be paid to him immediately.

The British Boxing Board of Control promptly served notice of appeal, but the fact that they were not prepared to accept the court verdict clearly rankled with Justice MacKinnon. As it turned out, the board were successful in having the verdict reversed by three appeal judges – Master of the Rolls, Lord Hanworth, and Lord Justices Romer and Slesser – leaving Jack with the £260 to share with his parents. However, he kept the £500 awarded by Justice MacKinnon from the original hearing.

Doyle walked away from the court with his legal team an embittered man. He felt he had been shamed and ridiculed by the sport's governing authority, besides being deprived of what he considered to be his rightful purse. 'The money I came out with was a mere pittance,' Doyle later told the author. 'It was a disgraceful amount of money to give any heavyweight championship contender. There were reports in some newspapers later that I received the balance of my purse – £2,740 – but I can assure you that I did not. The board were conveniently standing by the appeal rule and that was it.'

Doyle told reporters after the appeal that he was 'completely fed up with British boxing and the shabby treatment I received from the board'. He announced that he was going to try his luck in the US and campaign for a world heavyweight title fight, as well as continue with his singing career.

Before leaving, he would honour his contract with one more fight in Britain and in March 1934, knocked out Frank Borrington of Derbyshire with a mighty right-hander after 83 seconds of the first round at London's Royal Albert Hall. In August, he returned to his native land to celebrate his 21st birthday with a massive bash in a Dublin hotel, where several hundred guests got through bottles of champagne like it was going out of fashion. Whatever his financial situation, Doyle always seemed to have money for fun and games.

Doyle was a big hit on his US tour in 1935 in more ways than one. He knocked out his first three opponents in one, four and two rounds respectively, before getting himself mauled by a 6 ft 6 in. Baer by the name of Buddy, the younger brother of Max Baer, who had just lost his world heavyweight title to James J. Braddock. It was all over in less than three minutes. The Irishman had been battered to the canvas three times before referee Billy Kavanaugh mercifully intervened, although Doyle claimed he was fouled on the first knockdown by a hook delivered well below the belt.

From then on, Jack's boxing career went downhill faster than a toboggan on a snow-covered slope. After infrequent appearances in British and Irish rings over the next eight years – in which he had only seven fights, losing four, all inside two rounds – he hung up his gloves. In any event, he had long lost interest in the ring. In one of those defeats, against the Londoner Eddie Phillips in 1939, he was counted out on the broad of his back in two minutes and twenty-five seconds of the first round, with his eyes wide open, fondly gazing up at the ring lights as if to say, 'What's the point?'

In the meantime, he had continued his singing career and kept his name in the Hollywood gossip columns by making two movies and going through two disastrous marriages plus a succession of extramarital affairs with various actresses and socialites. Playboy Jack also had wild drinking sessions with hell-raiser Errol Flynn and a punch-up with Clark Gable, who claimed Doyle was seeing his girlfriend and future wife Carole Lombard behind his back. Was it any wonder that the Gorgeous Gael made hot copy for reporters? However, Doyle's singing career had more stops and starts than an old banger that has seen its best days on the road, and looking back, it's said today that he made more show business comebacks than Frank Sinatra.

After his last fight in 1943, Jack sadly turned to the degrading spectacle of all-in wrestling before being warned that he risked serious injury if he continued. By 1947, the former heavyweight star was sleeping rough in Dublin, usually in the back of a derelict car in a city backstreet. He later moved to London, where he lived out the final years of his life. He divided his time between his shabby little room in Paddington and his local bar around the corner, where he would buy drinks for his cronies with money he got from the dole or won on the horses. Or better still, somebody might buy him a drink, a not infrequent occurrence.

Strangely enough, Doyle's name was linked at that time with the glamorous British movie star Diana Dors, although he insisted he only had eyes for his regular Irish lady friend Nancy Keogh, who would later walk out on him. Jack hit rock bottom in 1966 when he was hauled before a local court for stealing a block of cheese from a local supermarket and fined £5.

Jack was always good for a song, and he managed to pick up a few pounds singing in pub cabarets. He also sold his story to newspapers but always with a new twist and a different angle. In an interview with the author in the 1970s for the *Dublin Evening Herald*, he was very dismissive of boxing standards of the time, saying that he felt that the sport had taken a turn for the worse. What he would have thought of the current era with its multiplicity of world titles decided by the so-called alphabet boys does not bear thinking about.

'The men of my day would have mopped the floor with the current champions,' he said. 'There aren't enough hungry fighters around, and, as you know, hungry fighters are tough fighters. In the 1930s, you had great men like Joe Louis, Max Schmeling, Tommy Farr and so on. Take the two current top heavyweights, Muhammad Ali and Joe Frazier. They aren't in the class of Louis or Rocky Marciano.'

Asked how he thought Jack Doyle at his best would have fared against Ali or Frazier, he waved his right hand dismissively: 'If I caught Ali in the right spot, he would have gone down. No doubt about that. As for Frazier, the winner would have been the one who landed first, and don't forget that the great Jack Dempsey said I had the best right-hand in the business.'

Sadly, on 13 December 1978, Doyle died in St Mary's Hospital, Paddington, aged 65. A heavy drinker all his life, the cause of death was cirrhosis of the liver. He used to say he would die a pauper, and he seemed destined for a pauper's grave had it not been for a kind-hearted Irish soldier of fortune who had once befriended him in London.

Joe Faye set the wheels in motion for Doyle's emaciated body to be taken back to his home town of Cobh in Co. Cork for a decent burial. Amid scenes that would have been remarkable at the funeral of a head of state, thousands lined the streets to pay their last respects to the Gorgeous Gael, and a wreath in the shape of a boxing glove was placed on his grave by the local ex-boxers' association.

Jack Doyle was not forgotten in the end. It was a pity he could not have been remembered as a great star of the boxing ring. His was a wasted talent. He had it all and threw it away. What a shame.

BIBLIOGRAPHY

No work of this nature would be possible without recourse to the many fine boxing books, extensively researched and well written, which have enhanced and continue to enhance the sport. So, if you can buy, borrow or beg any of them which you do not already possess, your knowledge of the Sweet Science will have been richly improved as they are all highly recommended.

BOOKS:

Allen, David Rayvern, *Punches on the Page: A Boxing Anthology* (Mainstream Publishing, Edinburgh, 1998)

Anderson, Roger, *The Fighting Irish: Inside the Ring with Boxing's Celtic Warriors* (Mainstream Publishing, Edinburgh, 2004)

Blewett, Bert, *The A–Z of World Boxing: Authoritative and Entertaining Compendium of the Fight Game from its Origins to the Present Day* (Robson Books, London, 1996)

Brenner, Teddy, *Only the Ring was Square* (Prentice-Hall, New Jersey, 1981)

Collings, Mark, *The 100 Greatest Boxers: The Ultimate Boxing Who's*

Who to Settle Every Argument and Start 100 More! (Generation Publications, London, 1999)

Corbett, James J., *The Roar of the Crowd: The True Tale of the Rise and Fall of a Champion* (G.P. Putnam's Sons, New York, 1925)

Cottrell, John, *Man of Destiny: The Story of Muhammad Ali/Cassius Clay* (Muller, London, 1967)

Downes, Terry, *My Bleeding Business* (Stanley Paul, London, 1964)

Fantuz, Guiliana V., Malfatto, Ivan and Argentin, Gino, *My Father: Primo Carnera* (SEP Editrice, Milan, 2002)

Fleischer, Nat, *Black Dynamite*, Vol. III (The Ring, New York, 1938)

Fleischer, Nat, *'Terrible Terry': The Brooklyn Terror* (The Ring, New York, 1943)

Fleischer, Nat, *The Heavyweight Championship: An Informal History of Heavyweight Boxing from 1719 to the Present Day* (Putnam, London, 1949)

Graziano, Rocky, *Somebody Up There Likes Me: My Life So Far* (Simon & Schuster, New York, 1955)

Gutteridge, Reg, *Uppercuts and Dazes: My Autobiography* (Blake, London, 1998)

Hannigan, Dave, *The Big Fight* (Yellow Jersey Press, London, 2002)

Haskins, James, *Sugar Ray Leonard* (Robson Books, London, 1989)

Hauser, Thomas, *Muhammad Ali: His Life And Times* (Simon and Schuster, New York, 1991)

Heller, Peter, *In This Corner* (Robson Books, London, 1975)

Hughes, Brian, *Willie Pep: The Will o' the Wisp* (Collyhurst and Moston Lads Club, Manchester, 1997)

Johnson, Jack, *Jack Johnson is a Dandy: An Autobiography* (Chelsea House, New York, 1969)

LaMotta, Jake, *Raging Bull: My Story* (Prentice-Hall, New Jersey, 1970)

Lane, Mills, *Let's Get It On: Tough Talk From Boxing's Top Ref and Nevada's Most Outspoken Judge* (Crown Publishers, New York, 1998)

Liebling, A.J., *The Sweet Science* (Grove Press, New York, 1956)

Lonkhurst, Bob, *Gentleman of the Ring: The Life and Career of Jack Petersen* (BL Associates, Hertfordshire, 2001)

McCallum, John, *World Heavyweight Boxing Championship: A History* (Chilton Book Co., Pennsylvania, 1974)

McGhee, Frank, *England's Boxing Heroes* (Bloomsbury, London, 1988)

McNeill, Jim, *That Night in the Garden: Great Fights and Great Moments from Madison Square Garden* (Robson Books, London, 2003)

McRae, Donald, *Dark Trade: Lost In Boxing* (Mainstream Publishing, Edinburgh, 1996)

Mayes, Harold, *Rocky Marciano* (Panther Books, London, 1956)

Mee, Bob, *Bare Fists* (Lodge Farm Books, Warwickshire, 1998)

Mullally, Frederic, *Primo: The Story of 'Man Mountain' Carnera, World Heavyweight Champion* (Robson Books, London, 1991)

Mullan, Harry, *Ring Wars: A Pictorial History of Boxing* (Parragon, Bristol, 1997)

Mullan, Harry, *Boxing: Inside The Game* (Icon Books, Cambridge, 1998)

Myler, Patrick, *Gentleman Jim Corbett: The Truth Behind a Boxing Legend* (Robson Books, London, 1998)

Naughton, William W., *Kings of the Queensberry Realm: Being an Account of Every Heavy-weight Championship Contest Held in America Under the Queensberry Rules, a Sketch of Every Contestant Who has Taken Part Therein, and an Account of the Invasion of Australian Boxers* (Continental Publishing Co., Chicago, 1902)

Newfield, Jack, *The Life and Crimes of Don King* (Virgin, London, 1996)

Odd, Gilbert, *Boxing: The Great Champions* (Hamlyn Publishing Group, London, 1974)

Odd, Gilbert, *Ali, the Fighting Prophet* (Pelham Books, London, 1975)

Roberts, James B. and Skutt, Alexander G., *The Boxing Register: International Boxing Hall of Fame Official Record Book* (McBooks Press, New York, 2002)

Steen, Rob, *Sonny Boy: The Life and Strife of Sonny Liston* (Methuen, London, 1993)

Suster, Gerald, *Lightning Strikes: Lives and Times of Boxing's Lightweight Champions* (Robson Books, London, 1994)

Taub, Michael, *Jack Doyle: Fighting For Love* (Stanley Paul, London, 1990)

Torres, José, *Stings Like a Bee: The Muhammad Ali Story* (Abelard-Schuman, New York, 1971)

Walsh, Peter, *Men of Steel: Lives and Times of Boxing's Middleweight Heroes* (Robson Books, London, 1993)

Webb, Dale, *Prize Fighter: The Life and Times of Bob Fitzsimmons* (Mainstream Publishing, Edinburgh, 2000)

Whiting, George, *Great Fights of the Sixties: Ringside Reports* (Leslie Frewin, London, 1967)

Wilson, Peter, *Ringside Seat* (Rich and Cowan, London, 1949)

Wilson, Peter, *The Man They Couldn't Gag* (Hutchinson/Stanley Paul, London, 1977)

Wilson, Peter, *Boxing's Greatest Prize* (Stanley Paul, London, 1980)

MAGAZINES:

Boxing Illustrated, Boxing International, Boxing Monthly, Boxing News, Boxing and Wrestling, International Boxing Digest, KO and *Ring*.

RECORD BOOKS:

Various editions of *Boxing News Annual, The Boxing Register, Irish Boxing Yearbook, Nat Fleischer's Ring Record Book and Encyclopedia* and *The Ring Boxing Almanac and Book of Facts*.

DVDS/VIDEOS:

Boxers (Marshall Cavendish Collection)
Boxing Classics (Clear Vision)
Boxing's Greatest Champions (Pickwick)
Fallen Champ (Columbia Tristar)
Fantastic Fights of the Century (Legend)
The Leonard v. Duran Trilogy (Castle Vision)
The 12 Greatest Rounds of Boxing (Arrow Films)
The World's Great Fights (Pickwick)

INDEX